THE DREAM OF ARCADIA

BY THE SAME AUTHOR

Published by E. P. DUTTON & CO., INC.

THE DREAM OF ARCADIA

American Writers and Artists in Italy
1760–1915

By Van Wyck Brooks

E. P. DUTTON & CO., INC.
NEW YORK, 1958

Library of Congress Catalog Card Number: 58-9597

AMERICAN BOOK—STRATFORD PRESS, INC., NEW YORK

To

BERNARD BERENSON

with affection

CONTENTS

PREFACE

"THE TRADITION of travels in Italy is perhaps the only one that is common to all schools." So wrote the painter Fromentin in *Les Maîtres d'autrefois;* and, thinking about my Americans there, I have had constantly in mind the writers and artists of other countries who were in Italy at the same time. What great European did not visit the peninsula during the nineteenth century, between the French Revolution and the first World War, the period that concerns me in this book? Yet, though one and all were governed by the same time-spirit, few were aware in Italy of one another's presence. I have found no evidence that any of the Americans of whom I write,—whether Washington Irving or Hawthorne or Fenimore Cooper, whether Howells, Mark Twain, the Jameses or Henry Adams,—fell in with any of these great men or were more conscious of them there than if they themselves had never crossed the ocean. Not a word of Stendhal or Heine, Gogol or Zola, Turgenev or Dostoievsky, Ibsen or Wagner. There were many good friendships between the Americans and the Italians of their time, but otherwise, with a few exceptions, they seem to have encountered only those who spoke their own language, Byron and Landor, for instance, Thackeray and Browning.

It was not merely the Americans, however, who flocked together in this way. Gogol, who regarded Italy as his "true homeland," seems to have known there only Russians and Poles, mainly the Russian painters in Rome, where he wrote *The Overcoat* and the greater part of his *Dead Souls.* All of Turgenev's friends in Rome, where he took lessons in drawing and painting during several months in 1840, appear to have been members of the Russian colony there, a retired hussar, a Moscow society woman and the young girl Chouchou with whom he fell in love. Dostoievsky, writing *The Idiot* in Florence, saw no one there except the new young wife who arranged to meet him every day, after the morning's work, in front of some great picture in the Pitti Palace. He would explain to her the ideas which the picture evoked in him; then the two walked on the river bank or stopped to look at Ghiberti's doors or strolled in the Cascine or the Boboli Gardens. Ibsen, who wrote *Brand* at Ariccia in 1865 and *A Doll's House* at Amalfi in 1879, fell in only, or mainly, with Scandinavians, just as Sigrid Undset's Jenny saw only Norwegians, Swedes and Danes in the Rome where she lived as a young art student.

Well, as Hans Christian Andersen said at a great Christmas party in Rome at which fifty Scandinavians were present in 1833, "The further the Swede, Norwegian and Dane travels from home, the louder sings the heart of each when they meet." Is this perhaps the case generally with men of all nations, so many of whom, both artists and writers, French, Dutch, Spanish, Portuguese, Austrians, Swiss, Rumanians and how many others, were, like the Americans, in Italy a hundred years ago? Ferdinand Gregorovius, the German historian of mediæval Rome, who lived in the city twenty-two years at a time when Burckhardt and Mommsen were also there, showed himself in his *Roman Journal* almost uniquely aware of the visitors from every other country. The American Minister, George Perkins Marsh, appears in this journal as "a quiet man of great culture" and the "celebrated Bayard Taylor" as "a serious, energetic and almost heroic-looking man." Then, in 1869, Gregorovius "met Longfellow at Princess Wittgenstein's. He has a fine head; striking features, liberal and open; white hair and a white beard—is entering on old age in full possession of his energies. Speaks German exceedingly well, as also all literary languages. His translation of Dante is extolled as first-rate."

It was Gregorovius who said, apropos of a resentful German of whom no notice had been taken, "What do we signify here? We are only like chaff or straw that is whirled through the streets,"—and what else could anyone expect in a city that for two thousand years has drawn to itself the genius of the whole Western world? The formidable Zola, "an enemy of the Church, but a straightforward enemy," as Pope Leo XIII called him, may have been received by the King and Queen during the five "ferocious" weeks when he was making his "vast inquest" there. But of what account was his young French priest who wished to revive the primitive Church, arousing a Christian love for the wretched and the lowly, and whose "New Rome" was condemned by the Index, while he himself was pushed aside as an insignificant intruder in that network of intrigues? Yet to those who asked for nothing what did Rome not give? "Rome is beautiful, wonderful, magical," Ibsen wrote in 1866. "I feel an extraordinary capacity for work and the strength of a giant-killer. I kept struggling with my poem [Brand] for a whole year before it took shape clearly. Then one day I strolled into St. Peter's—I had gone to Rome on an errand—and there I suddenly saw in strong and clear outlines the form for what I had to say. Once I had hold of it, I wrote from morning to night and finished it in three months."

Ibsen, who walked, with knapsack on back, all over the Papal States, often lay dreaming whole afternoons on the old Appian Way or among the tombs of the Via Latina. Thus came to life in him the drama with a Roman historical theme that he was to complete a few years later. The Appian Way gave Turgenev the theme of a poem when, driving back from Albano in an open carriage, he passed a tall ruin covered with ivy. He seemed to see, slowly rising above it in the moonlight, the laurel-wreathed head of Julius Caesar, surrounded by the ghostly shapes of Roman legions. But what spot in Italy has not given rise to some poem, some work of art, as in the case of Heine, for one, who "sang on the peaks of the Apennines" and whose five months in Lucca and Florence were, he said, the richest in his life? Then there was Wagner who, at Sorrento, bade farewell to Nietzsche, who, climbing up to Ravello on the back of a donkey, exclaimed there, "I've found Klingsor's garden," whom Liszt joined at Siena, where he played the third act of "Parsifal" while Wagner stood by the piano and sang it with him. In Venice, where he wrote much of "Tristan" and the "Meistersinger," Wagner found symbols in the sculptured lions that rearoused in him the will to work,—Venice where, like Browning seven years later, he was to die in 1882. There, fifty years earlier, George Sand, disillusioned with her "naughty boy Alfred," set out alone on her walking tour, dressed in a man's clothes, along the Brenta, with a knapsack, a big stick and plenty of tobacco, returning to write in Venice two or three books.

If I speak here of matters that all the world knows well, it is because they throw into relief the untold tale of the Americans who were in Italy also during these decades. "In Italy is she really?" said Mrs. Flora Finching, thinking of the land of grapes and figs, in the "interior monologue" in which, in *Little Dorrit,* Dickens anticipated Joyce by sixty years: "In Italy is she really? with the grapes and figs growing everywhere and lava necklaces and bracelets too that land of poetry with burning mountains picturesque beyond belief though if the organ-boys come away from the neighbourhood not to be scorched nobody can wonder being so young and bringing their white mice with them most humane, and is she really in that favoured land with nothing but blue about her and dying gladiators and Belvederes?" How many of the characters of whom I write might have found themselves partly expressed in Mrs. Flora Finching's rigmarole in the days when so many of them shared Wagner's "heart-hunger" for the land for which "beautiful souls will always be homesick"? In all these writers and artists from every other country I have seen my fellow-countrymen reflected, beginning with Stendhal, the fat little man with his Voltairean sangfroid, for whom "the charm of Italy," as he once remarked, "is akin to that of being in love." I am speaking of the days when Italy was still the Arcadia that it was for Poussin, for Goethe later, and perhaps especially for those who crossed the ocean from a land where Arcadia could only be a dream.

THE DREAM OF ARCADIA

CHAPTER I

THE FORERUNNERS

EARLY IN the summer of 1760, Benjamin West arrived in Rome. This young Pennsylvania Quaker had been encouraged by his friends to visit the fountain-head of all the arts, and, having saved money as a portrait-painter, he had sailed for Leghorn with letters to various Roman cognoscenti. At a certain point eight miles away from the walls and the gates of the city, he alighted from the coach, and, while the horses were baiting, proceeded on foot until he caught from an eminence a glimpse of St. Peter's. Near by stood a pile of ruins covered with ivy, and, hearing the tinkle of a pastoral bell, he turned and saw a peasant driving a few goats from a stony enclosure. Then, like another Balboa on another peak of Darien, he gazed over the Campagna, rapt in reflections.

For West was the first neophyte,—and the word quickly passed round Rome,—who had come from the American wilderness to study the fine arts. That afternoon, before he had time even to dress and refresh himself, the news had reached the ears of an English milord, who called upon him at his inn, inviting him to an evening party at which the blind Cardinal Albani was to be present. This great virtuoso, whom Winckelmann served as librarian, was celebrated for the delicacy of his taste and touch, and, feeling the head of the father of American painting, he asked if this young man was white or black. Then the principal Roman nobility and strangers of distinction who were there arranged to accompany the milord and his protégé on a tour of the sights of Rome on the following morning. They wished to see what effect the great works of art might have on the mind of a savage, and at the appointed hour a procession of thirty carriages, the most sumptuous in Rome, assembled for this purpose. The brilliant company, which included some of the most erudite men in Europe, set out first to see the Apollo Belvedere, for this was regarded as the most perfect of the ornaments of Rome and therefore the most likely to produce an effect. West was placed before the cabinet in which the Apollo stood, with the spectators ranged beside him, and it was then that he spoke the words "How like a Mohawk warrior!"— a natural phrase to be uttered by a man from the forest. There West had been taught by a band of Indians to use the colours, yellow and red, with which they painted their own primitive adornments, and, while his mother had added blue by giving him a piece of indigo, he had made a painter's brush from the tail of a cat.

With his calm, frank, open countenance, with the plain jacket and the collar of lace in which Angelica Kaufmann drew his portrait, West was a general favourite in Rome, where for four years he remained before, like Angelica herself, he went on to London. The most famous *improvisatore* in all Italy welcomed him at a certain coffee-house one evening, when the old man, who was called Homer, stood by the table with a guitar and asked on what subject he should recite. When West's friend said he was a young American who had come to study the fine arts, Homer said this was a new and splendid theme, and, unslinging his guitar, he drew his fingers over the strings, struck a few fine chords and began his chant. He sang of the darkness that for so many ages had covered

America before the seraph of knowledge had descended there from heaven, and he drew a picture of the wild beauty of mountain, lake and forest with the Indians in their sacrifices and their chase. Then Columbus appeared and the spirit of improvement, ever on the wing, alighted on the youth and led him to Rome, even as the star of Bethlehem had guided the Magi, and Homer concluded his chant with a prophecy and vision: "Methinks, I behold in him an instrument chosen by heaven to raise in America a taste for those arts that elevate the nature of man, an assurance that his country will afford a refuge to science and knowledge when in the old age of Europe they forsake her shores."

While West was to spend his life in London, as the court painter of George the Third, who gave him a studio in the palace and read Livy to him, suggesting suitable subjects for historical pictures, he was to fulfil this prophecy in part by becoming the master there of the whole first generation of American artists. For among his London pupils were Copley, the Peales and Gilbert Stuart, Trumbull, Washington Allston and Thomas Sully, along with the "American Vasari," William Dunlap. Meanwhile, in Rome, he was taken up by Raphael Mengs, the German, the director of the Vatican school of painting, the most respected painter,—a laborious eclectic,—at a time when the plastic arts were moribund there. Mengs's aim was to unite the expression of Raphael, the colour of Titian and Correggio's wonderful harmony of light and shade,—he was "like the bee, culling their various sweets from the different flowers," his biographer said, "in order to make its honey sweeter." He was the hero of artistic Rome, courted by students from all the world, Russia, France, Holland, Poland and Sweden, who had come, as he had come, to "form a just taste," as his father had said, "which was not to be obtained outside of Italy." But in Rome,—a great centre of music,—pictures were composed according to rules; the chief interest was rather antiquities than painting; and there were several cardinals who had collections of antiques while they kept musical protégés and singers. Mengs himself studied the paintings at Herculaneum, which had just opened its treasures along with Pompeii, where Winckelmann, who had arrived in Rome a few years before Benjamin West, had gathered the first fruits for Cardinal Albani.

This, in fact, was the great age of Roman excavations, and many of the well-known sculptures of the Rome of the future were dug up during these years when West was there and when he fell in with Raphael Mengs at the Villa Albani, where Winckelmann was writing his *History of Ancient Art*. For the German antiquary and the German painter were inseparable friends. There, in this villa, Winckelmann, the so-called prefect of antiquities in Rome, enjoyed a life "seasoned," as he said, "with intellectual pleasures," preaching at the same time the "ideal simplicity and calm greatness" that seemed to him the note of classic art. Nothing could have been more remote from the extravagance of the baroque, from the theatrical mannerisms and bravura of Bernini, who had been for so long the reigning sculptor, and Winckelmann's ideal, replacing this, was to rule for almost a century the world of sculpture. Canova was to appear soon; so was John Flaxman, the Englishman; and Thorwaldsen and many Americans were to follow these. The painter's world was governed by similar notions.

Like the *improvisatore*, Raphael Mengs was also struck by the advent of an American who had come to study art, and he urged West to make drawings of the best classical objects in Rome and then to see the pictures in Bologna and Venice. He suggested the tour of cities on which West embarked before he left the peninsula in 1764, the year in which Gibbon, musing in Rome, while the monks were singing vespers, conceived his plan of writing the *Decline and Fall*.[1] West, following the advice of Mengs, examined with great care the pictures of Correggio at Parma, and he went on to Venice for a similar study of Titian, Tintoretto and Paolo Veronese. All of these painters, because of their elegance and colour, appealed to an age of worldly splendour, but the great school that everyone praised and that West studied most carefully was the school of the Eclectics of Bologna. The German Mengs had followed them, and they were regarded as second to Raphael only as embodiments of classical clarity, refinement and grace. A hundred years later the French critic Taine was to call the Bolognese artists the product of an enfeebled generation, crushed by the Inquisition and exhausted by war, so that only sensibility and rhetoric were left them, and the world was largely to agree with Taine thenceforward; but to the end of the eighteenth century, and even to the middle of the nineteenth, the "wonders" of the Caracci were considered supreme. So was the "divine Guercino," as an English traveller called him,—whose elegance seemed to many almost French,—along with Guido Reni and Domenichino. For the rest, the American Quaker, who remarked that the Italians were "a calm, persuasive and pensive people," was elected to the academies of three cities, and this befitted the future president of the Royal Academy in England whose knowledge and taste were more eminent than his talent as an artist.

[1] This was also the year in which Dr. John Morgan, the "Founder of American Medicine," made his well-remembered tour of "Italia, nurse of the softer arts." Astounded by the perfection of the arts of the ancients, he wrote in his journal, "My soul is struck at the review, and the ideas expand." Presented to the Pope and the King of Sardinia, Dr. Morgan recorded his impressions of anatomical lectures at Padua and various Italian hospitals and medical schools.

A year after Benjamin West left Rome, another American, Henry Benbridge, arrived there to study with Raphael Mengs, —a young man of twenty-one who had come from Philadelphia and who was to spend five years in Italy and England. It was he who went to Corsica, commissioned by James Boswell to make a portrait of the patriot Pasquale Paoli, which was presently exhibited in London with great applause, and who was to spend the rest of his days as a popular portrait painter in Virginia and Charleston. Then a third American, John Singleton Copley, appeared in 1775 on a tour of Italy suggested by West, his master, who had written to him, "By that you will find what you are already in possession of, and what you have to acquire." West added, regarding the Renaissance painters, "Every perfection in the art of painting is to be found in one or another of their works," and he specified Raphael, Michelangelo, Correggio and Titian as the source from whence all taste in the arts had flowed. "All the others," he continued, "have formed their manner from these, so they are but second place painters." People in America thought of painting as no better than any other ordinary trade, hairdressing, tailoring, shoe-making or tavern-keeping, Copley observed in one of his own letters; and in fact a book published in Boston in 1786 classed "inside, house, miniature and portrait painters" all together.[2] Copley wished to see Italy in order to acquire that "bold, free and graceful style" which the dictates of nature could scarcely give him; and he felt that the Laocoön and the Apollo Belvedere left "nothing for the human mind to wish for." Then he copied a Correggio at Parma, commissioned by one of those

[2] As late as 1811, S.F.B. Morse, arriving in London, wrote that art was looked upon at home as "an employment suited to a lower class of people." He was surprised and pleased to find that in England it was a constant topic of conversation.—Morse, Letters and Journals, Vol. I., p. 46.

Englishmen who seemed almost as numerous in Italy as they were in Boston, so that he passed "from one town to another, as from Boston to Roxbury," with English houses to visit all the way. He was fortunate, for the inns were "abominably nasty," as Smollett had said a few years before, "enough to turn the stomach of a muleteer," even though cardinals, prelates and princes lodged there, and "the victuals were cooked in such a manner as to fill a Hottentot with loathing." It is true that the unæsthetic Smollett was also testy.

In Rome, Copley met Ralph Izard, the American envoy to Tuscany, whose portrait he painted there with Mrs. Izard and the sketch she had made of Roman sculpture, with the Coliseum in the background; and he accompanied Izard to Paestum, which had been discovered only thirty years before. Buried in ruins and overgrown, it had lain concealed for centuries until a wandering artist in 1745 found and sketched a few of the outcropping pillars, and after this the wild growth of plants and the soil were removed from the temples so that the large halls stood forth as of old. Since then the vines had grown up again, fig-trees shot up from the floors and violets and red stock sprouted in the crevices and clefts, as one saw in the etchings of Piranesi who, thirteen years after Copley's visit, drew the Greek temples just before his death. For these years of excavation were the years of Piranesi, who was sketching in the Forum when Copley and West were there,—while he directed a workshop for the restoration of antiques,—creating those imaginative views of Rome, architectural fantasies and visions, that tourists were to buy for generations. Who could forget his great piazzas, surrounded by palaces and domes, crossed with ruts, littered, unkempt, dusty, with huge golden coaches laden with lackeys passing by and vagabonds asleep against a column? Piranesi's prints were to be seen in Philadelphia, New York,

Charleston and Boston. To Copley, Paestum, "older than Rome ... with its singular style of architecture ... the first dawning of that science among the Greeks," was a place of as much curiosity in its fine bay along the shore as any he had seen except Pompeii.

As Anglo-American colonials, Copley and West quite naturally returned to England for the rest of their lives, while others, after the Revolution, naturally turned homeward with relics of "the softer arts of Italy." They brought boxes of perfumes, shaped like books, or statues for their gardens,—pagan goddesses, caryatids, nymphs and fauns,—or collections of prints and frames, one with a procession of muses that inspired home-made mantels in plaster or wood. Piranesi had published a pattern-book for mantel-pieces that also appeared in Philadelphia where a few merchants, travelling abroad, had picked up painted furniture that seemed to go with Palladian country-houses. But the statesmanly minds of the Revolutionary epoch, cultivated as they might be, were less concerned with art than with agriculture, sometimes because they had read Arthur Young's travels but mainly because they were building a nation at home. They were especially concerned with the contrast between America, where all was "young, vigorous and growing," as West said in Rome, and an Italy that seemed to be "old, infirm, decaying"; and Copley's friend Ralph Izard of South Carolina was typical of them all in his interests and tastes. A graduate of the English Cambridge, he was a lover of music who regretted that he found no opera in Rome, and he delighted in the beautiful bronzes that had been found in Pompeii and that "surpassed all imagination." He had seen the great collection of pictures at Düsseldorf and was sorry that he had not been able to see the Elector Palatine's collection at Mannheim, but, feeling deeply that there was "no freedom in any state in Italy," he was interested especially in soil and profitable fruit trees. He was concerned in Florence in 1774 with the planting of white mulberry trees at his Goose Creek plantation, and he studied the soil in Lombardy and Piedmont where the best silk was produced, hoping he might produce as good at home.

Thomas Jefferson, the minister to France who followed Benjamin Franklin when *le bon Quacker* was tired and wished to go home, had only "a peep into Elysium,"—Jefferson's phrase for Italy,—where he too was mainly interested in farming. He had been in love with a marble Diana that he saw in Beaujolais and he gazed "whole hours like a lover" at the Maison Carrée, for he never lost a chance to study the beautiful art of architecture, hoping to form the taste of his countrymen at home.[3] The "wonders of Roman antiquity" Jefferson was never able to see, though he visited the Certosa of Pavia that suggested his first designs for the University of Virginia at Charlottesville. Writing to Maria Cosway, the golden-haired Anglo-Florentine wife of the miniaturist Richard Cosway with whom he had spent so many weeks sightseeing in the outskirts of Paris,—where Cosway was always busy at his miniature-painting,—he recommended subjects for her to "consecrate to fame," among them a picturesque scene near Milan. It was "a castle and a village hanging to a cloud in front, on one hand a mountain cloven through to let pass a gurgling stream, on the other, a river over which is thrown a magnificent bridge," with rocks, olive trees, herds and so on. "I insist on your painting it," Jefferson wrote to the charming Maria, with whom he was obviously head over heels in love,—his *Dialogue of the Head and Heart* was a letter to her; but Jefferson, when he was not

[3] It is recorded that in 1787 the first born American architect, Charles Bulfinch, the builder of the Boston State House, was "moved to tears" when he first entered St. Peter's.

involved either in gallantry or architecture, was interested, above everything else, in rice. On his brief visit to Genoa, Milan and Turin, he also looked into the making of Parmesan cheese, but, hoping to forward the culture of rice especially in South Carolina, he toured the great north Italian rice-fields. He interviewed the owners and talked with the peasants, and, because it was forbidden to export the rice, he filled his pockets with the seed.[4]

At the moment when Jefferson was in Turin in 1787, Goethe had almost reached the end of his tour of the peninsula. For Goethe, who was thirty-eight years old, the hope of seeing Italy had been, as he said, a kind of disease, and this had reached such a height that he dared not open a Latin book or glance at an engraving of Italian scenery. For the rest, he was interested in virtually everything, in stones, plants, animals and agriculture, while, travelling at last in Italy, he was an example in his tastes of the general mind of this classical age of travel. He was devoted to architecture, Palladio and Vitruvius whose book left "glorious impressions" on his mind,— he read this author "like a breviary"; and at the same time, absorbed in the relics of ancient Rome, he had no sympathetic feeling for the Middle Ages. In Venice he delighted in Tintoretto and Titian, but for him the pre-Raphaelite world was barbarous or Gothic,[5] and he passed through Perugia without seeing Perugino and, visiting Assisi, he ignored Giotto. He

[4] Jefferson, who both read and wrote Italian, sent his young protégé William Short to visit all the Italian cities he had not been able to see himself. From Venice, Verona, Padua, Bologna and Rome, where he spent three months, Short sent Jefferson letters about everything he saw, from the making of wine and macaroni to the Pantheon and the Forum.

[5] Note, however, his letter from Padua, September 17th, 1786: "I have seen pictures by Mantegna, one of the older painters, at which I am astonished. What a sharp, strict actuality is exhibited in these pictures . . . Thus was art developed after the barbarous period."

had eyes there only for the Temple of Minerva. Guercino's little Cento meant more to him than Florence, where he "ran rapidly over the city." Three hours there were enough for Goethe, while Guercino, "intrinsically bold, masculine and sensible," pleased him as this painter pleased Byron later. Nor did Goethe have any interest at the time in Dante. He cared as little for the mystical as for the mediaeval, and in this he spoke for the eighteenth-century mind.

A hundred years later, an American writer, in a panoramic novel, carried one back to the very heart of this period in Italy when the heir apparent of Pianura,—which might have been Parma or Mantua,—visited the courts of Florence, Naples and Rome. Before she wrote *The Valley of Decision,* Edith Wharton absorbed into her pores the myriad details of this late eighteenth century civilization, reading Goethe, Goldoni, Gozzi, Dr. Burney and Arthur Young while she spent many springs wandering through the country. She evoked most vividly the old static feudal order, with the toiling serf and the heaven-sent prince or duke, the people living in unlighted hovels while comedies, cards and intrigue filled the days in the regal or ducal courts. There the drama was still alive, with the Venetian playwrights and Metastasio, the librettist, at the court of Vienna, and all through the century the musical world was active too with Pergolesi, for instance, and Cimarosa. But, like the plastic arts, literature was dead, or one might say it was paralysed in the network of academies that existed in every city from Turin to Palermo. As one saw in Edith Wharton's novel, the poet Alfieri was beginning to spread the ideas of the French Revolution, and the Illuminati, the bugbear of princes and priests, had begun to set the Italians dreaming of freedom. But this was only a dusk of dawn in the world of Erethrean shepherds, the Frigid, the Transformed, the

Wrapped-up, the Twisted, the Insipid, the groups of poetasters who looked to the Roman Arcadia upon whom they depended as the supreme arch-flock. At that time poetry led one over "vast meadows of green baize enamelled with artificial flowers among streams that did nothing but purl." So wrote the novelist Howells a century after. No one would listen to political problems at any of the Italian courts until the question of the last coin was settled, or the last bas-relief that had just been dug up, or the date of an intaglio, or some matter of counterpoint or of the construction of a line in Ovid. Or a question of the relative merits of Ariosto and Tasso. This was the world that Benjamin West had known in Rome and that was virtually unchanged four decades later.

CHAPTER II

WASHINGTON IRVING AND
WASHINGTON ALLSTON

FORTY YEARS had passed since Benjamin West departed from Rome when Washington Irving arrived there in 1805, in a vettura from Naples and Sicily which "the ancients so delighted in" and "where every step," he wrote, was "enchanted ground." Sailing down from Genoa, his ship had been seized by a privateer and a crew with rusty cutlasses, pistols and stilettoes, and this had predisposed him to see banditti everywhere when he had set foot again on Italian ground. But the pirates had released him when they saw the letters of introduction which this young man bore on his person, for Irving, already a man of the world, an engaging American of twenty-two, was taken up by the *grand monde* everywhere. In Genoa he had been presented to the cardinal archbishop and the doge, and among the first persons he met in Rome were Canova, Madame de Staël and the minister from Prussia, Baron von Humboldt. His elder brothers in New York had sent him on the grand tour for the sake of his education and for reasons of health. The ship on which he sailed from Genoa had been despatched to Sicily to pick up there for America a cargo of wines.

Irving, who was bent on learning to write, noted in his journal that "men discover taste and fancy in Italy." He remarked that the Italians "place gay flowers in their hats," and

13

how different were their "poetic fields" from "our honest American hills and dales where," as he added, "stubborn fact presides." As he entered Rome, he could not contain the crowd of ideas or emotions, or the wonder and curiosity inspired by this mistress of the world, and his eye roved rapidly from side to side, eager to grasp every object but continually diverted. Humboldt, the brother of Alexander, received him politely, and Prince Torlonia, the banker, invited him to a Roman *conversazione*. Visiting Canova's studio, he found the great sculptor at work on statues of the Bonaparte family, Madame Mère and Napoleon's sister Pauline, the Princess Borghese, as well as Napoleon, "naked in the style of the ancients," the so-called high style of Greece that Winckelmann had popularized with what he described as its "calm and noble beauty." Greece itself in Winckelmann's time had been a Turkish province that was virtually inaccessible to artists and explorers, and even the ruins of Sicily were still almost unknown, so that Winckelmann had seen Greek art in Roman copies only when he conceived his notion of ideal beauty. One should choose beautiful portions of different works, Winckelmann said, and reconstruct them harmoniously in a single figure,—the recipe also of Raphael Mengs in painting,—and this was what Canova had done when he replaced in sculpture Bernini's fantastic flourishes and operatic whims.[1] Canova was all grace and elegance, rather Italian than Roman or Greek, in spite of the cult of antiquity that he represented, and Irving must have found him sympathetic, for his own talent in prose was all elegance and grace. Irving shared the fashionable taste for the Bolognese Caracci, and for Guido Reni's "Aurora" and Domenichino, as

[1] Among travellers of the time, Irving was notable in being impressed by Bernini's churches,—though he said they were "overcharged with ornament,"—and his "most remarkable" St. Theresa.

well as for the "inimitable" Claude and Poussin. He conceived for Italian music a lifelong love.

For the rest, near the pyramid of Caius Cestius, Irving visited "a large field in which they bury foreigners," he wrote in his journal, the Protestant cemetery of years to come where famous poets were to lie near the author of *Two Years Before the Mast*. Then, one evening, he dined with Madame de Staël, astonished by the flow of her conversation and the searching questions with which she plied this young man who had come from the republic of the West. Irving had read her *Delphine,* but he could scarcely have known that she was collecting impressions for *Corinne,* the great *Kultur-roman* of these opening years of the century that was to be published two years later. This forerunner of *The Marble Faun,* and of George Eliot's *Romola,* as a vade-mecum of tourists in years to come, was a glorified guidebook to Italy, centring in the all-conquering muse who was named for the Grecian poetess, Pindar's rival. Multitudes thronged about Corinne, the most beautiful woman in Italy who was attired like Domenichino's sibyl, in blue over a robe of virgin white, tuning her lyre at the Capitol and improvising while the crowd threw laurels and myrtle at her feet. The greatest woman of her day, the cynosure of artists, who was to die at last of a broken heart, rejected by Lord Nevil for whose sake she defied the world, became for many a bluestocking the beau ideal. How far did not Margaret Fuller, for one, model herself on this poetess, this *improvisatrice* of an earlier Rome who refused to be judged by the common herd and travelled with Lord Nevil to Naples and Venice, ignoring the laws that were applicable to ordinary persons? With Nevil she discussed religion and art (airing the views of Lessing and Schlegel on which Madame de Staël descanted in *L'Allemagne*), visiting churches, palaces, tombs, exploring Rome, like Augustus Hare

—except that he walked while they drove in her carriage. Corinne, the cicerone, lectured her lover, that young man of "noble and foreign aspect." They visited by moonlight the Fountain of Trevi where, after a period of separation, she saw his face reflected beside hers in the water, and they visited the Coliseum also by moonlight, as every traveller in the future contrived to do.[2] It seemed to be always moonlight in this novel.

Irving, who talked with Madame de Staël on still another occasion in Rome, might well have met the original of Lord Nevil also, another American, a rich young man who spent many years in Italy and France, the first American archæologist. The son of a "signer" from South Carolina, John Izard Middleton had been educated in England, like Ralph Izard, at Cambridge, and he had often appeared in Paris, when Washington Irving was there, in the salons of Madame Récamier and Madame de Staël. Madame Récamier had given him a copy of Gérard's portrait of herself which he took back to Charleston when he returned for a while,—with his wife, the daughter of a Swiss banker living in Naples,—but he was not entirely pleased when Madame de Staël told him that the character of the lover of Corinne was drawn from his. For, with his imperious manner and his sensitiveness and fine mind, Lord Nevil was indecisive, nervous and timid. Middleton himself, leaving Cambridge, had soon gone to Italy where he explored the so-called Pelasgic ruins, the rock-cut tombs of

[2] "The sun of Italy should shine on festivals, but the moon is the light for ruins. Sometimes through the openings of the amphitheatre, which seems to tower to the clouds, a portion of heaven's vault appears like a dark blue curtain. The plants that cling to the broken walls all wear the hues of night. The soul at once shudders and melts on finding itself alone with nature. 'Ye solemn scenes,' cried Corinne, 'how are the storms of passion calmed by nature, who thus peacefully permits so many generations to glide by!' "—Madame de Staël, *Corinne*.

Valmontone, the remains at Palestrina, and the great walls of the "Cyclopean region." Of these he made water-colour sketches that appeared, with his own text, in the *Grecian Remains in Italy* of 1812, drawings that were found to be accurate by photographers later.[3] The first contribution made by an American to the knowledge of classical antiquity, as Charles Eliot Norton said of Middleton's work, this book, appearing in the last years of the struggle with Napoleon, which filled the public mind, was virtually ignored.

Did Irving fall in with John Izard Middleton? At least he had met in Paris another artist who painted his portrait there, John Vanderlyn from the Hudson river, a protégé of Aaron Burr, whom Irving encountered again when he appeared in Rome. The only American who was trained in France as a follower of David when his contemporaries were studying in England with West, Vanderlyn was to spend two years in Rome sketching in a life-class with students from Germany and Holland, Sweden and Denmark. Washington Allston worked there beside him, the only other American artist in the city. Vanderlyn, who lived in the former house of Salvator Rosa, made a few copies in the Vatican also, and it was in Rome that he painted the "Marius Amid the Ruins of Carthage" that was exhibited in Paris in 1808. There, in the Salon, examining the pictures, Napoleon pointed to it and said to the director, "Give the medal to that one." Vanderlyn drew his figure of Marius from one of the Pope's guards, taking the head from a bust of the general in Rome, and everyone recognized in the scene the ruins of Hadrian's villa and those of the Claudian

[3] W. J. Stillman, for one, the American consul at Rome from 1861-1865, who was struck by the extraordinary accuracy of Middleton's drawings. Of Stillman's own photographic studies of the Pelasgic walls, Norton said that they were "probably more thorough than those of any other living archæologist."

said, at a time when such things could be said in praise, that Allston was a painter born to renew the sixteenth century. To another friend he wrote that Canova had spoken to him of Allston "in very warm terms of admiration" regarding the "facility and exquisitiveness with which Allston modelled,"— for Allston worked at sculpture also in Rome.[6]

Coleridge left Rome hastily, fearing that Napoleon might blockade England. Besides, though Americans were free to travel, the Corsican Ogre had given orders to arrest all British subjects who were at large in his dominions. The travel-writer Joseph Forsyth, seized in Turin by the police, spent eleven years in a French prison. As for Washington Irving, he had already quitted Rome, leaving Allston to remain for three years longer, but the friendship of Coleridge, Allston and Irving was to be renewed when Allston returned to England, where Irving was living. Whether as "a poet, a painter or a philosophic analyst," in Coleridge's words, Allston was always dear to this English writer who published a series of essays in a Bristol journal in order to assist his American friend; and it was while visiting Allston, who was ill at Brighton, that Coleridge read Irving's *Knickerbocker*. This was the book for which Allston drew two illustrations. Meanwhile, in Rome, Irving and Allston had been constantly together, rambling among ruins and olive groves or under the pines of the Villa Borghese or at the Caffé Greco where the artists foregathered. Together they visited the galleries, and Allston showed Irving the masterpieces,—ignoring other pictures,—the works that moved him as a painter. He was especially devoted to Poussin

[6] "To you alone of all contemporary artists does it seem to have been given to know what nature is—not the dead shapes . . . but the life of nature revealing itself to the Phænomenon, or rather attempting to reveal itself."—Coleridge to Allston, *Unpublished Letters*, Vol. II, pp. 152-154.

and Claude, who was full of the calm grace of the Italian landscape. Allston had been impressed, on his way to Rome, with the truth of Turner's Swiss scenes which Ruskin, who was not yet born, was to celebrate in time, but his own work was always to savour of Raphael, Giorgione, Correggio, Titian, of whom one caught glimpses in it here and there. Irving remembered how Allston was moved by Michelangelo's Moses, by St. Peter's, which they entered with mute reverence and awe, and by the Apollo Belvedere, a "sudden intellectual flash," as Allston described it, "filling the whole mind with light and light in motion." Rambling with Allston about Rome, visiting villas and terraced gardens, in the bland air, under the serene sky, Irving, who was so soon to return to study law in New York, asked why he should not stay in Rome and become a painter. At home he had taken drawing lessons, and, with a little talent, or more than a little, he had almost a passion for landscape painting. Among these palaces, statues, fountains and beautiful Italian scenes, he dreamed of remaining there with Allston as companion.

But this was for a moment only. Irving was soon on his way. He was eager to get back to Paris for a course of lectures, and he travelled through wild romantic passes of the Apennines, —missing both Florence and Venice,—to Bologna and Milan. He liked to think the roads were infested with robbers, and it was true that crosses nailed on the trees marked certain spots where travellers had indeed been robbed and murdered. Perhaps it was then that he conceived the picture in *Tales of a Traveller* of an English travelling carriage, "an epitome of England, a little morsel of the old island rolling about the world," drawn by half a dozen horses. Within was the portly citizen with his wife and his daughters, and a landaulet followed with their luggage. One saw, from the Italian road, the bluff-looking face of the master in his gingerbread travelling-cap looking out of the window, the trunks, portfolios and dressing-cases and the beef-fed servants, looking down from their heights with contempt on this foreign world. There were the fine fresh young ladies just out of boarding-school and equipped with boxes of water-colours, busily sketching, enchanted with the savage scenery, so like what they had read about in Mrs. Radcliffe's thrilling tales of horror. Then they saw the fierce whiskered faces peering over the rocks and the carbines and stilettoes gleaming among the bushes.

Of course, there were scenes like this on many of the Italian roads with English milords driving through the country, or prosperous art-loving self-made men like Ruskin's father, the sherry-merchant, who was to be seen there later with his wife and his son. There were undoubtedly bandits like those with whom Irving filled the tales that he was to write in Paris in 1824; and, while Fenimore Cooper pooh-poohed them,[7] Hawthorne, as late as the fifties, escaped a robbery only by a week or two. Then there was the French writer Taine, who was prevented for a month from visiting Paestum even in 1864, and who wrote in his book *Rome and Naples*, "Everywhere brigands. Nobody speaks of anything else." But how did it happen that writers referred to them so often when travellers in the eighteenth century so seldom mentioned either brigands or the ghastly inn-keepers of whom Irving wrote, true as it was that Winckelmann had been robbed and murdered, on his way north, at Trieste?

It was the Gothic mood, coming into fashion, that caused the literary eye to select these scenes, and Washington Irving's

[7] "The marvels about banditti and assassins are enormously exaggerated . . . A man of ordinary prudence may go from one extremity of the country to the other with very little risk."—J. Fenimore Cooper, *Gleanings in Europe—Italy*, Vol. II, p. 235.

Tales of a Traveller was to popularize further a state of mind of which *The Castle of Otranto* had been the germ. Walpole had created, years before, the Gothic castle of romance, with its sensational machinery of moonlight and wind, its battlements, towers, trap-doors and underground vaults; and when Mrs. Jameson exclaimed in her *Diary of an Ennuyeé* in 1826, "O for the pencil of Salvator, or the pen of a Radcliffe!" she fully expressed the temper that Walpole had evoked. These were the years of Lady Morgan's *Life and Times of Salvator Rosa,* the Neapolitan painter who had lived in the Abruzzi, joining one of the companies of bandits there amid "rocks, caves, fogs, dens and shades of death," and whose wild and gloomy imagination so fascinated the English mind that most of his pictures were to be found in England. Moreover, everyone read *The Mysteries of Udolpho,* which coloured the general view of the Italian scene, for one could not but share the terrors of the young French noblewoman who had been shut up in the vast Italian castle. There, in the heart of the Apennines, silent, lonely and sublime, surrounded with shaggy steeps and precipices, listening to the wind among the pines, Emily, within the mouldering walls, heard the wolves howling in the woods outside. Mysterious figures appeared on the ramparts, mysterious lights in the corridors, and there were apparitions everywhere, with tracks of blood upon the stairs and strange sounds from the vaults where deeds of horror were no doubt committed. Montoni may have been himself a captain of the bandits whom Emily thought she saw among the rocks, and he still kept his troop of bravoes in these desolate and solitary mountains.

Irving, who shared with Washington Allston a taste for ghost-stories and robber-tales, as well as for the romantic trappings of mediæval castles, had been predisposed to see in Italy during this early visit the scenes that appeared later in his writings. Moreover, in Genoa he had actually witnessed the execution of a bandit, and he had seen over the gate of the town of Terracina an iron cage containing a murderer's skull. At the inn there,—an excellent inn, as a matter of fact,—later travellers, like Longfellow, "expected to see"[8] what Irving had imagined in *The Inn at Terracina*, on his drive up from Naples to Rome,—something sinister, at any rate, if not the actual bandits who were in league with the inn-keeper in Irving's tale. There Irving had placed the belated travellers, the old Polish count and his beautiful daughter, followed by the Spanish princess and her son, all of whom were besieged in the night, in this little ancient lazy town, by the formidable band of mountain robbers. It goes without saying that the Polish girl, in the presence of the young Spaniard, sang to her guitar a Spanish romanza that had "something of love and melancholy" in it, while the bandits, who were ultimately foiled, were picturesque in the extreme,—Salvator himself could scarcely have done them better.

For Irving's pictorial imagination loved to dwell on these dashing types that were to appeal also to Byron, especially the bandits on their mountain heights, among wild rocks and rugged oaks, that appeared in so many paintings and illustrations of the moment. It pleased him to describe their muscular figures, with pistols thrust into their sashes of silk and a handkerchief thrown loosely about the neck, with conical hats that streamed with ribbons and with brightly coloured breeches, leaning perhaps on a carbine, surveying a valley. He seemed to be sketching them for a picture that he would have liked

[8] See also the remark of James Russell Lowell on his first visit to Italy in 1851. Spending the night at Terracina, he found it "nothing like what I expected to see . . . The inn is one of the least cutthroat looking places I ever saw."—Lowell, Letter of 1851.

to paint in their indolent noontime repose on a woody summit, perhaps with a flock of white goats browsing beside them. They were among the types whom one soon saw on the Spanish steps, models waiting for the painters, and many American artists were soon to gather there with feelings that were more or less coloured by Irving and Allston.

CHAPTER III

THE SCHOLARS

WHEN THE roads of Europe were opened again, with the defeat of Napoleon, who had raged over the continent for so many years, travellers from all the world appeared again in Italy and, among these, a number of American scholars. Along with the merchants, they were struck by the contrast between prosperous America and the fallen magnificence and languor of the Italian scene, where all things visible were in disrepair, cracking, crumbling, peeling, rotting, and everything semed to speak of an irrecoverable past. "The moral and intellectual grandeur of Italy" was "mutilated and faded," a certain tourist observed in 1817; "her civil and political institutions" were "exhausted and decrepit," [1] and, driving through the country one could see that agriculture had made no progress whatever since the days of Cincinnatus. The same implements were in use that one found in ancient bas-reliefs, the shepherds were the very type of the mythical Pan and the husbandman drove through the furrows the old plough of Virgil's time, dragged by four white oxen, yoked abreast. The rude wains were drawn by buffaloes on the Roman Campagna. Entering Italy one turned instinctively from what *is* to what *was*, another traveller presently remarked, and the change from America,

[1] *Rambles in Italy in the Years 1816-1817*, by an American, Baltimore, 1818, p. 3.

26

said a third, was from movement to repose, from hope to memory, for the country had "sunk into a state" that was "half slumber and half despair."

It was not the Americans only who spoke in this manner of Italy, which Lamartine described as "the land of the dead," and various Italian poets and prophets were to raise their voices presently against the degradation of their country. Vittorio Alfieri, a child of the French Revolution, had done so by implication in his plays, and the early odes of Leopardi struck a patriotic note that found an echo later in Mazzini's writings. The nation did not yet exist. Italy, as Metternich said with contempt, was "only a geographical denomination," and Austria held the peninsula, controlling it through the despots who ruled its principalities, grand duchies and kingdoms. The organized old European regime, standing behind Austria, meeting at the Congress of Vienna in 1815, affirmed that Italy, as a nation, should not exist, and what Alfieri remarked of Piedmont might have been uttered of all the states,—"No high thing could be done or said" there. The police of Rome had a special surveillance for "the class called thinkers," inasmuch as ignorant people were easier to govern, and the Duke of Modena forbade his subjects even to read Dante because he had denounced the rule of tyrants. The Austrian emperor, addressing the professors of the University of Pavia, said, "Remember that your duty is to form not learned men but obedient subjects," and his minister Metternich, calling himself a spider spinning a vast web, ridiculed the Italian "cry for liberty and reform." Several decades were to pass before Mazzini's question, "Are we to have a country?" had a positive answer when those whose motto was "Italy shall be" unseated the petty tyrants who denied the possibility of the nation's existence.

For the young American scholars who visited Italy during

these years, questions of this sort had only an abstract interest, and the first stirrings of the Risorgimento were scarcely manifest as yet when George Ticknor, for one, arrived in Rome. Ticknor, who had been sent abroad to study the modern languages of which he was to become a professor at Harvard, bore with him letters of introduction to numbers of eminent persons from Thomas Jefferson, who was retired at Monticello. Having studied in Paris and Germany, he was on his way to Spain when he spent in Rome the winter of 1817–1818, engaging a professor of architecture to explain the principles of his art and an archæologist to guide him about the ruins. This may have been one of those antiquarians, abounding in the city of the Caesars and the Popes, whom Washington Irving described in one of his tales and who "relished a building as an Englishman relishes a cheese . . . the more mouldy and crumbling it was" the better. Irving, whom Ticknor had encountered in Paris, enjoyed these cicerones and their pleasure in the "crusts and cheese-parings" of an architectural past, as he delighted in the picturesque that also appealed to the painters whose eyes could not have enough of the "decrepit" and the "faded." But Ticknor, who was not seriously concerned with the politics of Italy, cared only for the history of the ruins, not their visual effects, while, a courtier bent on knowing the world, he spent his evenings at Madame von Humboldt's, at Lucien Bonaparte's or the salon of Madame Merè. For Napoleon's family continued to live, long after Waterloo, in Rome, the traditional home of fallen grandeur. Ticknor lost no opportunity to talk with Napoleon's sister, the Princess Borghese, with her uncle Cardinal Fesch, Thorwaldsen and Canova,—who received every travelling foreigner, mallet in hand; and he was present with a party of Germans on the anniversary of Martin Luther's burning of the papal bull.

There Bunsen made a speech and Niebuhr wept. At a private audience the Pope praised the principle of toleration as if it had been a doctrine of his own religion, and he told the young man that the time would come when America, growing so rapidly, would be able to dictate to the old world.

Then, dining at Naples with an old archbishop, Ticknor spent several evenings with a dozen cognoscenti, assembled in the salon, who read aloud from Poliziano, or one of the tragedies of Alfieri, or a new pamphlet on Pompeii. He heard more of Alfieri, much more, in Florence, in the salon of the Countess of Albany who had been his mistress, the widow of the old sot who had once been Bonnie Prince Charlie, a priestess now presiding over the temple of the poet. Portraits of her lover Alfieri hung on every wall, his books and papers were kept like the relics of a saint,—he who despised all priests as he despised all sovereigns,—and the countess asked Ticknor whether he did not think that England had really gained by the exile of the Stuarts. She seemed to like him better when, answering with an emphatic Yes, he did not shrink from the proof to which she had put him. Presently he called on Byron at his villa on the Brenta. Ticknor had met Byron in London two or three years before when the poet already thought of settling in Greece, but now he was full of another plan to visit the United States and stand in the spray of Niagara among the Indians in the forest. Byron must have been reading the travels of Chateaubriand, who had visited America before he came to Rome, where he had acted for a time as Cardinal Fesch's secretary and whither he was to return as ambassador of France. The English poet invited Ticknor to stay for a few days with him, and he gave Ticknor a copy of his poems with a letter to Ali Pasha and a splendid pistol to protect him when he went to Greece.

Of the "new Americans," as they were called,—partly because few of their stripe, well-bred, scholarly and cultivated, had been seen there before,[2]—two or three others, young men, friends of Ticknor more or less, also appeared in Italy during these years. William Hickling Prescott, later the historian, spent six weeks in Rome in 1817, driving down from the Alps with Horace and Livy suspended in the net of his travelling carriage. He passed over the battlefields of Gonsalvo de Córdoba, recalling the days of Ferdinand and Isabella, the subject of Prescott's first historical work, and, fresh from his classical studies, he was soon to take up Italian to which he devoted a good year. He was to employ an Italian in Boston to read to him, every morning, Tasso, Ariosto, Alfieri, Poliziano, Petrarch, while, half blind already, he studied the *Divine Comedy* which his friend Ticknor had carried all over Europe. With Ticknor he corresponded about all these matters, discussing the question of Laura's real existence and the reason why the *Inferno* was so much read.[3] Meanwhile, actually with Ticknor in Rome was the future professor of Greek at Harvard who devoted himself to the study of antiquities there. Edward Everett, who had spent two years at a German university, also saw much of the Bonapartes, who received in the evenings, and the Princess Borghese, who showed him her diamonds and

[2] At this time virtually all Europeans had very vague ideas about the United States. George Bancroft, in Rome in 1821, was asked by a bookseller of what country he was. "An American from Boston," Bancroft replied. "Ah," said the bookseller, "I have a large book in my shop about Boston." This turned out to be a history of Hindustan. "Forgive me," said the bookseller, "a little mistake. I took Hindustan to be Boston."

[3] "Human nature is so delightfully constituted that it can never derive half the pleasure from any relation of happiness that it does from one of misery and extreme suffering,"—Prescott to Ticknor, 1824.

For the *North American Review*, 1824 and 1831, Prescott wrote two long essays, *Italian Narrative Poetry* and *The Poetry and Romance of the Italians*.

precious stones, struck this young man as a great coquette.[4] He went to see Byron too, sending him first some Harvard rhymes in which he mentioned the poet with respect, and Byron gave Everett letters to Greece and a set of all his published books containing corrections in his own handwriting.

These were the days when Byron was casting over Italy a spell that for two generations enchanted tourists, who could not enter the Coliseum without declaiming the poet's lines or stand for a moment unByronized on the Palatine hill. From the hour when, virtually an outcast, he left England in 1816 to the day when he went to Greece in 1823, Byron lived in Milan, in Venice, at Ravenna with the Guicciolis, at Pisa, then near Leghorn,[5] and in Genoa at last. He moved from town to town with his servants and his cavalcade, ten horses, eight dogs, five cats, three monkeys and an eagle, rising with *Childe Harold* to a pinnacle of fame, turning out tragedies along the way, investing the historic sights with a new magic. Who could look at the tomb of Cæcilia Metella, the Pantheon, the Dying Gladiator without thinking of what Byron said about them?— though he had so little feeling for the painters whose work made Italy the great museum of Europe.[6] In Switzerland he had fallen in with Shelley, an English fellow-reprobate who had joined him near the Euganean hills, and finally at Pisa,—

[4] Pauline Bonaparte's "languishing glances," directed towards another young man, caused Keats in 1820 to give up his walks on the Pincian hill. They brought him "intolerable thoughts of beauty and desire."— Sheila Birkenhead, *Against Oblivion: the Life of Joseph Severn*, New York, p. 122.

[5] It was there that the Kentucky artist William Edward West painted his portrait of Byron (1822). West, who had studied with Sully in Philadelphia, also painted portraits of the Countess Guiccioli, Shelley and Trelawny, with the black eyes and general air of a brigand.

[6] "Of painting I know nothing, but I like a Guercino."—Byron, Letter of 1816. Byron also said that he "loathed the infernal din" of Rubens's pictures and "spat upon" all the pictures of saints that glutted the churches of Venice.

with Leigh Hunt, another Liberal who was under a cloud,—where the three published a magazine together. Then, taking a villa on the coast, Byron received another young man who had met him on an American frigate in the harbour.

Byron had come aboard at Leghorn and a young lady on the ship asked him for the rose that he was wearing; then, making a magnificent exit, he was followed by George Bancroft, who rode on horseback to his villa. Bancroft himself, in sheer exuberance, had leapt off his own boat and swum two miles back to land. He had set out for Italy with a commission from Lafayette who had enlisted him in the cause of Italian liberty, and he brought copies of Lafayette's speeches to be secretly published in Italy, a cause that was sympathetic also to Byron. The poet had joined the Carbonari, the so-called charcoal-burners,—he had become one of the "good cousins,"—with the Countess Guiccioli's father and brother, attending their clandestine meetings in the forest near Ravenna. Bancroft stayed to lunch with Byron and Teresa Guiccioli, and they discussed "the things that are proper to be discussed," he wrote, "in the company of a very pretty woman." They talked, in other words, about music and *Lalla Rookh,* and Byron said again that he thought of going to the United States and bidding farewell forever to Europe. Then Bancroft diverted the conversation to literature, telling him how, on his own visit to Weimar, Goethe had praised the English poet. Byron was obviously pleased to hear of Goethe's good will, and he said this would go far to sustain him in the face of the abuse he was receiving from England.

Bancroft, to whom Byron gave the latest cantos of *Don Juan,* set out on horseback again with a pack-mule for his luggage, riding to Marseilles where he caught the packet that was to take him home after his long travels. But one can imagine

with what zest he, like the other young scholars,—Ticknor,
Everett and Prescott, all of them from Harvard,—witnessed the
Roman scenes that in a way they had known by heart in a day
when Latin was the general and paramount study. They had
all been drilled in Roman history from Romulus to Caesar,
and the marble busts in the Vatican and the Capitol were as
familiar to them as the heads of Washington and Franklin.
Everyone knew the Laocoön, the Antinous, the Discobolus and
the figure of Minerva musing under her helmet; while all
about lay the ground on which Caesar, Cicero and Brutus
had walked and the Flavian amphitheatre, the "Niagara of
ruins." There were the arches of Constantine and Titus, the
ruins of Domitian's villa, Sallust's garden, and one could spend
hours guessing at what spot the chasm opened and Marcus
Curtius leaped in with his horse. Or where the blood flowed
from the thirty wounds in Caesar's breast and the rivulet from
Virginia's bosom, stabbed by her father. There was the Appian
Way, hedged with flowering myrtles and orange-trees laden
with fruit, and beyond there was Tivoli among the scenes that
Horace pictured in his odes where Corinne had had her villa
facing the temple. The great *improvisatrice* had hung in the
grottoes Æolian harps, adding music to the perfume of the air.
Then there was Frascati where, under the pines, Cicero had
once pursued his studies, and not far off was the Lake of
Nemi and the sacred wood surrounding it where Diana restored Hippolytus to life. There was the spot where Cicero
was supposed to have been killed, and there was Pompeii, near
Naples, where the private life of the ancients revealed itself
for travellers to see,—the pictures that kept their original beauty,
the amphoras decked for a festival, the flour to be kneaded
into cakes, the tracks of wheels that brought antiquity suddenly
before one's eyes.

Among such scenes these young Americans felt all the "entusamusy" that Byron himself derided and professed to despise, he who liked to laugh at the drivel he inspired, while he preferred to be treated as a man of the world. He had been riding about Rome at the moment when Ticknor and Everett were there, galloping over the Campagna to the Alban hills and sitting for a statue by Thorwaldsen who was impatient with his pose and told him not to pretend that he was so unhappy. Then two years later, in 1819, the poet Shelley appeared in Rome, where he found the Coliseum overgrown with fig and olive trees and wide fields within the city walls. The gardens of the palaces were like wild woods of cypress and pine, and, as he wandered among them, Shelley took up again the composition of *Prometheus Unbound*. His little son William, dying in Rome, was buried where he was to lie himself near the pyramid of Caius Cestius, close to the spot where John Keats was also to lie, the poet who had come to Rome in 1820. Joseph Severn brought him in order that Keats, as he put it, would not have to march up to the battery alone, for the little poet with the glowing eyes, a medical student when they first met, had only a few months to live when they left London. Together there Severn, the painter, and Keats had visited picture galleries and the Elgin marbles that had been brought from Greece, and in Rome they lived at the foot of the steps in the Piazza di Spagna, the "Ghetto of the English," as it was called. At the Babuino end the piazza was filled with great travelling carriages, parked side by side under tarpaulin covers, kept by the English families who were flocking to Rome. Keats was able to walk a little on the Pincian hill near by and sometimes rode about on a small pony. His mind was as full of Greek images as the mind of John Gibson, the sculptor, who said to Severn that Rome was "the university of Art" where art was the principal subject of thought and conversation. Severn was to remain there for twenty years after Keats's death, and later he returned as the British consul.

Already the Spanish steps, on which Keats's room looked out, were the meeting-place of all the artists' models, who were costumed as brigands, sages, martyrs and who lounged there waiting for artists to carry them off to studios near by. There were pilgrims with scallop-shells, kerchiefed contadinas prepared to pray at some painter's wayside shrine, bandits off duty, with conical hats and bushy beards, Holy Families appropriately grouped already. There were theatrical assassins, Judases, Bacchuses, young St. Johns, shepherds in cloaks of goatskin or buffalo-hide, with the hair turned outward, looking like antique satyrs, white-bearded Eternal Fathers and fierce-eyed peasants from the hills who had come down for the winter for a chance to pose. All these types swarmed on the steps, above the boat-shaped fountain, or at the top by Santissima Trinità de' Monti that stood on the site of the ancient garden of Lucullus in a Rome where every sixth person was a priest or a monk and the air was full of the musical clamour of bells.

This was "that central clime" of which Hawthorne was to write, "whither the eyes and heart of every artist turn, as if pictures could not be made to glow in any other atmosphere, as if statues could not assume grace and expression save in that land of whitest marble." How many were drawn there, like Goethe, "weary of the North," or Winckelmann who, after twelve years in Rome, could no longer endure the cottages of his own country—the sharply cut roofs and the narrow valleys,—Winckelmann who had once thought of begging his way down from cloister to cloister, pretending he was ready to adopt the faith of Rome. How many Americans like Rembrandt Peale could say that, from boyhood, Italy, their reverie by day, was the torment of their dreams at night and who were to follow Benjamin West, Copley and Washington Allston to the city where artists felt at home. There, on the Pincian hill, or in the Via Sistina, or the Via del Babuino just below, Guido Reni and the Caracci had lived in little villas, and so had Salvator Rosa, Claude and Poussin. Turner first appeared in Rome in 1819, urged to do so by a fellow-painter who said that no one else could render the atmosphere of Tivoli and its "milky sweetness." Turner painted at this time his large "Rome from the Vatican," and he made there hundreds of sketches and watercolours.

Meanwhile, for a number of years already, a group of German artists had established themselves in Rome, the Nazarenes, so called because they wished to revive the early Christian life and mind and incidentally the early Christian painters. Converts from Protestantism, reverting to the Romish faith, they hoped to recover the earnestness of the primitive artists, feeling that the pure springs of Christian art had been diverted and sullied by the false pagan artists of the Renaissance. Correggio had painted the naked Antiope, Titian painted Venus and others painted St. Agnes as a mere pouting child or a merry carnal Magdalen exposing her breast, while Giotto's great theme was the life of St. Francis, Ghirlandajo's the life of the Virgin and Fra Angelico painted the life of Christ. True art, the Nazarenes felt, sprang from religion, and they preached the superiority of the artists who came before Raphael to those who had lost the mediæval spirit. They wished to put an end to the cult of the Bolognese painters, Guercino, Domenichino, Guido, the Caracci; and with Overbeck, joined by Cornelius and others, they too lived on the Pincian hill in the former monastery of San Isidoro, restoring in a spirit of religious fervour the neglected art of fresco and cultivating the hard outlines of the primitive artists. Overbeck himself, a saintly man, simple as a child, ascetic in appearance and character, solemn in his gestures, wore a long priestly sort of dress. He painted New Testament subjects and the lives of the Virgin and the saints, while his figures were like the dryest of the old Sienese artists. But, with their pale cold tints, they had no touch of the Sienese colour which Overbeck considered too sensuous for spiritual art.

These painters were to be remembered later not so much for their actual work as for the point of view they represented at a time when the primitives were either ignored or thought of as "like Chinese pictures, where all is so stiff and hard." [7] The primitives were considered quaint at best, and when the Italians brought back to Italy the pictures that Napoleon had carried away they left Fra Angelico's "Coronation of the Virgin" behind. They did not regard it as worth their pains to reclaim this great picture which was to remain as one of the glories of the Louvre; nor did they bother to bring back the Cimabue or the Giotto, the Simone Martini or even the Botticelli. The anti-mystical, anti-mediæval, classical taste of Winckelmann and Mengs still reigned over the world of connoisseurship, though Giotto was praised now and then as the founder of modern pictorial art and occasional kind words were bestowed also on Ghiberti. For the great sculptors of the early Renaissance were looked upon as Gothic too,—it was felt that even Michelangelo departed too far from "ideal beauty," [8]—and it was not until

[7] Hans Christian Andersen, *The Improvisatore*.

[8] The anonymous American, a cultivated man, who wrote *Rambles in Italy*, 1818, reflected the fashion of the moment when he said that Canova was the only sculptor since Phidias and Praxiteles to "inherit the taste and genius of these great masters." Michelangelo's energy was "sublime," but he "departed too much from the model of ideal beauty," and after him with Bernini and his followers sculpture degenerated into

Ruskin popularized the new point of view that the English-speaking world adopted it. The Nazarenes inspired not only the English Pre-Raphaelites thirty years later but the mind of Alexis François Rio, the Frenchman who met them in Italy and set out to give the world a new interpretation of Italian art. Like Chateaubriand [9] in reaction against the French Revolution and the rationalistic spirit of the eighteenth century, he had studied the paintings in the catacombs along with the primitive painters before he wrote *The Poetry of Christian Art*. "Does art breathe the religious spirit?"—not "Is the picture well painted?" was the question that Rio always asked, and, popular in England at about the time of the Gothic revival and the Oxford Movement, he was to inspire Ruskin more or less directly. Mrs. Jameson spread his doctrines,[10] and so did Lord Lindsay in *Sketches of the History of Christian Art*, praising those "neglected relics of an earlier, a simpler, and a more believing age" that "lie concealed under . . . the pictorial iniquities of the last three centuries.[11] Lord Lindsay celebrated

---

affectation and mannerism. This American writer was simply repeating what scores of European critics said, not least in ignoring Niccola Pisano, Donatello, Benedetto da Maiano, etc.

[9] Chateaubriand, however, ridiculed the Nazarenes, saying it was the *thought* of their time that believed, not the painting of the early painters. The Nazarenes said that Raphael degenerated and became a pagan in his later manner. "Be it so," Chateaubriand replied. "Let us be pagans like the Raphaelite Virgin; let our talent degenerate and grow enfeebled as in the picture of the 'Transfiguration'."—Chateaubriand, *Mémoires d'outre-tombe*, Vol. IV.

[10] Mrs. Jameson, who was very influential, insensitive as she may have been, remarked that her meeting with Rio in Paris (1844) was "the great event" of her life there. She visited the Louvre with Rio. John Gibson said he owed his start to Mrs. Jameson's praise in her *Diary of an Ennuyée*.

[11] "What a scene of beauty, what a flower-garden of art—how bright and how varied—must Italy have presented at the commencement of the sixteenth century." Lord Lindsay deplored the sacrifice after that time of hundreds of frescoes of Giotto and "other elders of Christian art . . . great and good men," that were then existing.—Lord Lindsay, *Sketches of the History of Christian Art, 1846*, Vol. II, pp. 389-390.

the Giotteschi, Niccola Pisano and Fra Angelico, and it was this book, largely, that led Ruskin to realize what a "blind bat" and "puppy" he had been at first. Henceforth Ruskin was to preach the gospel of art as great only when it expresses the spirit of religion and only in the masters who appeared before art was engulfed in what he called the "pride" of the high Renaissance.

This aesthetic revolution was to affect in time the mind of every writer on art and every traveller in Italy. Meanwhile, the artist's innocent eye, looking for the picturesque, found it in the Italian scene on every side, in much that degraded the country, from the social and political point of view, as well as in the ruins, mediæval and ancient. With Joseph Severn for a while in Rome lived Frederick Catherwood, an Englishman,—forgotten in England but known in America later,—who made the superb illustrations for John Lloyd Stephens's travel books about the Central American Mayan ruins. As an architect's apprentice in London he had heard much of Piranesi whose work led him, in 1821, to Rome, whence he went on to Sicily and Greece, to Karnak, Luxor, Thebes and Arabia Petræa, always drawing ruins. It was Catherwood's archæological drawing of Baalbec that first made these ruins widely known, but he found among Piranesi's scenes the style he later followed in his drawings of Guatemala and Yucatan. Well he knew, for instance, the desolate Baths of Caracalla where Shelley had wandered a year or two before him, among the "mountainous ruins," the "flowery glades" and the "dizzy arches suspended in the air." There, in the dark recesses, Maldura hovered in Washington Allston's Italian romance, *Monaldi*. Feeling in his misery that his own fortunes were akin to these ruins, Maldura "inhaled a kind of savage refreshment from walking over the wrecks of these proud piles."

Catherwood became in time an American architect and engineer. Meanwhile, the American painters began to arrive in Italy, only, however, in twos and threes before the eighteen-thirties, when Rome took the place of London as their European centre.

CHAPTER IV

THE SCULPTORS

THE SCULPTORS came early. There were portrait-sculptors, makers of busts, carvers of tombstones and mantelpieces from Boston, Vermont, New York, Kentucky, Ohio. Some of them had learned their trade as stonecutters or plaster-moulders, modellers of waxworks, urns or figureheads for ships,—like Hawthorne's Drowne of the wooden image; and they suddenly appeared, singly, and presently in scores, some of them settling in Rome, others in Florence. They almost rivalled the portrait-painters in these pre-photographic days when there was no good marble to be found at home and when there were no bronze-foundries or professional models. These were the sculptors who made the statues one later saw in city squares and in parks and public graveyards in the American cities,—where no one ever remembered the names of the artists,—created when, as someone wrote, "We always show people the cemetery" on drives through Mount Auburn, Laurel Hill or Greenwood. That was the day of the "firsts," moreover, the first American professional sculptor, the first equestrian statue, the first sculptural group, produced in the "great university of sculpture,"— William Roscoe's phrase for Rome,—or in Greenough's "dear, mind-your-own-business, beautiful Florence."

How many sculptors were there? There were certainly all but a hundred between 1825 and the Civil War time, most of them simply mechanics in the "statuary business," in a money-making trade, as one of them said. Provincial, conventional workmen, they were fertile in inventions, a pointing machine to be used in the making of busts or a lathe for reproducing irregular forms. One of them undertook to modernize the primitive method of quarrying and moving the marble at Carrara by organizing a stock company and building a railroad to take the place of the men who tugged the heavy marble sledges. In general, they befitted a time when, as Greenough remarked, "Our good folk think statues can be turned out like yards of sheeting"; but others, like Greenough himself,—Horatio Greenough,—might have said, "No merchant traffics in my heart." Sometimes their main thought was to set some stream of beauty flowing in the dry land they had left at home. Perhaps, as boys, they had astonished their fellow-villagers in Vermont by modelling the Recording Angel, colossally, in snow, or, like Canova himself, in his village boyhood, shaping a dog or a lion in sugar or butter. Artist and artisan alike were patronized by statesmen who obtained commissions for them from the nation or the states, in these days of the rapidly expanding and flourishing republic; and occasionally the statesmen were cultivated men like John Quincy Adams who took pleasure in addressing the sculptor in lines of their own.[1] Some of these artists shared Thorwaldsen's feeling,—and Winckelmann's before him,—that they had never existed before they saw Rome, that they had been "born" on the day when they entered the city, the "Mecca of the art world," as one of them called it, "the dream-land of my imagination." The great

---

[1] See John Quincy Adams's apostrophe to Hiram Powers:
"Artist! may fortune smile upon thy hand!
Go forth, and rival Greece's art sublime;
Return, and bid the statesmen of this land
Live in thy marble through all after-time!"

Danish sculptor himself had been there to greet them with his big heart and his helpful eye and hand.

Horatio Greenough, the pioneer, the earliest of all the aspiring brood, had first arrived in Rome in 1825, and there he lived for several months in the former house of Claude Lorrain, near those of Salvator Rosa and Nicholas Poussin. Below the Pincio, Thorwaldsen lived, in Piranesi's old house, with blocks of marble lying about in the great studio garden, overgrown with aloe, mallows and wild roses. The studio itself, with its rows of marble goddesses and gods, recalled the Vatican gallery of antique sculpture. Thorwaldsen, the reigning sculptor since the death of Canova in 1822, carried on the style of the Greek revival, with the repose and serenity that Canova had reintroduced in his search for Greek simplicity and beauty. Thorwaldsen had followed Canova in his busts, statues and bas-reliefs. In a Rome swarming with archæologists, where classical antiquities were being disinterred on every hand, all the sculptors were bent on creating Greek mythological figures, Ganymede, the Three Graces, Apollo, Adonis. The Englishman John Flaxman, a generation earlier, had formed the style of his outlines on Greek vases, and the work of the Welsh gardener's son John Gibson, who had studied with Canova, resembled that of the "Phidias of the North." The younger sculptors venerated this Danish artist whose mind was fixed on the heroic age of Greece and the graceful fancies of Anacreon and other Greek poets.

Such was the style established in Rome at the moment when Greenough arrived there, and all the American sculptors followed this more or less for at least another generation. They were predisposed to follow it because the American revolution had been largely conceived in the spirit of the ancient republics, one of the reasons why travelling statesmen, as late as the day of Saint-Gaudens in Rome, commissioned busts of Greek and Roman worthies. Demosthenes and Cicero were favourite subjects, and Horatio Greenough's colossal figure of the father of his country was to look like a Roman general, unhappily naked.[2] But Greenough, whom Thorwaldsen encouraged, was to undertake this work when he had settled in Florence a few years later, after a visit home to Washington and Boston, where he had grown up in a cultivated household. As a boy he had cut with a penknife in plaster a copy of a Roman coin, a stonecutter had shown him how to use a chisel, and he had learned how to model in clay from an encyclopædia before he fell under the influence of Washington Allston. For Allston had returned to the huckleberry pastures of Cambridgeport, where, with a window facing a garden, stood his "lone studio of New England," as a compassionate observer characterized it. There he continued to emulate the old Italian masters with subjects taken from Europe and the literary past, writing the novel *Monaldi* about an artist like himself who wished to revive the style of the *cinquecento*. Monaldi's rival, the poet Maldura, was also in love with Rosalie, who sang the songs of Pergolesi, and the novel took one back to the student days when Allston had seen so much of Coleridge and Wash-

[2] Greenough's "Washington," commissioned by Congress, thanks to the efforts of Fenimore Cooper, was, like Canova's "Napoleon," unclothed. Greenough is supposed to have had in mind the legendary figure of Olympian Zeus.

Greenough followed in some degree Canova's conception of Washington in his colossal statue in the capitol of North Carolina. This was a theatrical sprightly Italianate figure dressed in Roman armour, now only to be seen in the plaster cast at Canova's birthplace, Passagno; for the statue was burned with the building soon after it was installed in 1821. It had been commissioned on the advice of Jefferson, who said "old Canove of Rome" was the person to do it. At the time it was no doubt the greatest work of art in the country. Jefferson later brought over Italian marble-cutters for the buildings of the university at Charlottesville.

ington Irving. The courtly painter's conversation was wise and sympathetic, and Greenough, as a student at Harvard, had been constantly with him. Greenough thought of Allston as an eagle tied to a roost, for there was so little of the atmosphere of art about him, but he said that Allston, advising him to go to Rome, had taught him how to discriminate, think and feel.

When, returning to Italy, he settled in Florence, where he was to live for twenty-five years, Italian had long been Greenough's favourite language, and meanwhile he was saved from despair by the novelist Fenimore Cooper, whom he called "a father to me in kindness." It was "glorious Cooper" who gave him his first large commission, a group of two little boys who were taken to task for their nudity when they were first exhibited in Boston. For America was even more prudish than England, where there existed "a fatal horror of whatever partakes of the nude," as an English well-wisher of John Gibson put it. Greenough was known also for his busts of Cooper and Cooper's friend Lafayette, of Francis Alexander, the Boston painter, and the Marquis Capponi, the historian, Prescott's correspondent; but this outspoken masculine man, ardent, with a large mind and heart, was "cunninger in talk" than with his chisel. So said Emerson, who met him in Florence in 1833; and, although this great man was scarcely at home in the world of plastic art, he spoke for the sculptor's countrymen a hundred years later.

For Greenough was an original thinker in talk and in writing alike, the first American at least to announce the theory of functionalism and the doctrine that "form follows function." In incidental essays he pleaded for schools of design in America, observing that American manufacturers would have to design with distinction if they were to compete with French and English importers; for in England and France they had ransacked Italy and Greece to find new forms for their looms and their pottery and fabrics. Wedgwood, for one example, used Flaxman's designs. But Greenough's chief idea was that, in architecture, the outward form should express the internal functions and that buildings should be adapted to their position and uses. In Washington he had shuddered at the Smithsonian's battlements and towers, struck by the unfitness of this sombre pile, and he was annoyed by the wooden Gothic structures that bore so little relation to the real life of the country. Why, moreover, those meaningless attempts to domesticate the Parthenon, compelling banks, taverns and hotels to look like temples instead of looking like taverns, hotels and banks, forcing the functions of a building into a general form instead of discovering a form that expressed the functions. It was preposterous, Greenough thought, to adopt models merely for the sake of the eye or association instead of following "Greek principles, not Greek things," the principles that were so well expressed in the bald Yankee farmhouse that seemed to belong to the ground on which it stood.[3] The American sailboat and trotting-wagon were closer to Athens, Greenough said, than modern adaptations of Greek buildings. In short, America must invent forms of its own to suit its own needs and its own climate.[4]

[3] Thomas Cole's painting, "The Architect's Dream" (1840), was a perfect expression of everything to which Greenough objected. The architect lies asleep on the top of a huge Ionic pillar, while all about him, in his dream, rise Greek and Roman temples, an Italian palace, a pyramid and a Gothic church. The dream was realized in Mrs. Trollope's famous bazaar in Cincinnati, which had an Egyptian portico, Grecian pillars, Gothic windows, a Turkish dome and the tower of a Norman castle.

[4] Greenough's definition of the obelisk has been much quoted as an example of the meaning of functionalism. The function of an obelisk, according to Greenough, is to call attention to a memorable spot. "It

There were architects a century later for whom Greenough's words were holy writ, and in this way he survived not only his fame as an artist but the fame of his contemporaries in American sculpture. For one, there was Hiram Powers, who was also in Florence and whose reputation for a while was all-European, —"the first sculptor of his age," as a Florentine authority called him, "without a rival," said Thorwaldsen, "in the making of busts." "The entrance of Powers upon the field," this patriarch of sculptors said, "constituted an era in art"; and replicas of "The Greek Slave," about which Mrs. Browning wrote a poem, were bought for great houses in England and Russia. Powers even represented in his busts the "porosities of the skin," a perfection that seemed incredible to good critics of the time, and Queen Victoria admired this "fair stone" that shamed the "strong" by its "thunder of white silence," in Mrs. Browning's poem. Its nudity was warranted harmless when it was shown in London, and a committee of clergymen in Cincinnati agreed that it could be shown there without scandal, as an emblem not only of the Greek point of view but of the Greek revolution that was associated with Dr. Howe and Byron. When Powers's "Eve" was exhibited, people reminded themselves that the mother of mankind, among the flowers, had unquestionably been naked "and was not ashamed," and it was understood that there was no need to fear it would introduce "foreign indelicacy among our women." It was largely in reference to Powers and Greenough that Landor wrote to Emerson, "Sculp-

---

says but one word, but it speaks loud. If I understand its voice, it says 'Here!' and says no more."

A typical New Englander, Greenough disliked what he called the "silliness" of Borromini as well as the "meaningless splendour" of St. Peter's. But if he had heard the remark of an American cardinal that St. Peter's is intended to be "the theatre of the Church," he might have found this splendour functional also.

ture at the present day flourishes more than it ever did since the days of Pericles, and America is not cast into the shadow by Europe."

Yet Hawthorne was right enough when, a few years later, he suggested that Hiram Powers was really a mechanic, much as he enjoyed this "great man" whom he liked "all the better because he did not put his life wholly into marble." There was no doubt whatever about the lifelikeness of Powers's busts,—of Andrew Jackson, Webster, John C. Calhoun, the Grand Duchess of Tuscany and many another,—but there was no poetry in his composition and manual dexterity was Powers's leading trait as a practising artist. A Yankee from Vermont, he had grown up in Cincinnati, where he had worked in a clock-factory and repaired wax figures for a broken-down showman who might have been Artemus Ward; then he had been employed by a local museum in which he invented automata that represented the damned in the infernal regions. In this mechanical apparatus the life-sized figures emitted smoke, groaning and rattling their chains in a terrifying fashion, as in some vision of Dante suggested to Powers by Mrs. Trollope when she too had lived in Cincinnati. In Florence, Powers amused himself by inventing tools and gadgets, a Jew's-harp with two tongues, an open file that was of great use in finishing the surface of marble, a machine for punching holes through iron, a remedy for burns, a clever new method of curing complaints of the chest. He devised a plan for laying the Atlantic cable far better than the method that was tried and failed, and he liked to talk about flying-machines in the carefully preserved Yankee twang that pleased and amused Hawthorne in the eighteen-fifties.

It was rather Powers's character than his statues and his

busts that many, like the Brownings, found delightful,[5] for his talk was fresh, original and full of bone and muscle and his ideas were square, tangible and solid. Hawthorne, who said all this, was always glad to listen to the mill-stream of Hiram Powers's talk, whether about the buckeyes of Ohio, the hunters of the West or the dangers of blood-transfusion and the effects of draughts. Powers, in his linen blouse, a sculptor's cap on the side of his head, grey, bald, with his large eyes and impending brow, was, Hawthorne said, both delicate and tender, massive and rude of surface as he looked. Of the human eye, he remarked that it did not depend for its expression upon colour but only upon the form and action of the surrounding muscles, and he said that royal personages, as he had observed them while making their busts, had a certain coldness of demeanour peculiar to themselves. They had been taught from infancy that they were apart from the rest of mankind, and this surrounded them with an atmosphere through which ordinary human electricity could not pass. Powers was convinced that he alone was worthy to touch marble, so that he was at sword's points with other sculptors of every epoch and degree, and he thought the faculty of making busts was extremely rare and beyond the reach of Canova, Greenough or Gibson. He annihilated the poor visage of the Venus de' Medici (for which Hawthorne despaired of expressing his own admiration), and he showed his own busts of Proserpine and Psyche to prove

[5] "Mr. Powers, the sculptor, is our chief friend and favourite. A most charming, simple, straightforward, genuine American—as simple as the man of genius he has proved himself to be . . . The sculptor has eyes like a wild Indian's, so black and full of light you would scarcely marvel if they clove the marble without the help of his hands."— 1847. *Letters of Elizabeth Barrett Browning*, Vol. I, p. 222.

"Not only Americans turned to Powers. A Mr. Leighton, an Englishman, brought his son (later Lord Leighton) to him, to know whether to make an artist of him. Powers replied, 'Sir, you have no choice. He is one already.'"—Giuliana Artom Treves, *The Golden Ring*, p. 155.

that everything was right with them as everything was wrong with the unfortunate Venus. For the rest, he was resourceful in dealing with American business men. He had a pillory by the studio door where he displayed the bust of a patron who had been slow in paying, labelled "Delinquent."

While Powers and Greenough lived in Florence, most of the sculptors gathered in Rome about the living Thorwaldsen and the memory of Canova, although it contained a "smothering accumulation of treasures," as Powers had said when he first saw it. Rome oppressed Powers. He felt as if he had been "riding in an express train through a cane-brake" and had been "called upon to number the reeds"; and he doubted if he could have preserved his courage labouring and striving amid such an overwhelming crowd of artistic products. But others were happy to live in a city where the studios were open to one another and the sculptors generally gave and received advice. Meanwhile, the painters were gathering there, turning away from London, where Benjamin West had attracted so many pupils, and, among the first, Robert Weir who had lived with Greenough when he was in Rome in 1825. Weir had stopped in Siena, where he found Pinturicchio's frescoes "very exquisite," in advance of the taste of the time,[6] and he had made sketches for Dante's *Inferno* before he spent three of his months in Rome copying the frescoes on the ceiling of the Sistine Chapel. He was appalled by the "fogs of stench and heaps of filth" in the "ruinous, dirty, religious, irreligious city" that was nevertheless so full of beauties; and, like most Protestants of the time, he was both piqued and shocked by the spectacle of a beautiful young girl becoming a nun. "The

[6] To Joseph Forsyth, whom Byron and Shelley both read and who expressed the general taste of the time, these frescoes had been merely "a series of gaudy gilt pictures."

beauteous maid who bids the world adieu" was a favourite
subject of poets [7] as well as of painters; for it had all the
picturesque interest that clung to the monastic dress, the
floating veil of the religious and the iron grating. It somehow
suggested a scene from an opera or a play, and for many
Americans, visiting Italy, the whole country was like a stage,
while the Italians seemed to them like actors playing parts in
some poetic dream.

So felt the novelist Catharine M. Sedgwick, among the
peasants in the north, the old women with gay ribbons and
flowers in their caps, the girls in their gypsy-like hats with
spreading brims, and she felt this all the more when the King
of Piedmont appeared on his horse with servants in scarlet
liveries and officers attending. What a scene, moreover, was
the train of coaches passing on the road, drawn by mules
flaring with tinsel and jingling with bells, and ornamented
with towering collar-pieces, conveying the domestics of the
newly made King of Etruria, returning by this circuitous route
to Spain. There were the contadinas in their corsets of red silk,
with their embroidered petticoats and necklaces of coral, bearing a basket of grapes or a pair of live chickens, and the monks
with bare feet and tonsured heads following an ass with a bell
that was carrying provisions to the convent. There were the
pilgrims, too, in their long coloured garments, with shaggy
beards, cockle-shells and sandals. Even the approach to Italy
seemed like a backdrop on the stage, as one slid down towards
Lombardy through a pass in the Alps, catching a glimpse of a

[7] See, for instance, "The Nun," a canto in Samuel Rogers's *Italy*, the
long prosaic poem that everyone read in the thirties and forties and
that almost replaced *Childe Harold* as a favourite of tourists. One of
Robert Weir's most ambitious pictures was "The Taking of the Veil."
    In later years, Robert Weir, the father of J. Alden Weir, was
Whistler's teacher of drawing at West Point.

campanile, then pink houses, vines and lakes, white long-horned oxen and the blue sky.

In Rome, what Chateaubriand called the "fever of the ruins" naturally possessed most of the artists, along with the Campagna where this great writer wandered at night when he arrived as ambassador to the Holy See. On these waste lands where the plough-share of Cincinnatus had once struck, he watched his own shadow passing the moonlit aqueduct, remembering that Horace's Lydia, Tibullus's Delia and Ovid's Corinna had often crossed this untilled common-land. He knew all the little roads that had once been lined with villas, destroyed by Lombards, Saracens, Goths and Franks, with their pavements and their drains, their crops and their cattle; and he walked around the city walls reading the history of the European world in their various types of construction and architecture. He, moreover, expressed the feeling of all the landscape painters when he spoke of the beautiful lines of the Roman horizon, the gentle inclination of the plains in the foreground and the soft flying contours of the terminating mountains. All the surfaces, he said, united at the extremities by means of an insensible gradation of colours, and in such a way that one could not ascertain the point at which one ended and another began. This was the light one saw in the landscapes of Claude, and, although it seemed ideal and more beautiful than nature, it was indeed the light of Rome. The delicate clouds, like light chariots, borne by the wind with inimitable grace, suggested the appearance of the pagan deities under this mythological sky.

One can be sure that the American artists on the Campagna for years to come longed to catch the effects that Chateaubriand spoke of, the effects of the landscapes of Poussin too, perhaps with a ruined colonnade, a river, a forest on the left and a tower in the distance. They visited the rolling pastures and the cork woods to the west of the Via Flaminia that was Poussin's country, where one still saw the ancient fortified farm that figured in so many of his pictures. The painters delighted in sketching the solitary arch of an aqueduct with a shepherd and his flock gathered beneath it, and perhaps a golden thistle in the foreground, or the fallen columns and marble debris of the Roman Forum where mules grazed and cows lay on the turf. They observed a shepherd under a tree in the posture of Meliboeus with his naked legs stretched out as he leaned on his elbow, or a villager with a soft peaked hat and a timeworn cloak, lined with green baize, which he tossed carelessly over his shoulder. Or they were pleased by the sight of a girl, on the seashore, dancing, surrounded by peasants with flutes and tambourines, or a girl singing with another group, holding in her hand a chaplet of flowers that she seemed about to drop into the waves. But what did not serve the painters?—the grimy, narrow, dirty streets, the grey stone balconies hung with skirts and jackets, the yellow fruit of a lemon tree suspended over a mottled wall, the caps that were adorned with frayed peacocks' feathers. Or the crimson cords and tassels and the faded red waistcoats, or even the blind old creatures on the steps of the churches. They too were as picturesque as the groups of young priests who passed in their green or violet-coloured cassocks, or, for that matter, a flock of goats standing in a rocky cave or a blind girl among the ruins of Paestum. These were themes that painters loved in the days of what came to be called "drawing-room art."

Some of them enchanted Thomas Cole, the father of American landscape painting, who, arriving in 1831, spent four years in Rome and Florence. The last picture Cole was ever to paint was of an Italian pine, one of the trees he had studied

from the Pincian hill, and from the first his chosen masters
had been Claude and Poussin, with Turner whose work he had
seen in London. The founder of the Hudson River School
had walked all the way from Ohio when he settled in the
village of Catskill on the west bank of the river where he
found the dark forests that he loved, the winding streams and
wooded hills, the rocks and the waving trees and falling water.
He felt, with his friend the poet Bryant, that there was a
certain advantage in dealing with an unhackneyed nature that
was new to art, with virgin waterfalls and primeval woods, but
he saw these more or less through the eyes of Claude, whose
painting-room he occupied in Rome. He painted views of the
Arno in Florence [8] and the temples of Sicily and Paestum, of
which he made cork models in 1832, spending a night in the
solitudes there in a shelter for marsh labourers with robber-
like visages lighted by a single candle. Caravaggio should have
been there to paint the scene. In Rome, day after day, Cole
walked on the Campagna, sketching the Claudian aqueduct
and the Arco di Nerone, with the cascades of Tivoli and the
Apennines beyond, happiest with what Bryant called, on his
own visit in 1834, the vapoury splendour of the sunsets there.
Cole did his best to capture the violet-hued edges of the clouds
and the wondrous play of colours at the going down of the
sun, and there he painted "The Dream of Arcadia" that was
really the dream for a hundred years of all the travelling
American artists and writers. The time was coming when almost every American painter felt that a visit to Rome was
virtually a duty, when William Sidney Mount was said to
have "made Long Island his Italy," implying that Italy was
obligatory for everyone else.

[8] One of these Florentine views of Cole hung in the front parlour of
the house in Fourteenth Street, New York, in which William and
Henry James spent much of their childhood.

CHAPTER V

FENIMORE COOPER AND LONGFELLOW

H ORATIO GREENOUGH had been settled in Florence for
several years when Emerson spent a month there in
1833, and the tall, reserved, commanding sculptor with his
full beard and his greyhound was already a familiar figure in
the Florentine streets. He was soon to be a professor of sculpture in the Grand Ducal Academy, and Emerson was delighted
with the magnanimity of this "votary of the Greeks, impatient
of Gothic art," as he presently called him. In *English Traits*,
years later, he praised the aesthetic philosophy of this "great
man and glorious sculptor," Walter Savage Landor's phrase
for Greenough, the American who had something in common
with the English republican poet whose earliest hero had been
George Washington. He too was a votary of the Greeks while
both were devoted as well to the cause of Italian unity and
its leaders and prophets, Mazzini and Garibaldi, Landor's later
heroes, and Greenough's friends, the poets Niccolini and
Giusti.[1] Landor was one of the writers whom Emerson had
come abroad to meet because he had contributed to the forming of his own mind.

[1] Horatio Greenough made a statue that he called "Genius" for a
monument erected in Pescia to his friend Giusti. He also did a portrait bust of the Marquis Capponi, the statesman, the leader of the
Liberal party in Tuscany, the historian of the Florentine state, who
directed the Italian translation of Prescott's first historical work. Both
Capponi and Prescott were virtually blind.

It was Greenough who brought them together in the Villa Gherardesca, Landor's home since 1826, on the Fiesolan hills where he had often been seen wandering and composing as he walked. In this way Landor had created those "fruits of the open fields," the *Imaginary Conversations* that Emerson admired because of their classical form and nobility of feeling, and this writer for whom Latin was a second mother tongue had found in the ancients his models of behaviour. He was, it is true, a "mad Englishman,"—in Italy a proverbial phrase,— who had quarrelled himself out of his father's house and even out of England, and, turbulent and violent, given to rages, he had been expelled from Tuscany once for threatening to thrash one of the magistrates. But, kind as he was violent, both lordly and unruly, he was profoundly courteous and generous also, and Emerson, who dined and breakfasted with him, amid his "cloud of pictures," felt that this hero-worshipper should have been a soldier. Emerson noted also that he "shared the growing taste for Perugino and the early masters," and in fact this grand elderly schoolboy had formed, in advance of the critics, a feeling for the so-called primitive painters. His rooms were crammed with their pictures, mostly spurious but with great names, and the story was told that, meeting a tailor with four small panels on a Florentine street, he had offered a handful of silver coins for them. The pictures might have been Botticellis for all that anybody cared, and the tailor, who had bought them for a few coppers, thought the English milord was out of his wits. But it was not safe in Landor's presence to praise a picture on his walls because he at once forced you to accept it.

Emerson, who presently went his way, was almost as indifferent to the painter's art as the poet Byron had been before him, though he remarked of Florence that "no man has any

idea of the powers of painting until he comes hither." At
least he looked at pictures, which Byron could scarcely be said
to have done, and he remarked in his journal, "I make a con-
tinual effort not to be pleased except by that which ought to
please *me*." Moreover, of Brunelleschi's dome he said that it
was "set down like an archangel's tent in the midst of the city,"
—few lovers of architecture could have rivalled that,—as he had
regretted in Naples that America built such mean churches
instead of the "sublime old temples" that he saw there. He
had said too in the Naples museum that it was "more than
meat and drink" to see so many princely heads and heroes. As
a worshipper of greatness, he was drawn to Michelangelo
whose Moses and Pietá recalled to him Plato's doctrine of the
archetypal forms.[2] He was moved profoundly by the literature
in art, by its symbolism and philosophic meaning, while, like
most of the English and American writers of the time, he had
small interest in aesthetic matters.

Florence, the "Etrurian Athens," had harboured in 1828–'29
a writer who felt these questions a little more keenly, not because his aesthetic sense was much more developed than Emerson's but because he had intimate friends who were practising
artists. James Fenimore Cooper had grown up with an eighteenth century taste that found the cathedral of Pisa a "droll
medley" and Giotto's campanile "finical," but he had been
thrown closely with painters and sculptors,—unlike the Bostonian Emerson,—whom he had followed sympathetically in stu-

[2] "When I see these fine objects I think of Plato's doctrine of the
original forms that are in the Divine mind. These things take a place
that seems to have waited for them in our own minds. They are almost
recognized, as Fontenelle said of new truth."—Emerson, Letter of April
21st, 1833.
   In Emerson's study in Concord always hung henceforward a copy of
Michelangelo's "The Three Fates." This had been made for him by
William Allen Wall, a New Bedford artist with whom he travelled
from Naples and walked in Rome.

dios and museums. One of these good friends was William Dunlap in New York, and he was also Horatio Greenough's "national benefactor and literary hero." In Paris, Cooper had spent hours in the Louvre with Samuel F. B. Morse, watching and even advising him as he made copies, perched on a high stool beside him and telling Morse how to "lay it on," just as if he himself had been a painter. Morse, like so many artists of the time, paid for his second tour in Europe by obtaining commissions for copies to be made there, but he also painted in Paris the picture of the Louvre that Cooper suggested to him and persuaded him to do. At that time Cooper had been writing *The Prairie* in Paris. There Morse took daily walks with him and helped him to choose pictures to buy, for Cooper developed rapidly a liking for pictures; but his real passion was for scenery, the passion that made him, as Balzac said, "the school of study for literary landscape painters." One saw this passion in many a page of his *Gleanings in Europe—Italy*. Driving down through the Simplon Pass, with his wife and daughters, in the family calèche,—and an old cuirassier of Napoleon's army as postillion,—he had often sat on the coachman's box to study the Jura mountains and marvel over the mists that clung to them. Neither Turner before him, nor Ruskin after, felt more "toosey moosey,"—Cooper's own word,—for scenes of this kind.

The most litigious of men, as quarrelsome as Landor and up to the neck usually in lawsuits, Cooper had also, as Greenough said, an "open, frank, generous nature" that was tranquillized for a time in the Italian scene. "Italy is the land to love," he said after spending nearly two years there, the only country that his wife had ever known him to leave "looking over the shoulder," the country that was the furthest removed from the money-getting mania where the common people excelled in grace of mind. Nations in their decline, he felt, enjoyed more happiness than nations that were advancing, like his own country, where the itch of incessant activity rasped one's nerves; and Cooper, who had no respect for what he called property patriotism, found grander scenery in Italy than he had known at home.[3] He delighted in the lights and shadows of the misty mountains, the grey villages stuck like wasps' nests against the slopes and ravines, and there more than ever he was able to indulge that "old passion for fine skies" that he shared with Thomas Cole and the poet Bryant. At Naples he climbed up to the castle of St. Elmo a dozen times to see the effect of a Neapolitan sunset, as enthralled as any landscape painter with the charm of the Italian sky of which so many poets had also spoken. Then, seeing nature with a fresh eye, he noted in the Bay of Naples the dominance of purple and blue as compared with the greens and greys of the American coast. Cooper indulged in Italy too the old sailor's passion for the sea that found expression in so many of his novels, *The Water Witch*, for one, which he wrote in Sorrento after exploring the coast in a felucca from Leghorn. He wrote this book in a little study on the terrace of the Casa Tasso, the supposed birthplace of the poet which he rented for the summer; and there, like another American novelist, Francis Marion Crawford, later, he looked out from the cliffs over Capri and Naples. Like Marion Crawford too, he explored the bay there, and the Gulf of Salerno below it, in a six-oared pinnace.

[3] "I can safely say, I have never seen any twenty miles square of Lower Italy, if the marches and campagnes be excepted, in which there is not more glorious scenery than I can recall in all those parts of America with which I am acquainted. Our lakes will scarcely bear any comparison with the finer lakes of Upper Italy; our mountains are insipid as compared with these, both as to hues and forms; and our seas and bays are not to be named with these."—Cooper, *Gleanings in Europe—Italy*, Vol. I, p. 154.

Cooper, who had spent a winter in Florence, where he wrote *The Wept of Wish-ton-wish,* and was about to spend a winter in Rome,—"stupefied as a countryman who first visits town, perplexed with the whirl of sensations and the multiplicity of the objects,"—was so famous at this time that every novel he produced was published simultaneously in thirty-four European cities. Castles were placed at his disposal and he found his name known in country inns and post-offices in small Italian towns,—he was better known on the continent than he was in England; [4] while, in the course of the seven years that he spent in Europe, he wrote novels also in Dresden, Berne and Paris. Moreover, he printed them wherever he was, going to Marseilles on one occasion to find an English compositor who could set up his work in a Florentine printing-office.[5] Meanwhile, an embattled republican, he studied the political institutions of the various European countries. The mildest and justest governments in Europe were "theoretically despotisms" in which, as he said, "concessions of natural right" were granted by the government to the people, whereas in the American republic, a true republic, they were granted to the government by the people; and he wrote *The Bravo,* a historical novel, in order to show the abuses and the disregard of human rights this led to. During a spring in Venice he read several books on the history of the city and investigated the prisons before he wrote it, intending in *The Bravo* to present

[4] In 1842, when Francis Parkman stayed in a monastery in Rome, he carried with him a copy of Cooper's *The Pioneers* "as a reminder of fresh air." Parkman found in Modena at his hotel an Italian translation of *The Last of the Mohicans,* and he said that in Italy and Sicily he had seen translations of nearly all of Cooper's novels.

[5] Cooper tried to have *The Water Witch* printed in Rome, but, after long negotiations, the censor forbade this unless the book was in great part rewritten.

a picture of the social system of one of the European "soi-disant republics."

Cooper's friendship with Lafayette, of whom in Paris he had seen much, was largely the result of a common political conviction; for Lafayette's aim was to create a new French republic based more or less on the American model. With Lafayette, whom he persuaded to sit for one of Greenough's busts, Cooper became engrossed in the cause of the Poles, who rose in rebellion against Russia in 1830, and he acted as chairman of the American committee in Paris to aid the Polish insurgents and the Polish exiles. Samuel F. B. Morse was an active member of this committee, and Cooper, who had met Morse in Paris, presently met him again in Rome where the painter continued his copying in the Vatican museum. There too Morse painted the portrait of Thorwaldsen, an old man now, that ultimately found its way to Copenhagen, while he walked in the hills round Subiaco with his painting equipment on his back sketching shepherds and peasants, towers, trees and gorges. Morse, who had found the career of an artist hard and unrewarding, had come abroad to escape from poverty and cares. It was on his voyage home that he conceived the invention of the electro-magnetic telegraph.

Meanwhile, Cooper became intimate in Rome with the poet Adam Mickiewicz, who was soon to publish *Pan Tadeusz*, after which, virtually ceasing to write, he was to devote himself to what he described as "realizing poetry in life." A friend of Mazzini, who called him the greatest of living European poets, he was a conspirator for the rest of his days, the heir of Kosciuszko, who was dear to Cooper,—like Lafayette,—as a figure of the American revolution. Cooper, on his white horse Chingi, rode constantly with Mickiewicz, roaming over the Campagna and among the ruins, and the Polish poet spent so much time with the novelist and his family that their friends thought he was going to marry Cooper's daughter. He was drawn to Cooper, whom he called "that star of the other hemisphere who sweeps across [ours] like a comet," whom he found so good-naturedly simple and unpretentious and who was read in Poland more even than Scott. Cooper noted that visiting scenes of the early persecutions of the Christians in Rome always recalled to Mickiewicz the sufferings of the Poles.

It was just at this time, 1829–1830, that Rembrandt Peale, the painter, appeared in Rome, where he witnessed the coronation of Pope Pius VIII. There Charles Bonaparte, the American ornithologist, received him at his villa near the Porta Pia, while Peale reckoned that there were about three hundred art students in Rome from almost every country at least in Europe. After the day's work, with their whiskers and chin-tufts and their babel of tongues, they thronged, in a cloud of smoke, the Caffé Greco. Rembrandt Peale remembered that in 1786, when he was eight, one hundred and thirty Italian paintings had arrived in Philadelphia. These were the first so-called old masters that had ever been seen there, and they were deposited for sale in Charles Willson Peale's exhibition room where they were shown to the public. Rembrandt raced home from school to watch his father stretch and mend them, ravished himself by the Venetian colours, enraptured by the strange designs and subjects; then he and his father sat down together over Pilkington's dictionary, reading the lives of the artists, a moment when Rembrandt Peale conceived a longing to visit Italy and a love that was never quenched for the art of painting. But he was fifty-one when he first saw the peninsula.[6] Visit-

[6] "The idea that my dreams of Italy were never to be realized seemed to darken the cloud which hung over the prospect of death itself."— Rembrandt Peale, *Notes on Italy*, p. 5.

Peale observed that the walls of the Sistine Chapel "painted by

ing Europe twice, he had been detained in Paris painting for his father's Philadelphia museum portraits of Houdon, the sculptor, David and Bernardin de Saint-Pierre, who dedicated his memoirs to this "Rembrandt of America." In Rome he painted Thorwaldsen of the blue eyes and the patriarchal locks and a second portrait of Cuvier, the naturalist. Peale had brought with him the portrait he had made of Washington, with the Phidian head of Jupiter above him; and he exhibited this in Rome and Florence, where the Grand Duke and his courtiers came to see it.

The young poet Henry Wadsworth Longfellow had visited Florence a year before, and there he had seen his first *improvisatore*, reciting, with emphatic gestures, the invasion of Italy by Hannibal and, following this, the battle of Navarino. Nine different subjects were then presented to him with a list of rhymes written on a sheet of paper to which he was expected to adapt his themes in a style that recalled the Homeric bards, simple and open as it was with many repetitions and digressions. But here the Italian guitar took the place of the Greek harp. A piano accompanied the *improvisatore* in the salon of Joseph Bonaparte's daughter who played "Yankee Doodle" herself to please the young American. Longfellow's New England father, eager to forward his education, had sent him to Europe to prepare to teach modern languages, and Longfellow had come to Italy by way of Germany, France and Spain on the tour that he was to record in *Outre Mer*. Like Henry James and Howells many years later, he lodged in the Piazza Santa Maria Novella, where, in the church near by, Boccaccio had placed the opening scenes of the Decameron. Longfellow wrote

---

various artists of merit in their time, and now much injured," offered "nothing worthy of notice." No doubt, in 1830, all the other artists in the Caffé Greco were of the same opinion. None of them would have cared a fig for either Botticelli or Perugino.

in Italian a sonnet on the Ponte Vecchio and the Arno that twisted like a dragon underneath it. In Spain he had met Washington Irving, who was planning his life of Columbus there, and it was Irving's *Sketch Book,* which he more or less followed in his own book, that had aroused in him the desire to travel. To Longfellow's youthful imagination the old world was a kind of Holy Land, and he too had longed to muse over the scenes of renowned achievement and loiter among ruined castles and falling towers. Like Irving, he wished to lose himself in the shadowy grandeurs of the past, the remains both of antiquity and the Middle Ages that so excited and piqued the romantic mind; and sometimes by diligence, sometimes on foot, he had wandered with a knapsack on the Loire and listened to the guitar on the Guadalquivir. Meanwhile, he collected for his book thirteenth-century fabliaux, old Spanish devotional poems and legends of the Moors.

Travelling from Florence to Rome, Longfellow, like Goethe, walked part of the way, rambling, for instance, on the shores of the Lake of Bolsena, carrying in his pocket *Childe Harold* as a sort of guide-book. To a friend he wrote, "You may imagine me sitting in the shadow of some olive grove, watching the rising moon and listening to the song of the Italian boatman or the chimes of a convent bell," and he certainly shared all the feelings of Thomas Gold Appleton, his brother-in-law, who caught his first glimpse of Rome five years later.[7] Well he knew

[7] From the summit of Soracte, 1834: "My eye caught instantly, far in the blue distance, amid the sparkle of its palaces, that illustrious dome which Buonarotti hung in air . . . I cried out to Percival as he came running up, 'The Niobe of nations, there she stands!' We chose a flowery seat and gave way to the intensity of our feelings. For a long silent hour we were indulging in the excitement of the situation, calling up all those bright things that make Rome the most interesting city on earth. It is not sentiment, it is not an artfully stimulated ebullition of romance, but awe and sublime joy which every student must feel when looking his first upon the 'lone mother of dead empires.' "—*Life and Letters of Thomas Gold Appleton,* p. 190.

that "awe and sublime joy which every student must feel when looking his first upon the 'lone mother of dead empires.'" In Rome the effect of the ruins upon him was "almost delirious," as he said, and so was the effect of the beautiful Julia, the Italian girl with whom he fell in love in the Piazza Navona. Julia was one of three musical sisters who lived there under the same roof with him. Like the author of *The Marble Faun*, Longfellow delighted in the dancing groups on the lawns, in the groves of the park of the Villa Borghese, moving to the music of tambourines, as in some picture of Poussin, or, if they had been immobilized, on a Grecian urn. Longfellow also witnessed the ceremony of a young girl taking the veil, and he made what Hawthorne later called the "inevitable" visit to the Coliseum by moonlight.[8] Studying Dante every night, he

[8] It is related that Fanny Appleton,—later Longfellow's second wife,—who was in Rome as a young girl in 1836, was so determined to see the Coliseum by moonlight that she would not look at it by day. It was soon after this visit to Rome that she first met Longfellow in Switzerland.

"Later still the moon shines through the arches and softens and hallows the ruins [of the Coliseum]: an owl plaintively hoots from the upper cornice, and from the grove near by you hear the nightingale's heart throbbing into song; voices are talking under the galleries, and far up a torch wanders and glimmers along the wall where some enterprising English party is exploring the ruins. The sentinel paces to and fro in the shadowy entrance, and parties of strangers come in to see the Coliseum by moonlight."—W. W. Story, *Roba di Roma*, p. 234.

"We drove to the amphitheatre and found, to our surprise, nearly a dozen carriages drawn up before the entrance. I thought the number of visitors would kill the solitude, but they only enforced the vastness and grandeur of the pile. Their voices were at times heard as from a far mountain, and their torches, as they burst from under some gap, poured a shower of light upon the old haggard arches, their red play forming picturesque effects of *chiaroscuro* that contrasted with the coldness of the moonlight. The effect from the moon was that all was light or all shadow; the ribs of the seats running down to the arena seemed restored, the seats were in shadow, and the simplicity and force of the contrasts accorded with the sublimity of the structure. The contrast of the present and the past was full of poetry, thus to be contemplating, under a melancholy moon, in mournful silence, the arena which once rang to the applause of thousands peopling its stately walls."—*Life and Letters of Thomas Gold Appleton*, p. 195.

made another inevitable visit to the tomb of Tasso in Sant' Onofrio. There, in the convent adjoining the church, between evergreen oaks and orange trees and with all Rome under his eyes, Chateaubriand dreamed of continuing his memoirs near the death-bed and tomb of the poet, invoking as he wrote the genius of glory and misfortune.

Longfellow and Chateaubriand were in Rome at the same time and they might have met in Sant' Onofrio. Meanwhile, after a violent illness, Longfellow went to regain his strength to the village of Ariccia in the Alban hills. This was a favourite resort of foreign artists where, nearly forty years later, Ibsen wrote *Brand,* and one saw them perched on their camp-stools at every picturesque point of view with paint-boxes on their knees and white umbrellas to shield them from the sun. There, between the Alban Lake and the Lake of Nemi, Hippolytus and the nymph Egeria were supposed to have dwelt, and there Longfellow read Italian poetry, threw stones into the lakes and idled in the woods of the Chigi park. Seized with the artist-mania himself, he sketched the trunk of a hollow tree, the spire of a distant church and a fountain in the shade, while, during this month of villeggiatura, he had long talks with the monks in the monastery there.[9] He observed a little band of pilgrims, clad in white, with staves and with scallop-shells and sandals, passing through the village, winding along the brow of the hill with slow and solemn pace on their way to the shrine of Loreto. They sang, as they moved, a mournful hymn, like Christian and Hopeful on their journey to the Delectable Mountains.

[9] This was no doubt his first intimate glimpse of the monastic life. Later Ruskin said (in *Modern Painters,* Vol. V, chapter 20): "Longfellow, in his *Golden Legend,* has entered more closely into the temper of the monk, for good and for evil, than ever yet theological writer or historian, though they may have given their life's labour to the analysis."

Longfellow lived in a Roman family with George Washington Greene, whom he had first encountered in Marseilles and who became his life-long friend in Italy and later at home when Greene at last returned to settle there. This grandson of Washington's favourite general, of whom he wrote a biography, was to spend twenty years in Italy, where he married an Italian girl and became the American consul in Rome and a favourite of all the American travellers there. Everyone confided in the sympathetic Greene, with whom Thorwaldsen spent many mornings and who recalled in *Biographical Sketches* his memories of Fenimore Cooper and Thomas Cole. He recollected Cooper's remark, "There is no place where mere living is such a luxury as Italy," of which for many years he himself planned to write the history that was never written. Greene took Cole to the catacombs and sat with him while he sketched the city looking down from Sant' Onofrio, and he remembered how Thorwaldsen, standing a long time before Cole's work, said with heartfelt enthusiasm, "A great artist! A great artist!" This was at some time during Cole's second visit to Rome, when he painted the old ilexes in the Villa Borghese, the pines of the Doria Pamphili and the Appian Way. In Rome he repainted the allegorical "Voyage of Life," and he talked to Greene about his "Course of Empire." The friends visited together Palestrina, where Marcus Aurelius had once had a villa, and Tivoli where Horace had read Homer in the shades that he loved.

Longfellow too unfolded to Greene the plans he had formed for his life and showed him from what deep cisterns he had learned to draw, and from that day, as Greene recorded, "the office of literature took a new place in my thoughts." This was at Naples where the two spent a few weeks together, visiting the tombs of Virgil and Sannazaro. Longfellow was to return in later years to Italy, the subject of several of his poems and Harvard lectures,—the land of the poet's "predilection" as of the artist's "necessity" and for all "the land of dreams and visions of delight." [10] Later it was Longfellow, translating Dante, who made America "the new Ravenna of the great poet," as an Italian writer said, after this poet had succeeded Ticknor as a lecturer on Dante at Harvard, to be succeeded in turn by Lowell and Norton. But that was thirty years later in another country.

[10] "The mind resolutely refuses to associate anything disagreeable with Italy. Horace may speak of winter firesides and Soracte white with snow,—but the imagination is not chilled. Dante may speak of the snow and sleet of the Apennines, . . . but our fancy does not feel them . . . To the imagination, Italy always has been, and always will be, the land of the sun, and the land of song; and neither tempest, rain nor snow will ever chill the glow of enthusiasm that the name of Italy excites in every poetic mind. Say what ill of it you may, it still remains to the poet the land of his predilection, to the artist the land of his necessity, and to all the land of dreams and visions of delight."—From one of Longfellow's Harvard lectures, 1851, quoted in Samuel Longfellow's *Life of Henry Wadsworth Longfellow,* Vol. II, p. 200.

CHAPTER VI

FLORENCE

I T WAS a remark of Horatio Greenough that "a proud and savage concentration is sometimes necessary here." He was referring to Florence where, as the years advanced, the so-called American colony grew in numbers [1] in a city so small that, as Landor said, a cabbage-girl's voice in the midst of it might be heard at all the extremities. Landor himself, who had lived apart in his Villa Gherardesca, had left Italy for England, only to return for the last six years of his life, but American travellers were beginning to stream through this oasis of Tuscany that seemed to them so beautiful and so careless and gay.[2] They were enchanted with the old nobles' towers, the madonnas at street-corner shrines, the flowers that were sold in stacks and sheaves, the soft violet hills that encompassed the city; and they carried away from the Ponte Vecchio caskets, lockets, table-tops and Psyches, Hebes and Graces in alabaster.

[1] "Americans are for the most part merged in the English," Catharine M. Sedgwick wrote at a time when New Englanders formed perhaps the majority of American travellers. "One of our party said to an Italian, 'But we are not English.'—'Ah, no, but English Americans—all the same.' "—*Letters from Abroad*, Vol. II, p. 68.

[2] "It is pleasant to see how affectionately all the artists who have resided here a little speak of getting home to Florence. And I found at once that we live here with much more comfort than in Rome or Naples. Good streets, industrious population, spacious, well-furnished lodgings, elegant and cheap caffés. The Cathedral, the Campanile, the splendid galleries and no beggars, make this city the favourite of strangers."—Emerson, *Journals*, April 29th, 1833.

When George Ticknor returned to Florence in 1836, he lived in the old rooms of Alfieri where, years before, the Countess of Albany had shown him the poet's manuscripts before her palace was let out for lodgings. Ticknor had come down from Dresden with a letter to the Grand Duke from his friend Prince John of Saxony, the Dante scholar, whose Accademia Dantesca became in time the model of the Dante Society in the American Cambridge. The Grand Duke, giving him an audience and questioning him about the United States, took notes, while he talked, like a German student, and, asking Ticknor where he thought it the greatest good fortune to be born, asked "Why?" when Ticknor answered, "In America." Ticknor's reply was that he thought it was more "elevating" to live in a country where the people shared in the affairs of government, and he observed that the Grand Duke "blushed a little but made no answer," possibly thinking this American had gone too far. As it happened, the Grand Duke, technically a despot, was the most liberal of all the Italian rulers, eager, moreover, to forward the interests of scholarship and art, such as the uncovering of Giotto's portrait of Dante. This was the joint work of an American, Richard Henry Wilde, Bezzi, an Italian, and Seymour Kirkup, an English artist, a friend of Blake and a London tradesman's son, who had come to live in Florence about 1822. A curious character who had been present at the burial of both Keats and Shelley in Rome, he was to figure later in three books of Hawthorne, and he lived in a ruinous old house, facing the Arno, that had once been a hospice of the Templars. His painting-room had been an abode of Ariosto. A hermit with a long beard and a glittering eye, he was supposed to be a necromancer, and his dusty, disorderly rooms were crowded with demonological writings and a great collection of Dante manuscripts and books. He was convinced that the poet often appeared and spent an evening with him.

It was Seymour Kirkup's claim that Dante himself had revealed to him the whereabouts of the Giotto portrait in the Bargello, and it is true that he made the tracing of this portrait, so often reproduced, before it was repainted. But actually Wilde, a lawyer from Georgia and an ex-member of Congress who spent four years in Italy about this time, had found in the Florentine archives the illuminating statement that confirmed Vasari's mention of its existence. Planning a *Life and Times of Dante,* of which he wrote mainly the "times" alone, —the manuscript itself was never published,—he had entered "like an American woodsman" the forest of the archives, with his axe, so to speak, on his shoulder, eager but untrained. Finding this clue, he called upon Bezzi, who obtained from the Grand Duke permission to remove the whitewash that covered the portrait, and it was Bezzi who brought in Seymour Kirkup to make the tracing.[3] Two years later, Wilde published another book "concerning the love, madness and imprisonment of Torquato Tasso," a lawyer's argument to prove that Tasso had merely feigned madness when his passion for the Princess d'Este was discovered. This was the book that Robert Browning

[3] What appears to be the true story of the Giotto portrait is related in T. W. Toch's *Dante in America,* 1896.

Among the pioneers of Dante studies in the United States was Dr. T. W. Parsons of Boston. Parsons spent a year as a young man in Italy in 1836, and a copy of his translation of the Inferno, 1843, was placed under the cornerstone of the monument to Dante in the Piazza Santa Croce. In one of his poems he spoke of

> "Dante's lines
> Which, when my step first felt Italian ground,
> I strove to follow, carried by the spell
> Of that sad Florentine whose native street
> (At morn and midnight) where he used to dwell,
> My father bade me pace with reverent feet."

reviewed in 1842 in what turned out to be an essay on the poet Chatterton. Browning, with his interest in the analysis of character, praised Wilde's method of handling his material, and he followed this method with Chatterton to reveal the true nature of a man whom the world had also misunderstood.[4]

Charles Sumner, the young Boston lawyer who was in Italy in 1839, interested himself in the studies of Richard Henry Wilde, finding for him at Ferrara some manuscripts of Tasso and various papers in Venice connected with Dante. Sumner, later the senator, had come to Europe for three years to study continental jurisprudence, and he had found in Italian the most masterly study of criminal law that had been produced in a generation. In Rome he saw much of Longfellow's friend, the consul, Greene, with whom he spent four days at Palazzuola as guests of the Franciscans in the monastery where they felt like "hermits hoar in solemn cell." That was the site of the ancient Alba Longa, and impenetrable forests surrounded the monastery, with Cicero's favourite residence Tusculum discernible on one side while behind rose the mountain dedicated to the Latial Jove. At Tivoli, Sumner lay on the ground with the *praeceps Anio* before him in the very Tiburtine grove that Horace had pictured, and, reading there the first book of the odes, he suddenly realized how apt was the poet's language. In Rome, during the hot months, he studied Italian literature, rising at half past six and throwing himself on a sofa with a little round table near by, covered with books. Breakfast came and went, and his reading went on till five or six when he dined under a mulberry tree in a garden. Then Greene arrived and they walked to the Forum or out of one of the gates of Rome,

[4] Longfellow included eighteen of Richard Henry Wilde's translations of Tasso in his anthology *The Poets and Poetry of Europe*.

sometimes sitting for hours on a broken column, calling to mind all that had happened there.[5]

In Florence, Greenough read to Sumner a few of the essays on art that had so interested Emerson six years before, essays that were to affect the taste of Greenough's fellow-countrymen, —American architects especially,—a hundred years later. But they could not compare in this respect with the writings of a young Englishman who was to appear in Florence in 1845 and who affected profoundly,—and not in matters of taste alone,—the outlook of the English-speaking world. John Ruskin spent many mornings in Santa Maria Novella, seated, sometimes astride, on the desks of the choir, left alone there to do what he liked while he wrote a critical account of Ghirlandajo's frescoes. Nobody disturbed him, for no one at that time, he said, had ever so much as heard of Ghirlandajo,—even the most learned travellers were ignorant of him,—and from these frescoes he was learning, as he wrote later, "the fine personalities of the Florentine race and art." Then he was let into the sacristy to draw the Angelico "Annunciation," for he was excited by Fra Angelico also. The monks allowed him to sit close to the picture, working as long as he wished, while they went on rinsing their cups and folding their copes.

Ruskin had loved the peninsula ever since, at thirteen, he had read Rogers's *Italy,* with vignettes by Turner, but not till he was twenty-six had he begun to realize that Poussin, Teniers and Canaletto were not the real old masters. He was a convert to

[5] "This was my day's round . . . I read Dante [in four editions], Tasso's 'Gerusalemme,' the 'Decameron' of Boccaccio, the 'Rime' of Politian, all the tragedies of Alfieri, the principal dramas of Metastasio,—some six volumes,—the 'Storia Pittorica' of Lanzi, the 'Principe' of Machiavelli, the 'Aminta' of Tasso, the 'Pastor Fido' of Guarini, and much of Monti, Pindemonte, Parini, the histories of Botta, the 'Corbaccio' and 'Fiammetta' of Boccaccio." He also read Manzoni, Petrarch, Guicciardini, Niccolini, Goldoni, Foscolo, etc.—*Memoir and Letters of Charles Sumner,* Vol. II, p. 115.

the painters who came before Raphael,—as opposed to the
painters in vogue who followed him,—and Rio and Lord Lindsay had convinced him that there had been a great age long
before the "harlotries" of the Renaissance. That the Middle
Ages, in fact, were "the only ages" he had seen when he was
in the midst of *Modern Painters,* and he had been won over to
the "perfect style" of the Gothic builders of Italy and France
and the world that he was to celebrate in *The Stones of
Venice.* That was a world, he felt, of pure faith and domestic
virtue, unlike the infidelity and corruption that followed, and
in Florence he was "more than startled" by Giotto's tower.
Cimabue dawned upon him, with Fra Angelico, Perugino and
other Italian primitives who were coming into notice; for, far
from being the first to appreciate these painters, he was merely
more eloquent in expounding them than any other writer.
He had believed, before he discovered "Christian art," that
Turner was the greatest of all painters, and, interested in
geology and botany too, he had revelled in the Swiss Alps and
the scenes of "supernatural loveliness" that Turner had
painted. He wrote marvellous pages on clouds, mountains
and rocks, on the deep blue of the Rhone and the beryl-
coloured water of the Lake of Zurich,—pale aquamarine crystal
he said this was,—at a time when the cathedral of Siena had
seemed to him "every way absurd,—over-cut, over-striped, over-
crocketed, over-fabled." But now in the Campo Santo at Pisa,
where he put up a scaffold over the frescoes and drew outlines
of the stories of Abraham and Job, the conversion of S. Raniero
and the Triumph of Death, he found the whole doctrine of
Christianity so painted that a child could understand it, and
that, he felt, was all one needed to know. He was to preach
henceforth that all true art is sacred art, that art itself could
never be divorced from religion, that, as he said later, "things

done delightfully and rightly are always done by the help and in the spirit of God."

Later, Ruskin lost his faith in the Protestant doctrines of his youth, while he could not accept Catholicism; but, like Tolstoy, he was to be drawn to what he described in *Præterita* as the "dutiful and kindly hearts of the laborious poor." This regard of his for "simple and unlearned men" led him to see in the Renaissance nothing but decay, the pride of learning and science and of brilliant technicians and men of the world, who had lost the integrity and grace of the earlier artists. Meanwhile, Ruskin always wrote as if any whim of his must be the eternal truth for everybody; and for countless readers from that time forth the Post-Raphaelite artists were dethroned and Raphael himself became something less than a god.[6] What Taine called the "grand orchestra piety" and the affectations of the Bolognese school began, gradually at least, to go out of fashion, and living artists were affected by Ruskin's pronouncements. Some of them tried to express in their work the moral principles that Ruskin saw as underlying the work of the primitive painters, while others, even in the forties, were already in rebellion against what they called Ruskin's "sanctimonious cant." [7] Meanwhile, the new taste for mediæval art,

[6] The general feeling regarding Raphael of the mid-century world was well expressed by the American George S. Hillard: "This [the 'Sposalizio'] in Milan was the first picture of Raphael I had ever seen, and such an occurrence is a red-letter day in the calendar of life. It is like the first sight of Niagara—of the dome of St. Peter's—of the summit of Mont Blanc. It makes us for a time impatient of all inferior sensations." -Hillard, *Six Months in Italy*, 1853, p. 12.

[7] See *Ernest Carroll, or Artist-Life in Italy,* by Henry Greenough, Horatio Greenough's brother. In this book the artists in Florence in 1847 feel that Ruskin has done more harm to art than all other critics could repair. This was precisely because of his exquisite style, "so full of sophistries and contradictions." They regard Ruskin as a traitor to art because he decried the great Renaissance painters.

In one scene in the book, a number of artists are skating, during a winter evening, on the frozen Arno. Two of them have made a scare-

which this writer had largely created, led travellers henceforth to visit the mediæval towns that had been ignored in the days of the old Grand Tour, the so-called earlier classical age of travel. Everything had been stereotyped then; no one discovered neglected remains; no one thought of revaluing works of art. Tourists in general had visited only certain great cities, Venice, Milan, Naples, Florence and Rome, but Verona now ceased to be mainly the city of Romeo and Juliet as Padua ceased to be thought of as Portia's city. Or Assisi, in the eighteenth-century manner of Goethe, as the city of the Temple of Minerva. Travellers began to stop now at Cortona, Perugia, Orvieto, Siena, towns of which the guide-books had once said that they presented "few objects of interest"; and Italy, once Byronized, was rapidly to be Ruskinized with the rise of a new variety of aesthetic feeling.

Robert Browning, who arrived in Florence in 1848, shared Ruskin's taste for the early painters and sculptors.[8] He was naturally sympathetic with this aspiring springtime art, and he showed in *The Bishop Orders His Tomb* that he felt as Ruskin felt about the worldliness and decadence that came later. Browning, in fact, had shown his interest in the dawn of the Renaissance when he had first visited Italy ten years before to prepare for the writing of his poem about Sordello, the troubadour who had been one of the forerunners of Dante. In

---

crow, stuffing a figure wearing a hat, an effigy of this "ass of an English critic." They all skate about the figure, which they cuff and kick as they drag it over the ice.

[8] "But at any rate I have loved the season
         Of art's spring-birth so dim and dewy.
    My sculptor is Nicolo the Pisan;
         My painter—who but Cimabue?
    Nor ever was man of them all indeed
         From these to Ghiberti and Ghirlandajo
    Could say that he missed my critic-meed."
                    —Browning, *Old Pictures in Florence*.

the hill-town of Asolo, where he was to stay in after years, he had heard a peasant girl singing a snatch of Sordello, and this was a first suggestion of the little silk-winder of *Pippa Passes*. He had written before he settled in Italy all his dramas with Italian themes and several poems about the Renaissance,—among them *The Last Duchess* and *Pictor Ignotus*,—together with *An Englishman in Italy*, the poem Mazzini translated and used in his propaganda of the Risorgimento. Mrs. Browning who, as a child, had wished to join Byron and fight for Greece, developed a passionate faith in the future of the country. She and her husband, republicans both, "by profession," as she said, saw Italy not as a museum but as living and hopeful.

The Brownings settled in the Casa Guidi near the Pitti Palace, and there they were to live for thirteen years until Mrs. Browning's death in 1861. They had eloped two years before when Mrs. Browning, an invalid, had not left her room for seven years, and, travelling to Paris, on their way to Italy, they had been joined by Anna Jameson. Browning had begged her to help his frail wife on the journey, and Mrs. Jameson, already interested in the Italian primitives, was to stay briefly with the Brownings in Pisa and Florence. Whether *with* or, as Ruskin said, "*without* knowledge or instinct of painting," she was, Ruskin added, "industrious and candid," and, devoting much of her life henceforth to the interpretation of religious art, she was to produce three or four standard handbooks. She was a tireless explorer of the Pisan Campo Santo, old churches, modern studios and art collections, making tracings for illustrations and drawing outlines, while she hunted out Titian's old house in Venice with its small neglected garden, not the supposed palace but the actual half-ruined dwelling. Many a reader in decades to come was to be awakened to the history of art by her *Memoirs of the Early Italian Painters* and her *Sacred and Legendary Art,* relating the stories of the apostles and saints who appeared in the works of the Italian painters and sculptors.

This short, round, competent, energetic and comely Anglo-Irishwoman had recently visited Canada, Lake Huron and Boston, where she had seen something of Channing and Washington Allston of whom she left an admiring and lively record. She was presently to go on to Rome, which she had visited years before as a governess in an English nobleman's household, and it is quite possible that her interest in the primitives was not without effect on Browning's taste. As for Browning and his wife, they were associated, more or less closely, with several Americans in Florence and in Rome,—Hiram Powers, the sculptor Story, Harriet Hosmer, Margaret Fuller, James Jackson Jarves and various others. To one of these Mrs. Browning seemed like the night-blooming cereus in her shuttered world of pictures, books and flowers, while Harriet Hosmer's "Clasped Hands of the Brownings" became for a long age to come a symbol of constancy in marriage. In fifteen years Robert Browning dined only once away from home, and he never visited the famous cities, San Gimignano, Pistoia, Volterra and others "of great interest," as he said, "to me," because "Ba could not go, and I could not leave her." Meanwhile like Landor earlier and like James Jackson Jarves, he picked up "hole and corner" pictures of the kind which the dealers had not yet discovered but which Ruskin and the English Pre-Raphaelites had come to admire.[9]

[9] "Robert has been picking up pictures at a few pauls each, 'hole and corner' pictures which the 'dealers' had not found out; and the other day he covered himself with glory by discovering and seizing on (in a corn-shop a mile from Florence) five pictures among heaps of trash; and one of the best judges in Florence (Mr. Kirkup) throws out such names for them as Cimabue, Ghirlandajo, Giottino, a crucifixion painted

Florence, said James Jackson Jarves, who came there to live in the early fifties, was "the world's capital of Bric-a-bracdom" where one could buy fragments of ruined temples, contents of long-buried tombs, mediæval seals and bits of armour. No other city had so many votaries and victims of ancient children's toys, toilet articles of Greek and Etruscan ladies, old china, discarded frames, snuff-boxes and what not; and Florence, moreover, was the art-market of the world where travellers bought pictures, sometimes because their taste had been first aroused there. As a mine of old copies and originals, Jarves wrote, it was as inexhaustible as the coal-pits of England, and there new copies were made in thousands of the favourite pictures of the moment.[10] Among these, besides Raphaels and Leonardos, were Sassoferrato's blue-mantled Madonna and the Mater Dolorosa of Carlo Dolci, for taste had not yet caught up with these sugared beauties.[11] One dealer told Jarves that he had sold twelve thousand pictures to England alone, while lumber-rooms were stored with them, tailors had galleries of their own and every Florentine gentleman had his heirlooms. The streets of Florence were all but lined with pictures, and

---

on a banner, Giottesque if not Giotto, but *unique,* or nearly so, on account of the linen material, and a little Virgin by a Byzantine master."—*Letters of Mrs. Browning,* Vol. I, p. 448.

[10] The artists had to await their turn before being permitted to copy the pictures. The Bostonian Thomas G. Appleton, an amateur artist, wrote from Florence in 1833: "I patiently (impatiently!) wait my day. Titian's mistress will soon be mine. As for the Pitti, only seven are admitted at a time; and an artist who is to copy some Salvators for Mr. Perkins has been waiting eight months. Pretty patrons of the arts! No art but that of procrastination."—*Life and Letters of Thomas Gold Appleton,* p. 167.

[11] Nor for many years to come. In Henry James's *Roderick Hudson,* the family of Christina Light had a Sassoferrato "from which we're inseparable," said Christina. "We travel with our picture and our poodle."

daubs were regilded and retouched, varnished and shipped to America as Correggios and Titians.

Jarves, born in Boston, had been sent for his health to Hawaii, and there he had edited a newspaper and written a history of the Sandwich Islands before he discovered for himself the world of art. He had known this only as a feeble exotic in the Western hemisphere except for the Mayan remains that he had seen, the temples and sculptures in Central America that John Lloyd Stephens and Catherwood had found, the magnificence of which he recognized at once. But what he called his first interview with true art at the Louvre had left him "oppressed, confused, feverish, uncertain" until, developing soon after Ruskin a taste in advance of the time, Jarves found that he was a born collector. There was no real expertizing then and works of the most famous men were sometimes picked up and bought for a handful of silver, a Titian discovered in a pile of dilapidated canvases, a Michelangelo sold by a rag-and-bone man. One painter found in a street market in Florence an angel of Leonardo and another found a Velasquez in the trash of a great villa, in fine preservation under its crust of dirt. It was known that the "Muse of Cortona," when first disinterred, being on slate, was used by a peasant to stop a hole in an oven; and only a few dollars were paid for the Madonna del Gran Duca. Others besides Jarves, Browning and Landor rescued these waifs and strays of art,—for instance, the Boston painter Francis Alexander, who had returned to live in Florence. Alexander had given up painting himself, and he spent most of his time touching up old pictures upon which he had happened, while every morning an array of "old masters" was strung up facing his house, all in various stages of disrepair. It was known that he had money to spend if only because, in his tall silk hat, he kept coins to distribute to the boys who followed him about, and the owners of the pictures watched intently the house across the way until Mr. Alexander appeared at the window. If he saw anything promising on the house-front opposite, he would descend, examine it and perhaps buy the picture.

At that time gold-background pictures were occasionally burned merely for the sake of the gold one found in the ashes. Jarves set out in search of the obscure works of Giotto's successors,—still regarded with contempt as barbarous or Gothic, —collecting the early Tuscan and Umbrian painters on which for several years he spent all his resources. He searched through monasteries, churches, palaces, invited to examine old family collections in which the dusty pictures in the musty rooms hung over ancient marbles and piles of lace, vestments of cardinals, relics of melancholy grandeur, sometimes finding pictures so dirtied and smoked in a convent that, for a few francs, the monks were glad to sell them. He explored many a dark retreat and he climbed miles of staircases, putting up, as he wrote to one of his friends, with filth, lies, fraud and disappointment. But the Jarves collection became in time a part of American folklore when, rejected as rubbish, it was placed at Yale only in default of the repayment of a loan, though it had the high approval of good authorities at the time who anticipated the praise of Berenson later.

Jarves had hoped to establish a gallery in Boston that would be "worthy of its intellectual claims," but the names of the early painters were scarcely known there at the time and Jarves was even regarded as a kind of impostor. Charles Eliot Norton and Charles Sumner tried to help him, but all their efforts went for nothing. He wished to illustrate in this collection, as in his book *Art Studies,* the development of painting in Italy and its "Christian inspiration," for he too was largely influenced by Rio and Lord Lindsay, but he also made a remarkable collection of three hundred pieces of Venetian glass which he gave to the Metropolitan Museum in New York. His father, Deming Parves, had been the inventor of Sandwich glass, and Jarves's intention in forming this collection was to suggest styles and methods to American workers. If the artistic life was to grow in America, examples of art must be carried there, he thought, inasmuch as art springs from art, not primarily from nature; and, like Ruskin and his own friend Norton later, Jarves was an aesthetic missionary. In Italy he liked to think of the great age when men of genius were employed even for common buildings, when every house and almost every stable was a monument of the talent of the architect and the taste of the owner, and he never passed Giotto's campanile without feeling his heart lightened, as if a celestial ray had descended upon him. His feeling for art of all kinds was acute, and he urged Americans of knowledge and means to form collections that would ultimately be open to the public. He fought against the "Art-knownothingism,"—the knowing only of what one sees at home,—that one found everywhere in the mind of the country, and he wrote, "We need art students who will . . . go on their backs and knees . . . to read the soul-language of the mightiest minds of Europe." An excellent critic and art-historian, Jarves was severe with the mere mechanical dexterity of the sculptors of the moment, including his countryman in Florence, Hiram Powers.

While Jarves's art books were intelligent and useful at the time,[12] another, *Italian Rambles,* was of lasting interest, for

[12] Jarves . . . "not only a most remarkable collector but an admirable writer and the first to my knowledge to write seriously about Japanese art in any European language."—Bernard Berenson, Letter of 1957.

It was years later, in 1876, that Jarves, still living in Florence, wrote *A Glimpse at the Art of Japan.* Jarves studied Japanese art in Florence with an Italian who had learned Japanese and Chinese in Paris.

this writer was one of the first travellers from abroad to visit small towns in the Apennines of which he left irreplaceable descriptions. Few even of the Florentines knew some of these mountain communities, although they were only a few hours' drive away, Pescaglia, in the Carrara hills, and Serra, for example, where Jarves had for a while a summer perch. There the peasants, unable to believe that he had come of his own free will, asked if he was contented with their rude mountains which had nothing to offer strangers but good air and good water, and they wished him all manner of enjoyment, while he, feeling that they deserved the most courteous words and deportment in return, was happy to have found such gentle neighbours. Their manners were aristocratic, as if the spirit of chivalry lingered among them, and the old women in their patched homespun were like noble ladies in low disguise, fulfilling vows of humility to chasten their souls. Their language was far superior to the vernacular of cities, with idioms and phrases savouring of the style of Dante, elegant and refined in construction and tone, though they had no schools, books or education; and in them, Jarves felt, lay Italy's promise of a power richer than that of her quarries, olives and vines. This mountain country of steep inclines, rugged chasms and towering cliffs where the castle of Udolpho might have stood seemed to Jarves the real kingdom of the peasant; and, as he studied the mountaineers, he joined in singing matches that reminded one of the contests of the ancient Greeks. He visited and described as well some of the better known cities, Cremona and Piacenza, antique cities of the plains, Lars Porsena's Chiusi, the heart of the old Etruscan domain, Ravenna, the impoverished capital of the Ostrogoths. He went to Loreto, three miles from Recanati with its seventeenth-century palace, Leopardi's birthplace, the house within sight of the Casa

Santa, one the shrine of fanatical belief, the other the abode of melancholy disillusion. They struck him as the poles of modern and mediæval thought.

Reading Jarves's *Italian Rambles,* one recalled in after times the horseback tour of Kenyon and Donatello when, setting out, in *The Marble Faun,* from the tower of Monte Beni, they rode through forgotten towns in the Apennines. There one could study among the mountains some of the old artists in spots where they were born and could still be seen in faded frescoes in dark chapels or when the sacristan revealed some treasured picture hidden behind a curtain.

CHAPTER VII

ROME IN THE FORTIES

IN THE course of the forties and fifties, a Roman winter be-came "the fashion," as the wife of one of the American sculptors said, especially perhaps with Bostonians who were sometimes eager to escape from "the frozen ocean of Boston life." For them the "Boston of Italy," [1]—Florence,—seemed too much like home, too gossipy and too smug in the American circles, and most of the artists, both painters and sculptors, pre-ferred to live in Rome, along with the scholars and writers, the reformers and students. The sculptor Story settled there, and John Lothrop Motley, Francis Parkman, Charles Eliot Norton and Theodore Parker were among many who stayed there dur-ing these decades. There came Samuel Gridley Howe with

---

[1] This phrase matched the phrase of the Florentine professor who called Boston "the Florence of America." W. W. Story said that Florence was a "sort of continental Boston,"—for this reason he did not wish to live there; while Margaret Fuller, also preferring Rome, said, "Florence is a kind of Boston with the same good and the same ill—and I have had enough of both. I do not like it . . . because it seems like home."

There was a vogue in Florence of amateur theatricals, managed a few years later by Anna Cora Mowatt. This was the "glamour girl,"—Mrs. Ritchie,—whose play, *Fashion,* an event in New York, she brought out again in Florence. There she directed charity performances of *The School for Scandal* and *The Rivals,* appearing herself with Mrs. Trollope as Mrs. Malaprop and Thomas Adolphus Trollope as Bob Acres. In Florence she wrote a novel, *Fairy Fingers,* about a young woman of her own world who defies convention and opens a dress-making shop.

Julia Ward Howe, like James Russell Lowell and his cousin John Lowell who had set out for the Near East with a cavalcade of twelve horses and an artist to make sketches. There lived for several years the "thoughtful" actress, the "celebrated female Romeo," Charlotte Cushman. Rome, in the mid-century years, was the refuge of expatriates that Paris was to become a generation later.

Of the sculptors, who came from all over America, some were "business artists,"—Jarves's phrase,—and some were backwoodsmen from the West, farmers' sons from up-state New York or Yankees like Paul Akers, who had grown up in Maine. There were several women sculptors, such as Harriet Hosmer and Vinnie Ream, who appeared in Rome a little later, or Emma Stebbins, who made the fountain, "The Angel of the Waters," that was set up in New York, in Central Park. There was the Negro sculptor Edmonia Lewis, and there was Miss Lander from Salem who was to make Hawthorne's bust, the lady with the narrow sallow face, sharp eyes and a long chin, whom Hawthorne's son was to remember. It was she who went fearlessly by night or day about the Roman streets, suggesting the "unhampered ways of life" of Miriam and Hilda in *The Marble Faun,* and she was to live to a very old age, as a sculptor and a painter, long enough to paint Pierpont Morgan. Charlotte Cushman, who galloped every day on her black horse over the Campagna,—accompanied by Emma Stebbins, her biographer later,—was a friend of all the women sculptors, and on their behalf she made war on all the sculptors of the other sex.

Many of the sculptors created by borrowing a hand here, a torso there or a bit of drapery from some figure in the Vatican, where the sculptures were shown in the evening by torchlight. The sudden flare brought out the expression of the statues and the contrasts of light and shade in a very striking manner, and the figures seemed to start into life before one.[2] Some of the artists worked in the Via Margutta, at the foot of the Pincian hill, which had rung for generations with the hammering of sculptors, and sometimes they went to Carrara to select blocks of marble that would be worthy of the images floating in their minds. Rome for them was a paradise of sculpture, with urns and busts, huge jars and broken caryatids scattered in every garden, and they all remembered the story of Michelangelo studying in the Forum at the age of eighty. In the evening the men gathered in the Caffè Greco where, in the Via Condotti, in the three smoke-darkened rooms, they talked at the small round tables.[3] There every day John Gibson arrived before sunrise for breakfast, sitting with a wax taper in his hand reading the newspaper over his coffee. Gibson had settled in 1817 in Rome, where he was to live for forty-eight years, creating his polychrome sculpture, Pandora or Venus or what not, with blue eyes, blonde hair and ivory flesh. Sometimes his figures had nets of gold about the hair. When he was criticized for

[2] The effect of torchlight or moonlight on sculpture was a frequent theme of writers from Madame de Staël to Henry James. The heroine of *Corinne*, with Lord Nevil, visiting Canova's studio, saw the statues by torchlight. See also in Henry James's *The Last of the Valerii* the effect of moonlight on the statue of Juno: "The beautiful image stood bathed in the cold radiance, shining with a purity that made her convincingly divine. If by day her rich paleness suggested gold, she now had a complexion like silver slightly dimmed."

[3] "The Caffè Greco, where artists meet and discuss subjects of art, pictures and statues, read the French newspapers and *Galignani*, and fill the air of the crowded little rooms with tobacco-smoke. There you may see every night representatives of art from all parts of the world, in all kinds of hats, from the conical black felt, with its velvet ribbon, to the stiff French stove-pipe, and in every variety of coat, from the Polish and German nondescript, all befrogged and tagged, to the shabby American dress-coat, with crumpled tails; and with every cut of hair and beard, from that of Peter the Hermit, unkempt and uncut, to the moustache and pointed beard of Anthony van Dyck."—W. W. Story, *Roba di Roma*, pp. 200-201.

colouring his work, Gibson always said, "Whatever the Greeks did was right."

Thomas Crawford, who had arrived in Rome in 1834, was the most important of the American sculptors, a marble-cutter from New York who had been known for his mantelpieces, with wreaths and flowers and graceful female figures. Crawford's caryatids might have been by Thorwaldsen, the hero whom he had studied in plaster casts and whose constant counsel was, when Crawford worked under him in Rome, "Mass before detail, mass before detail." Crawford, dreaming of goddesses and gods, read translations of the classics while he copied figures from the antique, rescued from poverty by Charles Sumner who arranged, in Rome, for the purchase of one of his works by the Boston Athenæum. He was soon taken up by various patrons and by politicians who obtained commissions for him in Washington and Richmond. Hiram Powers complained that Americans had little esteem for native work, elevating foreigners of no merit above their ablest countrymen, but rich men with imagination were at last appearing from Boston and New York with others like Mr. Leavenworth from "the banks of the Ohio." [4] Crawford was to be known for his statues of Washington and Jefferson, for his pediment of the capitol at Washington, for the bronze doors [5] and for the

[4] "You may be sure that I've employed a native architect for the large residential structure that I'm creating on the banks of the Ohio . . . Are we not told that the office of art is second only to that of religion? . . . My library, filled with well selected and beautifully bound authors in groups, is relieved from point to point by high-class statuary." —Mr. Leavenworth, in Henry James's *Roderick Hudson*.

It was Mr. Leavenworth who suggested to Roderick Hudson "a representation in pure white marble of the idea of Intellectual Refinement." [5] These bronze doors of the capitol, left half finished at Crawford's death, were completed by William Henry Rinehart, the Baltimore sculptor. This artist, who spent many years in Rome and Florence later, was known, like Powers, for his portrait busts at a time when it was

colossal "Armed Freedom" on the top of the dome of which he derived the proportions from the cross on St. Peter's. Like Powers he became the fashion, so important a man that a ship of war was sent over to Italy to convey his work; but most of it in after years embarrassed the beholder. Hawthorne, though he had no pretentions as an amateur of plastic art, expressed the general feeling of a century later. Visiting Crawford's studio after his death in 1857, he saw only "commonplaces in marble and plaster such as we should not tolerate on the printed page," true as it was that Thomas Crawford was at least more inventive than the prosaic Powers.

Crawford, however, had days of glory in the forties and fifties in Rome, where he employed an army of marble-cutters and where he occupied twelve studios that he was permitted to build among the ruins of the Baths of Diocletian. The studios, long and low, crowded with statues and busts, were called a whispering gallery when kings and queens and public men of all shades of political opinion met on this aesthetic neutral ground, so that Francis Marion Crawford, the novelist, who was a child when his father died, had known something of patrician Rome almost from birth. Thomas Crawford, who had married a banker's daughter from New York, might have been called rich in his own right, and he occupied the second story of the great Villa Negroni as a tenant of Prince Massimo, who lived below him. The family of the supposed descendant of Fabius Cunctator were lifelong friends of the Crawfords. The villa itself had been built of materials filched from the

---

fashionable to be "done by Rinehart." He was called "the last of the classicists," as Saint-Gaudens was called "the first of the moderns."

Crawford introduced in the bronze doors portraits of his family, and his son Francis Marion Crawford, the novelist, in Washington many years later, recognized himself in one of the children. Marion Crawford had been four when his father died.

great baths close by, and from the windows one overlooked the spot on which Nero stood fiddling, according to the legend, while Rome burned. It was a kitchen-garden now, belonging to Prince Massimo, filled with asparagus, artichokes and lettuce, and there was a fish-pond too, an orange-grove and gardens near by with cypresses that Michelangelo had planted. The summer-house over the gateway had been Joseph Severn's studio, and there Keats and Shelley had both come to visit him, while beyond was a wild waste of open fields and broken land leading to the church of Santa Maria Maggiore. The spot where Crawford lived and worked, and where his son Marion played as a boy, was covered in after years by the great railway station that Mussolini rebuilt in the nineteen-twenties; but in those days it was far out in the country. On moonlight nights the children saw foxes from the Campagna drinking from the basin of the marble fountain in the garden.

Meanwhile, the painters outnumbered the other groups in Rome. They were mostly artists, obscure then, who never became better known, with others who were famous but rapidly forgotten; and, distinguished or not, they were all governed by the same ideas and styles as the European artists of the moment. They were in search of the picturesque, as one saw in their beards and habiliments, with velvet jackets and hair romantically curled, looking for "subjects" in a scene where pictures that were already made met the eye at every turn. The painters with "Claude on the brain" haunted the Campagna, painting all day until twilight, willing to run the risks of the chill and the night-mist, hoping to catch a little of the wonder of the sunset; and they hurried in to pass the gates before these were closed in the evening, marvelling over the purple clouds behind the purpler Alban Hills and the mellow golden glow in the sky at the west. George Inness, who spent two years in Italy before he went to Barbizon, Christopher Cranch, John Kensett and Asher Durand,—like Thomas Cole earlier,—found Arcadia there; happily free in this Roman world from the vortex of politics and business that, as Cole said, was forever whirling at home. The eager fraternity of the brush were to be seen at all seasons of the year on every road that led into the Campagna, hastening to paint the Arco di Nerone and the other arches of the aqueducts where in summer flowers waved from every cranny. They sketched the ivied buttresses, the mouse-coloured oxen with their wide-branching horns, the little jingling carts laden with wine-casks,—perhaps with the dome of St. Peter's rising behind,—the shepherds leaning on their long staves, the lumbering wains, the wooden ploughs, the cork woods of Monte Mario, the chestnuts of Frascati. Every tree there was a perfect study, with "accidents," as the painters called them, of light and shade; and there were the magnificent sombre cypresses of the Villa d'Este and the water-fall at Tivoli foaming down the ravine.

Sometimes the painters went further afield, John Gadsby Chapman, for instance, who wandered all over Calabria with a party of friends, dressed in goatskins and wearing the un-tanned shoes of the peasants, sketching and painting on the way. Chapman noted the outlines of mountain ranges, mediæ-val towers, vine-laced terraces and rocky headlands, painting vintage scenes, stone pines in a valley, sunsets and sunrises, Paestum by moonlight. Albert Bierstadt and Sanford Gifford walked through the Abruzzi,—"the most Italian part of Italy," they thought,—with knapsacks on their backs, ending at Naples; and Christopher Cranch, both painter and poet who later translated the Æneid, found fine subjects for his land-scapes near Amalfi. He painted the mountains behind the town and a ruined castle by the sea, as well as Barbarossa's castle on the island of Capri. He too painted Paestum, so old that the temples were ruins even when the Emperor Augustus went to see them; while others along the coast were charmed by the lazzaroni stretched out in the sand, the fishing-boats, the water green as grass. Sometimes they walked from Rome to Sorrento with pistols in their belts to guard them in this brigand-infested region.

Of the other kinds of artists, there were some who painted biblical subjects, Ruth gleaning in the field of Boaz, Rebecca at the well, Naomi and her two daughters by marriage, while many painted from the costumed models a juvenile pifferaro from the hills, playing his pipes perhaps, or a blind girl of Pompeii, or a contadina holding a pitcher at a fountain, with the clean white triangle of a kerchief falling over her forehead. Or they undertook an ambitious theme like Renzo wandering by the river Adda, suggested by *I Promessi Sposi,* or a scene from Madame de Staël's romance of the Fountain of Trevi under the moon with the faces of Oswald and Corinne reflected in the water. Thomas Hicks, in the Via Margutta, the age-old centre of Bohemian Rome, painted a large "Italia," a rustic damsel with a mandolin and "a world of passion in her eyes," —to quote the phrase of one observer,—while, working on a portrait, he would talk about his childhood when he had learned the craft of painting a coach. His friend John Kensett climbed the hill over his studio every day to see St. Peter's in the sunset.

It was Thomas Hicks who painted Bayard Taylor, seated, in burnouse and turban, on a Syrian roof-top,—the "great American traveller" of the future who arrived in Rome in 1845 and lived there in an inn for mechanics and tradesmen. This inn faced the Pantheon, and a barrel of wine stood in a corner of the dining-room, with bladders of lard hanging among boughs in the window. The dark courtyard, filled with heavy carts, re-sounded with the neighing of horses and the singing of truck-men. Taylor, at the moment a poor young man, engaged in writing *Views Afoot,* walking all over Europe with a knap-sack,—"making a journey of penance," as the peasants sup-posed,—had crossed the Alps from Germany and spent four months in Florence before he continued his tramp to Siena and Rome. Naturally, he saw low life much more than high life, though in years to come as a traveller in almost every corner of the world,—from the Arctic zone to the White Nile and the hills of Loo Choo,—he was to see life on every level, comparing himself with those wanderers of the Middle Ages who seemed to be boundlessly capable of wonder and delight. This veritable innocent abroad, a Pennsylvanian villager, paid his way by writing for Horace Greeley's *Tribune,* unique among writers of travel at the time because in part he wished to show that one could see the world on a dollar a day.

The ablest American painter in Rome was undoubtedly William Page, an artist from Albany, a pupil of S. F. B. Morse, whose work was "the wonder of everybody," Robert Browning said,—"an earnest, simple, noble artist and man." [6] So Mrs. Browning remarked, writing to Ruskin, and her husband wrote to Harriet Hosmer, "Stick to him like a leech, for it is real life blood you will get out of him, real thoughts and facts, nothing

[6] "William Page painted a portrait of Robert like an Italian, and then presented it to me like a prince. It is a wonderful picture, the colour so absolutely *Venetian* that artists can't (for the most part) keep their temper when they look at it, and the breath of the likeness is literal. Mr. Page has *secrets* in the art—certainly nobody else paints like him—and his nature, I must say, is equal to his genius, and worthy of it."—*Letters of Elizabeth Barrett Browning,* Vol. II, pp. 170-171.

The portrait of Browning had turned so black fifty years later that the head had virtually disappeared.

W. W. Story called Page's portrait of Charlotte Cushman "the finest portrait, I think, I ever saw."

like sham and conventionalism. I carry in my mind all I can of his doctrine about the true proportions of the human figure, and test it by whatever strikes me as beautiful, or the reverse." [7] Continuing her letter to Ruskin, Mrs. Browning said, "I never saw such portraits from a living hand, but will the colour *stand?*" Unhappily, it did not. Page was perversely convinced that toning was not a result of time and that Titian's pictures were painted as we see them, so he undertoned his pictures at the outset, the consequence being that, generally, they turned black. By good luck, two of them survived to show how fine Page really was, the full-length portrait of himself and the portrait of his wife with the Coliseum in the background.[8]

Many an artist remembered later the stillness of the streets of Rome, where sometimes one heard only the plash of a fountain and where, from a studio in some old palace, one looked out on a garden with blossoming oleanders, oranges and roses. The little society of painters and sculptors sometimes gathered for expeditions to the ancient Præneste,—Palestrina,—or for an evening ramble among the Roman ruins, where perhaps they "set up a choral strain," singing "Hail Columbia!" as in Hawthorne's novel; or they went for a picnic to the Campagna over ploughed fields that were scattered with broken pottery and bits of marble. Occasionally one picked up in the furrows a small bronze statuette or a tourmaline from the ring of some ancient beauty; and every month or so someone dug out of a ruin a figure like the one discovered by Hawthorne's Donatello. There were several who saw the great statue of Augustus Caesar, which later stood in the Vatican, taken from the earth and laid upon trestles in the shed of a farmhouse on the road,— it had stood in the grounds of the villa of Livia Augusta; and

[7] Letter of 1854, in *Harriet Hosmer, Letters and Journals.*
[8] In the Detroit Institute of Arts.

others saw the great bronze statue of the young Hercules lifted from its bed of oyster-shells, with remnants of the original gilding still clinging to it. Nor was it unheard of to find a peasant lighting his pipe with steel and a flint that turned out to be a shoulder brooch of an imperial mantle, an intaglio perhaps of *pietra dura*. For the rest, the artists lived in hope that some travelling business man, catching the "art infection," might give them a commission, although most of the tourists, who were apt to be gullible, preferred a "genuine Guido" or a "real Titian" or a black patched-up landscape, a "real Salvator."

Among the young art students in Rome in 1844 was William Morris Hunt, later the painter, who was studying sculpture there before he went on to Barbizon virtually to live for two years with Jean-François Millet. Hunt, more perhaps than anyone else, was to turn the next generation of painters away from Rome and Italy and towards France and Paris; but he was working with the American sculptor Henry Kirke Brown when his friend Francis Parkman turned up in Rome.[9] Parkman had been sent abroad, like Prescott earlier, for his health, and he rode with Hunt to Subiaco and up the mountain to the monastery that was built over the cave where St. Benedict had lived. Together they visited Civitella where every stranger was called a *pittore* because only artists visited the town.

Parkman, already planning to write his history of French Canada, wished to study a Catholic civilization, and he was eager for clear impressions of the monastic life to which he was, in a way, temperamentally drawn. For he was the most austere of men, and he was also, as he said, "a little mediæval." In

[9] It is related of Hunt that about this time in Florence he saw on a table a copy of Mrs. Jameson's *Early Italian Painters*. On the margin, beside a passage on Correggio, Margaret Fuller had written, "And yet all might be such." Hunt said afterwards, "These words struck out a new strength in me. They made me set my face like a flint."

Sicily, on horseback, he had visited monasteries in the wild inaccessible mountains more than once, among them a luxurious Benedictine monastery where he dined on lampreys and game from the monks' preserve. In Rome he rode on a mule to another monastery, a few miles from Albano at Rocca di Papa, where the Passionists wore haircloth and lashed themselves with chains, for theirs was the strictest of monastic orders. They refused his request to stay for a few days with them, but he was accepted for a week's visit at another Passionist monastery, near the Coliseum, at Rome.[10] There the enormity of his disbelief horrified the monks, he said, and he left with "unimpaired prospects of damnation," while, remaining an anticlerical who became an agnostic, he was charmed by the romantic colour of the Catholic church. He met a number of Jesuits in Rome through a Boston cousin, Coolidge Shaw, a convert to Catholicism who was studying for the priesthood, and, in spite of his incredulity, he became convinced that the ceremonies of the Church had a "salutary effect on the mind." When he came to write the history of a Catholic country, this initiation in Rome was to serve him well.

At Naples, Parkman had fallen in with Theodore Parker, the Boston reformer, with whom he climbed Vesuvius and went on to Rome, while Parker declaimed Virgil and Cicero all the way, disapproving of the young man's wish to visit a monastery when a prison of the Inquisition still existed in Rome. Then he said he could not help looking at the Coliseum professionally as a fine place for preaching Parkerism, a variety of Unitarianism that won adherents through the English-speak-

[10] "I was led into a convent by the same motives that two years later led me to become domesticated in the lodge of the Sioux Indians at the Rocky Mountains, with the difference that I much preferred the company of the savages to that of the monks."—Quoted in Parkman's *Journals,* Vol. I, p. 101.

ing world for whom Parker was an American Savonarola.[11] Another reformer from Boston, Dorothea Lynde Dix, presently visited Rome on a tour of Europe, on her way to Constantinople, Syria, and Russia, inspecting mental hospitals everywhere. She was shocked by what she found in the hospital in Rome, and she persuaded the Pope to visit the asylum unannounced and inspect the wards that she had seen. The Pope then gave her a second audience, told her how distressed he was and thanked her for calling his attention to this sad situation; and before she left Italy a tract of land was bought for a new hospital and a special doctor was sent to Paris to study the advanced methods of the hospitals there.

Dorothea Dix was not the only reformer who carried a missionary zeal from Boston to Rome. Dr. Samuel Gridley Howe, appalled by the indifference of the rich to the poor, had opened a school for blind children of kindergarten age there. Dickens's *American Notes* had spread the fame of Dr. Howe, so that even the Pope asked him about Laura Bridgman, and there was a tinge of adventure and poetry in everything he did, a touch of the "romance of philanthropy," as Emerson called it. He had fought for the Greeks in their revolution and he had been imprisoned in Germany as a friend of the Poles. Aside from all this, a believer in phrenology, he studied in Rome the busts in the sculpture galleries, tracing out the proofs of this science of the moment, judging by their bumps and bulges and by their brows, high or low, the ancient worthies and deities of Rome and Greece. He found in the head of Jupiter the majesty

[11] Theodore Parker returned to Italy in 1860, and he died and was buried in Florence. It was on his death-bed there that he met the Anglo-Irish writer, who had long been his disciple, Frances Power Cobbe. It was she who edited Parker's collected works.

The association of Parker with Savonarola was perhaps largely suggested by his death in Florence at about the time when George Eliot published *Romola*, in which Savonarola played so important a part.

of intellect, and the head of Pallas was intellectual also, while Aphrodite's head was small and the organs of sensation predominated, as one might have supposed, over those of thought. The all-curious Mrs. Howe,—Julia Ward Howe,—who wrote poems in Italian and made speeches in French, studied Hebrew with a learned rabbi from the ghetto where he had to be within the walls by nightfall. This minor Margaret Fuller, more of the world and less of the mind, who was later a great founder of clubs for women [12] and for whom "causes" were the breath of life, was already an *improvisatrice* and a singer at musical parties that brought the Anglo-American visitors together.

Some of the artists living in Rome maintained their Calvinistic views unaltered in a city they regarded as pagan. There they were opposed to the artistic Bohemia and Catholicism alike, while their wives still lived as if Rome were a New England village, carrying jellies to invalid friends, just as they had done at home, and pumpkin pies to others who were homesick. But all kinds of Americans were turning up there in the eighteen-forties, among them two Brook Farmers, George William Curtis and Isaac Hecker, together with the Concord namesake of William Ellery Channing. Curtis, at Florence for a few weeks, had gone with the Brownings to Vallombrosa where Browning seated himself at the organ in the chapel on which Milton had played two centuries before, playing himself some hymn of Pergolesi. Isaac Hecker, who had been the community bread-maker at Brook Farm, was a convert already to the Catholic Church. The future founder of the Paulist Fathers, visiting in Concord, where he became a good friend of Thoreau, tried to persuade this other young man to go with him to Rome "without purse or staff, to prove that the dollar is not almighty"; but,

[12] The Circolo Italiano in Boston was one of these.

much as Thoreau approved of Hecker's mode of travelling, he did not wish to interrupt his own way of living. He had just returned from a week in the Catskills, "subsisting mainly on bread and berries and slumbering on the mountain tops," as he wrote to Hecker, who was twenty-five years old to his twenty-seven, and he was not as eager to walk where the saints had been before him as to continue his "Brahminical, artesian, Inner Temple life." On the other hand, the poet Channing, the great doctor's nephew,—the "sublimoslipshod" Channing, as Thoreau called him, "as naturally whimsical as a cow is brindled,"—seemed, in his *Conversations in Rome,* to associate himself with the Catholic who carries on the dialogue with the Critic and the Artist. The peppery discussions of the three, on Italian gardens, on Montaigne, on Claude, the Roman fountains, the Coliseum, might well have been a continuation, in this exotic scene, of the Concord conversation of the Sunday walkers.

CHAPTER VIII

ROME: W. W. STORY

WILLIAM WETMORE STORY had been haunted from child-hood by "dreams of art and Italy." Born in Salem but growing up in Cambridge, where his father had been the founder of the Harvard Law School, he had been a Boston lawyer who made repeated visits to Rome before he arrived to spend the rest of his life there. He had come over to study sculpture in 1847, and, stopping for a few weeks in Florence, he had met the Brownings, with whom he became intimate a few years later. The following year, on another visit, he had written to his friend James Russell Lowell, "How shall I ever again endure the restraint and bondage of Boston?"—where, as he said in another letter, "There is no such thing as flesh and blood . . . We love nothing, we criticize everything . . . The sky itself is hard and distant. The heart grows into stone." He had made up his mind, however, to break with art and Rome for a while, write Judge Story's biography and edit his works; then at last, sure of his talent, he took warning from Washington Allston's unhappy fate at home.[1] In the mid-fifties he

[1] "Allston starved spiritually in Cambridgeport; he fed upon himself. There was nothing congenial without, and he turned all his powers inward and drained his memory dry. His works grew thinner and vaguer every day . . . I know no more melancholy sight than he was, so rich and beautiful a nature, in whose veins the South ran warm, which was born to have grown to such a height and to have spread abroad such fragrancy, stunted on the scant soil and withered by the

settled in the Palazzo Barberini, where he and his family were to live for forty-five years.

Small and wiry, intensely alive, all animation and sparkling wit, a writer in verse and prose as well as a sculptor, Story was born to succeed too easily, some of his well-wishers thought, but who should have been happy if not he? [2] The palace, designed by Bernini and built from the quarry of the Coliseum, with a statue by Thorwaldsen outside, gardens and palm-trees, became, with the Storys, almost at once, an Anglo-American centre that travellers were to know for two generations. The sculptor converted one large room into a theatre with footlights where he presented plays, sometimes written by himself, and in one of these he acted with his friend Salvini who was so famous later as Iago and Othello. Salvini was just entering on the renowned career is which he made Anglo-Saxon actors seem cold and artificial. But writers and artists of every sort appeared in the Storys' rooms, from Alexis de Tocqueville to Thackeray, who took a great interest in the Story children and wrote for them, along with his own, the fireside pantomime, *The Rose and the Ring*. This was the comic fairy tale, with his own Twelfth Night pictures, about Rosalba, Angelica, Prince Bulbo and Blackstick,—and the Broccolis, Articiocchis and Spinachis,—that he read to Story's little daughter, sitting on the edge of her bed when she was ill.

Once Story gave a party for Hans Christian Andersen, who

---

cold winds of that fearful Cambridgeport. I look at his studio whenever I pass with a heart-pang."—W. W. Story, Letter to Lowell, quoted in *Washington Allston*, by E. P. Richardson, p. 155.

[2] "The most variously accomplished and brilliant person, the fullest of social life and fire, whom I ever met . . . He kept us amused and entertained the whole day long, not wearisomely entertained either, as we should have been if he had not let the fountain play naturally . . . Rich, in the prime of life, children budding and blossoming around him, with sparkling talents . . . who should be happy if not he?"—Hawthorne, *French and Italian Notebooks*, Vol. II, p. 173.

read *The Ugly Duckling* aloud to the children. Then Browning read *The Pied Piper,* and this was followed by a grand march through the spacious rooms, Story himself leading with a flute. Hans Christian Andersen had written in Rome *The Improvisatore,* in part his own life-story in Italian dress. Gawky and gaunt, with a singer's voice, fleeing from the cold north, he had pictured himself in Antonio, the Roman orphan who had lived with shepherds on the Campagna, in one of the decayed tombs there, largely to escape from his uncle Beppo.[3] Then he had been seized by bandits who took him to their cave where they fed him on buffalo cheese and asses' milk, as in some robber scene of Salvator Rosa, and meanwhile he was befriended by Prince Borghese and fell in love with the actress Annunziata. He made his debut at San Carlo in Naples as a masculine Corinne, an *improvisatore,* famous from Rome to Venice, from whose lips words flowed at any suggested theme, Titian, the catacombs, Tasso, immortality, Sappho. The great poet with his guitar visited all the historic spots from Florence to the fairy world of the Bay of Naples, and *The Improvisatore,* like the earlier *Corinne* and *The Marble Faun,* became for tourists a romantic vade-mecum.

It was Story's studio in the Via San Niccolò da Tolentino

[3] Beppo was the famous beggar, the "king of the Spanish steps," whose two withered legs were crossed beneath him. He stumped along on wooden clogs, moving only on his hands and knees. Beppo appeared in Story's *Roba di Roma,* in Hawthorne's *The Marble Faun* and in almost every other book about Rome in the mid-century.

"Yesterday morning I saw Beppo with the withered legs at his post on the stairs. His hair is quite white. He has got to be an old man, but his face is as jolly as ever, and he has the same wheedling voice with his 'Buon giorno, signore.' I deliberately stopped, opened my purse, took out a heavy two baiccho piece and dropped it in his hat, for the sake of old times. I told him it was ten years since I had seen him. I could as little have missed old Beppo in Rome, and on his old place, as I could have missed the boat fountain at the bottom of the Spanish stairs."—Christopher P. Cranch, Letter of 1858.

that Hawthorne presently described as the sculptor Kenyon's, and there stood the figure, "Cleopatra," that was shown with the "Libyan Sibyl" at the London exhibition of 1862. It was these that established Story's reputation in England, where he made for Eton College the bust of Shelley whom Leigh Hunt,[4] Severn and Landor had described to him. Later, convinced that the taste for sculpture was growing among the Americans and that they bought more statues than any other nation, he explained that the English cared more for painting because everything in England was saturated and washed in colour. The atmosphere, thick and humid, obliterated form, whereas the American atmosphere, tense and dry, revealing the outlines of everything, insisted on form. The distances were clear in America, the trees were etched against the sky. It was in connection with the studio of Story that Browning wrote a poem, *Eulogy of Sculpture,* and Hawthorne thought it delightful to escape to his creations from the "universal prettiness" of other sculptors; but his work seemed singularly dull and flat when, in after years, sculpture was disassociated from the anecdotal. He had worked for a literary age that liked to see in statuary illustrations of history or the picturesque, and he had to face another taste,—a distaste, one might rather say,—that was bred by other prepossessions.[5]

[4] "I shall always be glad that I knew [Leigh Hunt]. It was like touching an older generation of poets and writers. He showed me one day a lock of Milton's hair and said, 'Put your hand on it.' I did. 'There!' he said, 'you have touched Milton.' "—W. W. Story, *Conversations in a Studio,* Vol. II, p. 404.

[5] See Mrs. Henry Adams's remark on Story's sibyls—"all with the same expression as if they smelt something wrong. Call him a genius! I don't see it."—*Letters of Mrs. Henry Adams,* p. 95.

Henry James suggested, in *William Wetmore Story and His Friends* (Vol. II, p. 226) that he might have had better fortune if he had remained in Boston. For there "he would have had to live with his conception, there being nothing else about him of the same colour or quality . . . The 'picturesque' subject has by no means all its advantage in

But who had for the city of the Caesars and the Popes a more truly appreciative feeling than the sculptor and poet who wrote *Roba di Roma?*—"roba" meaning everything from rubbish and riff-raff to the most exquisite products of nature and art. "The soil and stain that many call dirt, I call colour; and the cleanliness of Amsterdam would ruin Rome for the artist." So wrote Story in this book, adding, with his native land in mind, "Nothing is so prosaic as the rawly new." He delighted in the grim, browned, rotted walls, their peeling mortar and their yellows and greys, the tumbling tiled roofs with their myriad lichens and the streets where, at every turn, one encountered nature, not conscious or prim but graceful, impulsive, free and simple. What made Rome good for the artist, he thought, was the careless out-of-door life where all poses were unsought, all groupings accidental and where, in the long damp alleys, at any moment one might meet a curly-headed young St. John or a Madonna. He wrote also about the ballad-singers, the street musicians, the popular games, the costumes that survived to please the painter, the beggars, the Campagna where one still picked up fragments of marbles and coins, or bits of terra-cotta from the ruins of villas. On every hand one found the relics of old pagan customs of which one had read in Ovid or Varro. Story quoted the dialect poems of Giovanni Belli, so close to the popular life and the pavements of Rome,—poems of which Eleanor Clark was to make so much in her book, many years later, *Rome and a Villa*,—and he described the Artists' Festival in the groves of Egeria in May when crowds assembled to witness the merrymaking. He had spent a season at Castel Gandolfo where, in the main palazzo, the upper ten

---

the picturesque country." It is true that the work of William Rimmer, the Boston sculptor who remained at home, was finer than that of any of the American sculptors in Italy.

assembled every evening,—the bishop, the syndic, the lawyer, the physician and so on,—and the young peasant girls, in their Albanese costumes, came, glittering with necklaces and earrings, to dance with their lovers. A barrel of wine was set up in a corner of the great hall, and all distinctions of rank and wealth were abolished for a few hours at least in a whirl of quadrilles, polkas and waltzes.

No one conveyed better than Story the much-talked-of Rome-sickness that drew the visitor back again and again, that drew even Hawthorne back, with all his distaste for the city, and led him to say, "No place ever took so strong a hold of my being." Story had been drilled in Roman history, like all the New Englanders of his time, and, knowing the Roman writers by heart, he half expected to meet Cicero and Horace as he went down the Appian Way. He saw the processions of victory winding through the Arch of Titus; and, driving through the Nomentian Gate, Story saw Nero in his flight, his underground hiding-place and his miserable ending. The ancient Roman characters who had been mere lay-figures in school became here like men of yesterday, and he felt in the Trastevere that these were the people who listened to Marcus Antonius and Brutus when the bier of Caesar was brought into the streets. Then, walking past the Albergo del Orso, he had seen rising before him the shape and figure of Montaigne who had once lived there; and he saw Alfieri looking out of the window of the Villa Strozzi to the villa where the Countess of Albany was waiting for him. He saw Tasso under the cypresses of the Villa d'Este and Benvenuto Cellini fighting on the walls of the castle of San Angelo and escaping from the tower; and he remembered that Cagliostro had lived in the Piazza di Spagna after the famous intrigue of the diamond necklace. It was Story's historic sense that gave a measure of interest to the various dramatic monologues that appeared among his poems, *A Roman Lawyer in Jerusalem, A Jewish Rabbi in Rome, A Primitive Christian in Rome* and many another. Marcus Aurelius, Leonardo da Vinci, the Duke of Urbino and Raphael were among the characters who appeared in Story's poems. If these had only a measure of interest it was because in their form and style they were obviously imitations of Robert Browning.

For Story, as a poet, was steeped in Browning, who returned the compliment by taking lessons in modelling from his American friend, working in the studio during a winter for three hours every day and "making extraordinary progress," Mrs. Browning said. Of her, Story made a bust, and the Storys and the Brownings were constantly together in Rome or Siena or Bagni di Lucca, where both families took villas for several summers. They went together on drives and walks, and evening after evening Story and Browning played and sang till midnight. Browning, in London, read the proofs of Story's *Roba di Roma,* making the necessary cuts for a handbook edition, and the two travelled later through Scotland together. Meanwhile, one of their common friends was Browning's "dearest Hattie," —"a great pet of mine and of Robert's," Mrs. Browning called her,—the sculptress Harriet Hosmer who had grown up in a suburb of Boston and who made the cast of the clasped hands of the Brownings. She was John Gibson's only pupil, and Gibson turned over to his "young miss" the old studio of Canova that adjoined his own, giving her books, engravings and casts to study while he watched over her with fatherly interest. The two were often seen breakfasting together at the Caffé Greco, while Harriet, as she said, was "sworn to celibacy . . . the only faithful worshipper of it." She "emancipated the eccentric life of a perfectly 'emancipated female' from all shadow of blame, by the purity of hers," as Mrs. Browning put it, working all day from six in the morning until she set out on horseback for her late afternoon gallop over the Campagna. She rode all over the city until she was stopped by the police because her appearance caused so much excitement, bent as she was on showing that a Yankee girl could do anything she pleased and ride or walk alone by day or night. With her wideawake manner, she was small and brisk, downright and straightforward, dressing like a man with shirt-front, collar and cravat and with a black velvet cap over her short brown curls.

Harriet Hosmer spent a summer with the Storys at Siena, and when she was in Florence she dined with the Brownings every night. Browning gave her lessons in Greek, and he wrote to her from Paris about his new friend Rosa Bonheur, "a glorious little creature with a touch of Hatty about her that makes one start." From Florence he wrote to her in Rome that he saw her image "on the queer chair, at the little end of the table, on the sofa, and in all old places of yours," adding, "We get on a little with our work, yet we had rather be idle and have you." At Rome, they went on picnics together, once to Albano with Frederick Leighton, all of them mounted on donkeys, winding past the monastery of Palazzuola. Climbing a hill, they emerged on Hannibal's old camping ground, near the sparkling lake of Nemi, "Diana's Mirror," guarding still beneath the blue water Caligula's enamel-decked barges. They spent two days at Albano. Harriet had brought Browning's poems in her travelling-bag, and she persuaded the poet to read aloud the whole of his poem *Saul*. Some time before, with a party of friends, she had ridden for a lark from Rome to Florence, travelling on horseback only after dark. As they rode, for three nights, Harriet studied the effects of the play of light and shadow on the silhouettes of trees, watching the moonlight on the turf in open spaces. Thirty years later she worked these effects into a design for one of her sculptures.

But how did it happen that Harriet Hosmer became, for so many years, one of the well-known popular sculptors of Europe? Perhaps at first the reason was that her studio adjoined Gibson's and the throngs who came to see his work were drawn to see hers. She exhibited in London, Edinburgh, Dublin and Paris, and she was decorated by the King of Bavaria and by the Empress of Russia, while the Prince of Wales bought her "Puck" for his rooms at Oxford. After the fall of the kingdom of Naples, the queen sat for her in Rome, and she spent a week at the castle in Germany where the king and queen lived, playing chess every evening with the deplorable "Bomba." What Fanny Kemble called Harriet Hosmer's "infinite fun" explained her popularity, at least a little, and her skilful mimicry of the ancient sculptors accounted for a great deal more in the days of the heirs of Canova and the Greek revival. The president of the Royal Academy said of her "Sleeping Faun" that if it had been discovered among the ruins of Rome it would have passed for Greek and one of the best, and Tennyson said of her "African Sibyl," "It is the most poetic rendering in art of a great historical truth I have ever seen." The Bostonians were delighted by the womanly modesty of Harriet Hosmer's "Zenobia," as well as by the sculptor's masculine courage, and they earnestly studied the admixture of Oriental and Grecian in the sculptured costume of this ancient sovereign. Just so, a few years later, the intellectuals of New York,—Bancroft, Bryant, Beecher, Bierstadt and others,—assembled to pay homage to the intrepid artist. In its aesthetic naivety the mid-nineteenth-century literary mind was almost equally marked in America and England.

Of the common friends of the Brownings and the Storys an-

other, a writer on sculpture, was the Boston art-historian
Charles C. Perkins, who had studied music in Germany and
painting in Paris and who was to live in Rome for several
years. It was he who bought Crawford's statue of Beethoven
for the Boston music-hall, where he himself occasionally appeared as a conductor, and he had become absorbed, meanwhile, in the study of sculpture in Italy which, as compared
with painting, was so little known. Italian sculpture had always been measured by the standard of the antique, a standard that did not exist in painting, and the great Italian works
of sculpture were not collected in galleries but were scattered
in streets and churches everywhere. There were few books on
the subject, and Perkins searched the peninsula, north, south,
east and west, drawing and collecting photographs in hundreds
of towns. Like Ruskin, he had read Lord Lindsay and Rio,—to
whom he dedicated *Tuscan Sculptors*,—and he was deeply
affected by their conception of Christian art and the greatness
of Niccola Pisano and his early successors. Then, studying in
Urbino, in the ducal palace that had been described in the
high Renaissance by Castiglione in the *Cortegiano*,—when artists, musicians and men of letters thronged there,—he prepared his fine *Raphael and Michelangelo*, treating these artists
conjointly to bring out their peculiarities by force of contrast.
Almost a century later, *Tuscan Sculptors* and *Italian Sculptors* [6]
were virtually as authoritative and living as when they were
written. Perkins was one of those gifted minds, deeply cultivated and mature, that mid-century Boston was producing in
numbers.

[6] These two works were later combined, abbreviated, largely rewritten
and published under the title *Historical Handbook of Italian Sculpture*,
1882. Perkins included in his *Raphael and Michelangelo* some of Longfellow's translations of Michelangelo's sonnets that had not yet been
published. He also wrote, in French, *Ghiberti et son École*.

CHAPTER IX

THE RISORGIMENTO:
MARGARET FULLER

THE THREE principal sights of Milan, from the traveller's point of view, were the "Last Supper," the cathedral and the novelist Manzoni, whom George Bancroft had called upon in 1821 before the appearance of *I Promessi Sposi*. After the great novel was published in 1825–1827 and Andrews Norton [1] of Harvard put it into English, American tourists sometimes read it among the scenes that it described in the Lombard capital or on Lake Como. There they pointed out the promontory where the priest met the bravoes in the opening scene, or perhaps, like Charles Sumner, in the public vettura, they found the "spontaneous tear" on their cheek as they read about Fra Cristoforo asking for pardon. Many a reader, moreover, saw in the story a sympathetic plea for the Risorgimento, although the more active workers for the great cause rejected Manzoni's doctrine of "Pray and wait." For the book was a moving indictment not only of foreign tyranny but of the degradation and oppression of the people. The tyrants in the book happened to be Spaniards, but they might have been Metternich's Austrians, the present rulers.

While most of the visiting Americans were too full of their

[1] The father of Charles Eliot Norton. Mrs. Andrews Norton translated Silvio Pellico's *My Prisons*.

dream of Arcadia to care whether Italy itself was alive or dead, this was not true of the sculptors Greenough and Crawford, who were passionately concerned for Italian independence. They felt as Mrs. Browning felt when she came to live in Florence and Walter Savage Landor who had lived there, and like James Jackson Jarves, who was not a "tourist Tory," for all his wonder over the Italian past. Jarves loved to think of the time when almost every hamlet, and certainly every town, boasted its artist, but he was not one of those amateurs of good old times whom one encountered now on every hand. He did not wish to persuade the peasants that when they were herded like swine, and begged at convent gates, they were better off. Moreover, he had seen too much of what he called "papal mis-rule" and "the ruthless tyranny and dirty state-craft of Austria in Italy." Jarves followed Mazzini as he followed Garibaldi, and even the frosty George Ticknor, in the course of two visits to Italy, sought out some of the heroes of the Risorgimento. He had spent several evenings with the young Count Confalonieri, before this Carbonarist was condemned to the Spielberg. Then, talking with Silvio Pellico in 1836, he too had called upon Manzoni. Within a few years, Margaret Fuller, Catharine M. Sedgwick and Julia Ward Howe,—politically minded all,— were drawn to the great movement.

Miss Sedgwick had known intimately the "Italian exiles" in New York whom she and her brothers were among the first to welcome, the patriots released from the dreadful Austrian prison on condition of perpetual exile from their native land. Among them were Confalonieri, Foresti and Maroncelli who supported themselves in America by teaching Italian, in Cambridge, New York or the Berkshires where several Sedgwicks began to study under these lively masters. Julia Ward Howe, as a girl in New York, had read Metastasio and Alfieri with a son of Mozart's librettist Lorenzo da Ponte, and she remembered Foresti and Albinola as having a "perfectly childlike delight in living." No wonder, after their long dreary years in prison where, forbidden to read year after year, they could only watch spiders on the walls spinning webs. Julia Ward Howe had studied Dante with Foresti, and, coming to Italy in 1843, she had looked up in Milan some of his relations. She had brought a letter from Catharine Sedgwick to Confalonieri, released from exile and prison but broken in health. Miss Sedgwick herself had found him in Genoa in 1839, and she had met Foresti's sister and Silvio Pellico in Turin, where he was acting as librarian for a certain marchesa. Short, slight, delicate and singularly sweet,—"a more shadowy Dr. Channing,"—the author of *My Prisons* was eager for news of his old companions of the Spielberg who were still in New York. She too saw Manzoni with his mother and his wife, all of them as grateful for her kindness to the exiles "as if," she said, "we had cherished their own lost children."

Miss Sedgwick, who was touched by the spirit of her Italian friends, was astonished by the restraints which the governments imposed here, so that without special permission one could not cross the frontiers of the mosaic of small Italian states. She was shocked also, like Fenimore Cooper and the poet Bryant, —in 1834,—by the contrast between "governments of opinion" and "governments of power" that had no concern whatever with the welfare of the governed, and by the presence everywhere of Austrian guards, heavily armed, in the midst of these peaceful populations.[2] The shameless corruption of the custom-

[2] Bryant, *Letters of a Traveller*, p. 22.

Cf. Mrs. Browning: "Ah, here's oppression! here's a people trodden down! You should come here and see. It is enough to turn the depths of the heart bitter. The will of the people forced, their instinctive affections despised, their liberty of thought spied upon, their material life ignored altogether. Robert keeps saying, 'How long, O Lord, how

houses, the hopeless dependence and poverty and the want of self-respect of the lower classes were enough to explain the apathy in which the peninsula lay bound until Mazzini's "Young Italy" brought it to life. The secret society of the Carbonari had long since been discredited by the failure of the risings it had led to, though various poets, Parini, Niccolini, Giusti, had worked on the minds of readers everywhere. Meanwhile, imprisoned as a Carbonarist,—with Byron and Tacitus in his cell, a Bible and a greenfinch as companions,—Mazzini had planned another movement which he promoted from London, while teaching a school for poor Italian boys there. He dreamed of a United States of Europe in which Italy's part would be messianic, for Italy was to take the lead in forming a new epoch for the human race, a collective humanity, in short, the religion of the future. The necessary first step towards this was the unification of Italy and the expulsion of the despots who ruled the eight states; and this was to be followed by a more or less socialist republic. Mazzini, who was always dressed in black,—"in mourning for my country,"—wrote pamphlets that were smuggled into Italy, appeals, manifestoes, concealed in bales of cloth and barrels of pitch, reminding the Italians of their former greatness, their present degradation and their radiant future.

In London, Mazzini lived near the house of the Thomas Carlyles, where Margaret Fuller met him in 1847 and where, like Jane Carlyle, she was deeply moved by his burning words, —"rose-water imbecilities" Carlyle called them. But she understood, better that Carlyle, that Mazzini's flights of mind were calculated to arouse young Italy's will, and she was soon to find herself, as one of Mazzini's lieutenants, in the thick of

long?' Such things cannot last surely. Oh, this brutal Austria."—Letters of Mrs. Browning, Vol. II, p. 114.

the Italian revolution. She had once exclaimed, "I must die if I do not burst forth in heroism or genius," and the cause of Mazzini gave this *exaltée,* at the apex of her life, an opportunity for which she had always longed. This was a day when, as Harriet Beecher Stowe remarked, there were no heroes like "the men who get up insurrections," when virtually every country in Europe was undergoing a revolution to establish the rights of humanity against the old order. Margaret was also to see much of Adam Mickiewicz, who might have been described as the Mazzini of the Poles. Now, coming abroad as a foreign correspondent for Horace Greeley's *Tribune,* she was to find in Italy a spiritual home. "Italy," she wrote, "receives me as a long lost child." Her preference had always been "for the Italian genius," as Emerson remarked in a memoir later.

The "Yankee Corinne," as she was called, who had modelled herself in a measure on the priestess of Apollo, Madame de Staël, had already played a conspicuous part in the flowering of New England before she realized her dream of a visit abroad. Brought up by her father, a member of Congress and a scholarly Boston lawyer, she had read Virgil and Ovid at six or seven, and she had seen it as her duty "to grow" when, as a young girl in Cambridge, she had risen every day at five in the morning. Her schedule had been severe, the piano before breakfast, then French, Greek and philosophy till twelve,—she took Latin for granted,—two hours of Italian in the afternoon, metaphysics and French literature, with interludes of writing in her journal. Plain in appearance but with a dashing air, she had early made up her mind to be "bright and ugly"; and, always the centre of an admiring group, she sought out the cleverest Harvard boys to talk philosophy with and study German. She carried on classes for young ladies, reading Dante with them,— the great new vogue in Boston in the early forties,—translating all the hundred cantos with the aid of the best commentaries and carefully studying Flaxman's designs as well.[3] With them she also read Petrarch, Tasso, Alfieri, and various French and German authors, composing three sonnets to Petrarch herself while she translated and published the *Conversations with Eckermann* of Goethe. In her own "Conversations" with older Boston ladies, on Greek mythology, the nature of beauty and what not, she glorified George Sand's heroines and their active protest against what she thought the indignity of a woman's lot. For the author of *Woman in the Nineteenth Century* was a fervent feminist and a searcher for "the *mot d'énigme* for which we are all looking,—how the poetical mind can live and work in peace and good faith, how it may unfold to its due perfection in an unpoetical society."

All this had made the imperious Margaret, with her magnetic influence, together with her contempt for the "broadcloth vulgar," a leader of the young at Brook Farm and elsewhere; and, with her habit of "ducking, diving or flying after the truth," she was a formidable literary journalist as well. She was aware of the new currents of thought in the European countries,—it was she who introduced Browning to American readers,—and she contrasted American literature and its "boyish crudity, half boastful, half timid," with the tempered manly equipoise of the best European writers. Meanwhile, at a moment when the Boston mind was developing an interest in the plastic arts, when Allston's pictures were shown at the Athenæum, followed by the sculpture of Greenough, Crawford and Powers and the great Brimmer collection of Italian

[3] "With what envy I looked at Flaxman's picture of Hesiod sitting at the feet of the Muse! How blest would it be to be thus instructed in one's vocation!"—*Memoirs of Margaret Fuller*, Vol. I, p. 153.

Margaret Fuller wrote a sonnet on Flaxman, and later, in Paris, she gave the poet Mickiewicz a set of Flaxman's illustrations of Homer, Hesiod and Dante.

drawings, she began to write on aesthetic matters also. When, as Emerson said, "Certain months seemed coloured with the genius of these Italians," when prints of Correggio, Guercino and the Sistine frescoes appeared on many Boston walls, Margaret was more than ever absorbed in Palladio's architectural drawings, Piranesi's etchings, Cellini and Vasari's Lives. More than ever too she dreamed of that "free life guided by fantasy" that seemed to her the note of her admired Corinne.

But Margaret Fuller's aesthetic interests were to be absorbed in turn in social and political interests when she met Mazzini, and this became still more the case when she encountered Mickiewicz, Fenimore Cooper's old friend who was living in Paris. She had in Paris too a memorable interview with George Sand, whose Consuelo had been an ugly duckling, not wholly unlike Margaret in her childhood, and Mickiewicz took her to call on Chopin, his fellow-countryman, who seemed, she wrote in a letter, "as frail as a snowdrop." Chopin played for Margaret and her "brother Adam," for so Mickiewicz called himself in the letters that he wrote her when she had left Paris and gone on to Rome. In Paris he was involved in a mystical circle that was not unlike the Transcendental circle which Margaret had known well at home, and as a professor at the Collège de France he had lectured on Emerson and circulated among his students copies of *The Dial*. For Poland he advocated sweeping reforms, equality of rights, freedom of speech, land-ownership for the peasants, rights for women,—resembling his friend Mazzini in much of this,—and he called Margaret "the only woman to whom it has been given to touch what is decisive in the present world and to have a presentiment of the world of the future." [4] She was "a true person," Mickiewicz

[4] Leopold Willicz, *The Friendship of Margaret Fuller d'Ossoli and Adam Mickiewicz*, 1947.

wrote to her again, and theirs was one of those encounters that "console and fortify." But she must not confine her life any longer to reveries and books, he said. The important thing for her now was to "live and act."

Margaret was to see this friend again in 1848 in Rome, where Fenimore Cooper had known him in 1830 and where he was looking now for the world revolution "to inaugurate the new era of freedom for the oppressed of the world." She was to assist him there in his organization of the Polish legion to fight against the common Austrian oppressor, but in the meantime she stopped to see Manzoni who seemed, she wrote, "to like to talk to me." However, she could not accept his Fabianism, for she needed "a more fervent hope, a more active faith," and she went on to Genoa to see Mazzini's mother, who led her out to the balcony of her son's old study. There she plucked two leaves of the scented verbena that grew in the window to send them to Mazzini in his exile. It was the spring of 1847 when she arrived in Rome. She was at that moment thirty-seven years old.

Not many weeks passed before Mickiewicz wrote to her, advising her not to leave lightly "that little Italian you met in the church," telling her that she should "liberate her spirit" by responding to her "legitimate physical needs." [5] She had told him about Ossoli, the impoverished marquis, slender, reserved and gentle, much younger than herself, whom she had encountered in St. Peter's, a devout anti-clerical Catholic who presently became her husband and the father of her child. The results soon bore out Mickiewicz's counsel, for Margaret's personality seemed to change over-night, as friends who had known her in Boston immediately noticed. One was Mrs.

[5] See the quotations from their correspondence in *The Golden Ring*, by Giuliana Artom Treves, p. 163.

Story, who was visiting in Rome, where she and her husband were to settle a few years later. Margaret, Mrs. Story said, had come off her "intellectual stilts," she was no longer arrogant, the pedant was transformed, she was everything that she had not been at home, sensitive, confiding, affectionate, generous and simple; and this was largely because she had followed Mickiewicz's advice to act and live, no longer in reveries and books but physically also. Besides, she had found her cause, the Roman revolution, and art, as she wrote, was no longer important to her, engrossed as she was in great historic events. Ossoli was a liberal in a papal family,—his brothers at the Vatican were members of the noble guard,—and he was deeply committed to the movement for unification and Mazzini's conception of the future. In quieter moments Margaret and Ossoli went for all-day picnics, carrying roast chestnuts with them as they set out from the city, finding bread and wine in some lonely little osteria and returning in time to see Rome gilded by the sunset.

Margaret had arrived when all Rome was rejoicing over Pio Nono's first measures of reform, when he pardoned his political adversaries, interested himself in night schools for the people and seemed to share the spirit of the Risorgimento. He went about every day on foot, visiting the poor in their houses, accompanied by a single priest, with no other guard; but this was only a momentary gesture and the Austrians were soon in control again, while every new act of repression sowed dragon's teeth. The general demand at first had been only for limited monarchies, but the cruelty of King "Bomba," the defection of the Pope and the meannesses of the Grand Dukes destroyed all hope of a possible peaceful transition. A radical revolution was under way, and Margaret found she was living in an "epoch," no longer in a "period," in the phrase of Charles Péguy fifty years later. Thinking, speaking, living "only what is Italian," she said, she realized that this was the time she had always dreamed of, secretly hoping to see it, and, already taking notes for a history of the time, she felt that she might be called to act in it as well. Every day Ossoli brought reports that were of use to her, all the more because he knew, from his own family, the papal side as he knew the liberal side from his associates and friends. They went to meetings of both sides together. At last, in 1848, when Louis Philippe fell in France and Metternich was crushed in Austria, the news came that the cities of north Italy were rising. Crowds gathered in front of the Palazzo Venezia, the Austrian embassy at that time, pulled down the double-headed eagle and burnt it in the street, while Polish refugees brought faggots to throw into the flames. Mickiewicz, who had come to Rome and whose Polish legion had been blessed by the Pope, stood by, looking on.

During that summer, Margaret, whose child was about to be born, set out for Rieti at the foot of the Umbrian mountains, a hive of ancient dwellings with red-brown roofs, decaying palaces and half-deserted churches. About it were olive and mulberry groves, and bridle paths, fringed with vineyards, led away across the fields to monasteries and villages in the hills. Margaret spent three or four hours a day walking or on donkey-back, while she continued to write her letters for the *Tribune,* quite alone, surrounded with peasants only, for Ossoli was obliged to remain in Rome. She was hard-pressed, desperately poor, anxious about the future,—where was she to live, in Italy, at home?—and the future of the child was a problem also. Its birth was irregular, no doubt. Her marriage had been kept a secret, ostensibly because of Ossoli's inheritance from his father, for the estate had not yet been divided and his marriage to a Protestant would have jeopardized this, he felt, in the papal courts. But, if this had been the only reason for concealing the marriage, why should Margaret have so dreaded the "social inquisition" in Boston? Yet in Italy they had nothing whatever to live on. Margaret was apprehensive, but she wrote to her mother, "Do not feel anxious about me. Some higher power leads me through strange, dark, thorny paths"; and meanwhile Körner's words rang in her ear,— "Though the million suffer shipwreck, yet noble hearts survive!"

From Florence, before she sailed for home, she looked back on the days when Mazzini arrived in Rome in 1849, entering the city on foot at night to avoid demonstrations and enjoy the quiet of his thoughts at this great moment. He had come at once to see her, staying two hours, and more than ever he seemed to her a great poetic statesman, a lover at heart and full of resource in action. He had lived for eighteen years in exile. Margaret, feeling that she was a part of this great drama of the Roman republic, felt also that she must see it played out to the end; and during the siege, when the Pope had fled and the troops of Napoleon III were bombarding the city, she was director of one of the hospitals there. In charge of the wounded, she cared for their peculiar tastes, carrying books to one, flowers to another, bringing them the news of the day, listening to their life-stories, reading to them and talking to them in the Quirinal also, the palace that was used for convalescents. In the gardens she walked with the wounded, one with his arm in a sling, another with a crutch, while the cannonade continued and shells fell about them. Her child was in Rieti, her husband was fighting, and Garibaldi was in command, with his red shirt of a gaucho of the Uruguayan pampas. Before the French entered the city and the Garibaldians withdrew, Mazzini, who escaped by a sailing vessel, had become an old man, white-haired and haggard. Twenty years were to pass before, once more in exile, he was to see Italy finally united.

Margaret, who had also escaped, with Ossoli, to Florence, surrounded herself with manuscripts, journals and books there, bent on finishing, before she sailed for home, her *History of Italy, 1848–1849.* She saw much of the Brownings and of Greenough and Powers, but she felt herself drawn back to America by what she called heart-weariness over the general triumph of reaction in Europe. With the fall of Italy she had lost much of her will to live; and besides, with her "man's ambition and woman's heart," she had undergone too great a strain. She sailed with dark presentiments of the shipwreck in which she and her husband and child were drowned together, feeling that the omens were all against their crossing the sea which Ossoli had been told would be fatal to him. On their last evening in Florence, passed with the Brownings, she had given a Bible as a parting gift from her child to theirs, "In memory of Angelo Eugene Ossoli." A strange prophetical expression, it seemed to Mrs. Browning, as she remembered the gloom in which they had parted and the truthfulness and courage of this extraordinary friend.

CHAPTER X

NORTON AND RUSKIN

IN THE middle eighteen-fifties, Charles Eliot Norton drove down to Rome in a well-built carriage, drawn by four horses,—"the pleasantest sort of conveyance," he wrote to a friend; and there, with his mother and sisters, amid the "dirt, ruin and malaria," he presently settled down for a long winter of study. He had recently visited India in connection with a trading firm, but, after steeping himself in Ruskin's *Modern Painters,* he planned to devote his life to literature and art. Often breakfasting with the Storys, or with Father Manning, the cardinal of the future who was sometimes there, or Harriet Beecher Stowe, who was writing *Agnes of Sorrento,* he saw much of the family of Mrs. Gaskell, with whom he went sightseeing and to whom he gave lessons in the history of Italian art. Preparing to write his own *Notes of Travel and Study in Italy,* he visited Orvieto, Ravenna and many other cities. He felt that to cultivate oneself was the best service an American could render at a time when men were so "ready to devote themselves simply to 'getting on' in lower ways."

Everything was going down, Norton felt, in Italy,—everything had been going down, in fact, since that "period of pure immorality," the Renaissance; and Browning had said to him years before in Florence that literature had sunk as low as art there. Or, for that matter, the character of most of the priests.

"Simplicity of taste and feeling" was evidently extinct there, while the popes seemed to prefer a "gaudy show,"—the statues of Bernini, Borromini's churches,—and Norton would have liked to see Rome "battered down" in a revolution, "if in that way we can get rid of these churches and these priests." He was reminded of Benares by all the glitter and superstition, and he shared Ruskin's opinion of the "vile taste and vapid design" of the interior of St. Peter's. At the same time he responded, with Ruskin, to the great art of pre-Renaissance times that appealed to their common instinctive puritanism. He was soon to set to work on a translation of the *Vita Nuova* that showed how unimpeachable was his own taste in fields in which he felt at home; and in the Vatican he singled out Fra Angelico's frescoes in the little square chapel of Nicholas V. He was impressed by the architecture of the twelfth and thirteenth centuries and the growth of the worldly spirit that gradually followed when, the more skilful the monuments were, the more they exhibited to him the absence of noble design and elevated thinking. Giotto, he was soon convinced, was, in thought and feeling, as far superior to the other Italian painters as Dante was to all the other poets; and if, in this, he was largely a follower of Ruskin, he was by no means a parasite. Ruskin, who was in his late thirties, eight years older than himself, was even to describe Norton as his "first real tutor," one who knew more of classical literature as well as English literature, along with the older French writers, than himself. It was Norton who introduced Ruskin to the *Fioretti*. But in aesthetic matters Ruskin was the master.

The two had met a year before when James Jackson Jarves, a shipmate of Norton's, had given him a letter of introduction to Ruskin; and, after a brief encounter in England, where Ruskin showed Norton his collection of Turners, they met again on a steamer on Lake Geneva.[1] Almost at once, as Ruskin said, Norton assumed over him "a kind of paternal authority and a right of guidance," though "always admitting his full power in its own kind," the kind of power that was giving him, throughout the English-speaking world, a virtually despotic position in the world of art. Highly emotional, petulant, wilful, the spoiled child of a rich wine-merchant and a tyrannous bigoted mother to whom he was devoted, this master of a glorious literary style was a half-mad prophet who was to become, in time, altogether mad. A manic-depressive, he saw himself as a hero in the Carlylean sense who was "more and more persuaded, every day, that everybody" else was "always wrong," convinced that the present race of mankind was "tramwayed, shamwayed, damn-wayed" and that he had been born to set it right. He wanted "to make the Italians industrious, the Americans quiet, the Swiss romantic, the Roman Catholics rational and Parliament honest," as he wrote once in a letter to Norton; while there was much of the infantile in this wonderful writer who could even be at times preposterously silly. His mother had forbidden him to marry his first love, the glamorous Spanish daughter of his father's partner, and since then he had never been able to fall in love with a full-grown woman and his ambiguous marriage had been annulled. He was infatuated with an Irish child named Rose La Touche, he spent long afternoons romping with schoolgirls, playing games of hide-and-seek and dancing with them; and, sometimes proposing to marry them, he lectured to them in a tone that was half goody-goody and half girly-girly. All this time he poured

[1] In her story *False Dawn*, Edith Wharton describes Ruskin as he must have appeared at about this time,—a young man with a light springing figure, a blue coat and swelling stock and a scar slightly distorting his handsome and eloquent mouth. Every remark he made to the young American in the story was "a many-faceted crystal flashing with unexpected fires."

out books, refractory, superb, perverse, profound, expressing in magical prose a world of notions. Ruskin, who had been a poet and could have been a painter, became both painter and poet in this other form.

During their long friendship, Norton was to use what Ruskin called his "rectorial power" to regulate this unsteady man of genius, and it seemed to please Ruskin to be treated as a child who had to be kept "strictly and busily at work." He was "affectionately submissive," as he was to write in *Præterita*, to Norton's "infinitely varied and loving praise . . . a constant motive to exertion," as he called it, grateful for Norton's "calm influence" upon him, coming from "that neighbourhood of rattlesnakes and bears," that "fearful American wilderness" in which Norton dwelt. They were to meet in Italy often in the years to come, and Ruskin could understand the American thirst for ruins and shadows as a relief from the "atmosphere of calculation." [2] The only difference between them was in their innate political faiths, for, with whatever socialist leanings, Ruskin was a Tory and one who had no interest in the Risorgimento; while, pessimistic as Norton was, he cared for the future of Italy as he defended republican ideas at home. His mother had translated Silvio Pellico's *My Prisons*, just as his father had translated *I Promessi Sposi*, and he had been brought up on the Risorgimento. Meanwhile, not yet the deity he was to become, Ruskin was a familiar sight in Italian churches where, with his courier and valet and men bearing

[2] "After the scraped cleanliness and business and fussiness of America, mildew and mould may be meat and drink to you, and languor the best sort of life, and weeds a bewitchment . . . The sense of despair which there is about Rome must be helpful and balmy after the over-hopefulness and getting-on-ness of America, and the very sense that nobody about you is taking account of anything, but that all is going on into an unspelt, unsummed, undistinguished heap of helplessness must be a relief to you, coming out of that atmosphere of calculation." —Ruskin, Letter to Norton, 1856.

ladders, he scaled façades and peered into the dark corners of chapels. He was always copying details of frescoes,—Giotto's at Assisi, for instance,—or drawing the sculpture on a font. It was his mission, he said, to teach people to see, and there was some justice in his claim of actually discovering this painter or that and establishing the supremacy of several of them.[3]

Norton had been prepared to accept Ruskin's view of the Renaissance and what he himself called its "degraded taste and debasing principles"; and, despising Borromini's "fantastic creations," he thought Bernini a fit expression of the papacy's "weakness and decline." He might even have shared Ruskin's feeling as a boy that the malaria on the Campagna was one of the natural consequences of the papal system. Norton felt he could "roast a Franciscan with pleasure"; and, for the rest, he seemed to share Ruskin's delight in the English Pre-Raphaelites who were among the heirs of the Gothic revival. For Norton himself Rossetti was to paint "Dante Meeting Beatrice," while Ruskin stood over Rossetti and told him how to paint,—"Please put a dab of Chinese white into the hole of the cheek and take all the pure green out of the flesh." Ruskin, whose parents had hoped that he would be a bishop, was nothing if not peremptory, a martinet of culture, just as the son of Andrews Norton,

[3] "I say with pride . . . that it was left to me, and me alone, first to discern and then to teach . . . the excellency and supremacy of five great painters, despised until I spoke of them—Turner, Tintoret, Luini, Botticelli and Carpaccio. Despised, nay scarcely in any true sense of the word, known."—Quoted in *The Life of Ruskin*, by E. T. Cook, Vol. II, p. 45.

But one might ask, When had Tintoretto not been known, and when had Turner been despised?

Ruskin did not discover Carpaccio until 1869, when the picture of St. Ursula sleeping reminded him of Rose La Touche. Ruskin's passionate preferences often sprang from a source that was very remote from the aesthetic.

Even among Ruskin's disciples, it became a standing joke to ask who was his latest "greatest painter."

the "Unitarian Pope," was himself to be at Harvard later. But it is not impossible that Norton admired Rossetti mainly because Ruskin had admired him first; for Norton disliked in Rome the German Pre-Raphaelites who also followed the masters of the *quattrocento,* Cornelius who was making a cartoon for a vast fresco in Berlin and Overbeck's similar works of "spiritual art." Norton disparaged not only their pictures but their motives in painting them, referring with contempt to Overbeck's fervour in trying to revivify the "meagre saints and mild madonnas of five hundred years ago." [4] What could be said of these pictures as works of today? They found their inspiration in the minds of men long dead instead of in the freshness and beauty of living nature. So Norton spoke of the Germans,—but was this not precisely what others said of Holman Hunt, Burne-Jones and Rossetti?

With all his fixed ideas, Norton found in Italy "the home of the imagination," nevertheless, for the Middle Ages were still in possession of it; and he had begun to make the studies of mediæval architecture for which he was known as a writer later. It amused him, as he walked about, to pick up bits of ancient sculpture that lay, unheeded, by the roadsides, a piece of a marble leg, for instance, that was half washed out of a bank, or a bas-relief of Leda lying in a cart-track. Watching men digging a trench near the Fountain of Trevi, he saw them turn up a handful of imperial coins; and his table was soon laden with broken inscriptions and fragments of mosaic that he had gathered in the city or on the Campagna. He was present at a convocation of the Arcadian Academy with a few sleepy old gentlemen, a few ladies and priests and two cardinals throned in old-fashioned gilt chairs at which an architect read

[4] Cf. Margaret Fuller's characterization (in *Things and Thoughts in Europe*) of the "galvanized piety of the German school, more mutton-like than lamb-like to my unchurched eyes."

a paper on the restoration of a church and a young priest read Latin hexameters on the Sacrifice of Isaac. Then a youthful countess who was descended from Ariosto recited verses of her own on Beatrice and Laura that brought the languid audience wide awake.

Norton who, like Fenimore Cooper and most of the earlier travellers, was deeply concerned with public life, found the condition of political affairs disheartening in Italy and especially in the moribund Papal States. There was no freedom of discussion as yet, all public spirit was stifled there, and he was depressed by the utter sterility and impotence of the Roman mind, the deadness of the Roman imagination. Decrepitude and inertia, he thought, could scarcely go further. Norton, struck by the air of neglect in the Protestant cemetery, felt that it ought to set Rome a good example,—for he had all the assurance of the puritan Brahmin,—so he had Keats's gravestone firmly reset and planted round it violets and myrtles. For the rest, since the fall of the Roman republic, the French troops were in control, marching up and down in squads and battalions, keeping order in the name of Napoleon III and the Pope, and, not until they were called away to fight in the Franco-Prussian war, was Rome to be open to the troops of the Italian kingdom.

James Russell Lowell, who was also in Rome in the fifties,— he had ridden the length of Sicily on the back of a mule,—was convinced, like Norton, that the Church there was moribund,[5] though he did not share Norton's hostility to it. He felt it was

[5] "I am more and more persuaded that . . . Romanism is a dead thing in Italy . . . The Papacy lies dead in the Vatican, but the secret is kept for the present, and government is carried on in its name. After the fact gets abroad, perhaps its ghost will terrify men a little while longer, but only while they are in the dark, though the ghost of a creed is a hard thing to give a mortal wound to, and may be laid, after all, only in a Red Sea of blood."—Lowell, *Fireside Travels.*

the only church that had been loyal to the soul of man and clung to its faith in the imagination, so that it would not give up its images and symbols, and he called it the mysterious enchantress who had known how to adapt herself to the weaknesses and the wants of human nature. Yet on Easter Sunday, not to be tempted by the "mockery of Pio Nono's benediction," he walked out to the Grotto of Egeria, avoiding St. Peter's. In Rome, time seemed to him of no account, and, face to face with the ancients there, he felt that the Americans represented the old Roman sentiment and power more truly than any other people. For their literature and art were also in a sense exotic, while their genius for politics and law, for colonization especially, and their instinct for trade and aggrandisement, all were Roman. With the Crawfords and his old friends the Storys, he went on picnics to Hadrian's Villa, where they sat on the warm stones and lunched in the shadow of the walls; and in Story's little theatre he made his debut on the stage, in the *Midsummer Night's Dream*, as Bottom the Weaver. In Rome he met Silvio Pellico, a Jesuit now, a little old man, bespectacled and withered.

As for Harriet Beecher Stowe, whose *Uncle Tom's Cabin* had appeared in almost every language, she could scarcely enter a shop unrecognized.[6] She too was drawn, like Lowell, and like so many Americans, to the symbolism and ritual of the Catholic Church, while she rejected all the rest, and she wrote the romance of *Agnes of Sorrento* after talking with

[6] "In Rome she visited the workshop of the brothers Castellani, goldsmiths, and admired their beautiful workmanship. One of the brothers handed her the head of an Egyptian slave, chiselled in black onyx, saying, 'Madam, we know what you have been to the poor slave. We ourselves are but poor slaves still in Italy. You feel for us. Will you keep this gem as a slight recognition for what you have done?' She took the gem in silence; but when we looked for some response her eyes filled with tears, and it was impossible for her to speak."—Annie Fields, *Authors and Friends*, pp. 171-172.

Father Manning whom she had met, with Norton and Story, in Rome. Detained, with her friends, by a storm at Salerno, she had begun to write it there; then, in Florence, she had been stirred by the history of Savonarola, who appeared in George Eliot's *Romola* three or four years later. She introduced in her own weak little novel not only the prior of San Marco but an artist-monk like Fra Angelico, and it pleased her to think that Florence had been a city of poets and artists with a gravity and earnestness that suggested her New England forbears. She saw Savonarola as an Italian Luther, and she entered deeply into his wish to restore the Church to the primitive apostolic simplicity in which she felt at home. Meanwhile, with Mrs. Browning she had long discussions of the spiritualism in which they both believed. D. D. Home, the spiritualist from Connecticut, had first appeared in Florence not long before, and he had carried away not only Mrs. Browning but Hiram Powers, Jarves and many others.

The "perfectly veracious Jarves," as Mrs. Browning called him, who had spent a night under the same roof with Home, testified that his four-poster bed was carried into the middle of the room and that shadowy figures stood beside his pillow. These figures, though not threatening, were extremely disturbing, but this was not unusual, for, in Home's presence, flowers moved through the air and books drifted from one table to another. Ruskin, an enthusiastic follower of Home, attended several of his seances, trying to communicate with Paolo Veronese. Mrs. Browning herself was converted during a visit to England, where everyone was talking, she said, about spirit hands and bodies that floated through rooms with tables and lamps. She wrote that Home "turns the world upside down in London with this spiritual influx," and there in Park Lane several seances were given in Bulwer-Lytton's house. "When people gather round a table now it isn't to play whist," said Mrs. Browning, and on one occasion spirit hands lifted a garland that lay on a table and placed it on this devoted believer's brow. Robert Browning, annoyed, stood helplessly by. Later he expressed his opinion of Home in *Mr. Sludge the Medium.* But Mrs. Browning said of the spiritualistic movement, "It grows, it grows."

The wizard, before he invaded Europe, had wandered from town to town at home, astonishing William Cullen Bryant and Thackeray, who saw Home perform at the house of George Bancroft in New York. "It is the most wonderful thing," said Thackeray who urged his friends in England to form spiritualistic circles and set tables tilting, and, within a few years, visiting Paris, at the invitation of Napoleon III, Home turned the Tuileries into a witches' Sabbath. So said the Princess Metternich who recalled that massive armchairs "flew from one end of the room to the other as if they were driven by a hurricane." The Emperor held an accordion that played of itself melodious airs, and the Empress Eugénie recognized her Spanish father's hand in one of the hands that Home materialized. Then the handkerchief that she was holding climbed into space. At one of Rossini's receptions in Paris, Home floated in a trance out of one window and floated back through another, while chairs on casters bowled along and a table sailed into an adjoining room and placed itself on top of another table. The widow of Balzac was converted at once, and when, with the blessing of the Czar, Home married a young Russian countess, Alexander Dumas went with him as the best man. In the Russian palace, every article of furniture took to moving about of its own accord, and a bell rose from a table into the air and rang as it drifted about the salon.

This was after Home had first appeared in Florence, where

the rumour went about that he held Black Masses, that he administered the sacrament to toads and raised the dead by spells and incantations. But an English lady said to him, "You are a greater event in Florence than an overflow of the Arno or a revolution"; and there the Countess Orsini's piano, as she was playing, rose in the air and balanced itself while she continued her playing. Seymour Kirkup, who had spent years searching for the philosopher's stone and who thought his "adopted" daughter,—his real daughter by a servant,—was a medium under the special patronage of Dante, made a drawing of one of Home's spirit-hands and arms in order to prove their actuality; and Hiram Powers examined closely the delicate ladylike phantom hands that appeared, in his house once, at the edge of the table. These two hands terminated at the elbow in a white mist. The Powerses, whose house had been a monastery, heard a violent scratching once that turned out to be the voice of twenty-seven monks—now spirits in distress,— who had once lived there, and who pulled so hard at Mrs. Powers's skirt that they broke the gathers. Hawthorne, talking with Powers later, felt there was a quality in the Florentine air that favoured transcendental speculation;[7] but, while he also felt that the miracles of Home were "absolutely proved," he could not force his mind to be interested in them. Later, the Yankee wizard settled down for a while in Rome in a studio that Story found for him. He asked Story to give him lessons as a sculptor. In the end, however, although he became a Catholic and the Pope blessed him, he was expelled on a charge of sorcery from Rome.

Some time before this, the poet Landor returned to Florence, involved as ever in quarrels and litigation, and he soon

[7] This was a heyday of Swedenborgianism also. Hiram Powers was a Swedenborgian; so was William Page, and Page, in Rome or Florence, converted George Inness.

quarrelled again with his wife who had continued to live there
and who turned him out of doors with a few pennies in his
pocket. More turbulent than ever, throwing dishes, throwing
whole dinners and even the cook, as everyone was told, out of
the window, the broken old man, now eighty-four, had wandered about the streets of Florence when Browning took him
under his protection. He brought the old poet to Siena, where
the Brownings and the Storys were spending the summer, and
Landor stayed for three weeks in the Storys' villa before his
own cottage was ready for him. In *Conversations in a Studio,*
Story related how Landor tottered in, a pitiable sight, dazed,
with his white hair straggling, another King Lear, and how he
rose at daybreak, while the servants were still asleep, and
strolled among the cypresses, composing verses. They were
Latin alcaics, mostly, which he read to the Storys at breakfast, "bombs that he threw into Louis Napoleon's camp," for
this lover of Italy was a friend of Garibaldi and the presence
of French troops in Rome infuriated him. He tried to sell his
watch on behalf of Garibaldi's wounded. Courteous, gentle
and generous when he was not in a violent mood, with "a
noble and capacious mind," as Story said, that had only "a few
cracks and flaws,"—surrounded to the last with paintings that
he said he could not live without,—he found in Kate Field a
new admirer and friend. An American girl of seventeen who
hoped to be a singer, extremely pretty, a pet of the Brownings
in Florence, Kate Field,—to whom Anthony Trollope referred
as his "most chosen friend,"—was also in ardent sympathy with
Garibaldi. In his sunny rooms in Florence overlooking a garden, Landor gave "kind Miss Field" lessons in Latin, several
times a week, month after month, and he addressed a poem to
her and gave her a relic of Rose Alymer who had died in
Calcutta sixty years before. "Whatever Landor may profess, the

thing he really loves is a pretty girl to talk nonsense with,"
Browning wrote to his friend John Forster in England; and
how pretty Kate Field really was one saw in the portrait that
Elihu Vedder painted of this girl who would have none of
him.

CHAPTER XI

ROME: HAWTHORNE

A YEAR before Hawthorne's arrival in Rome, his friend from the Berkshires, Herman Melville, had spent a month there in 1857, on his way back from the Holy Land at a time when, apparently written out, he felt that he had reached the end of his tether. Coming from the Orient with great expectations, he found Rome at first "oppressively flat," but, presently aroused, he went the rounds of the sculpture galleries and called upon John Gibson and William Page. Gibson was presumably the English sculptor "with dirty hands" whom he had already seen in the Caffé Greco, among the "rowdy-looking chaps" who were lost in the smoke there,—for Melville disliked the Bohemian as much as Hawthorne, who never even mentioned the Caffé Greco. He bought a copy of the bust of Antinous in the Capitoline museum, and perhaps he also bought in Rome the engraving that he later owned of Guido's supposed portrait of Beatrice Cenci. All the Roman picture-shops were filled with copies of this portrait, cameos, lithographs, pictures in oil or crayon. Beatrice "haunts one everywhere," Story wrote in *Roba di Roma,* "with her white turban and red eyes."

When he returned to New York, Melville gave a lecture,—reported but not published,—"Statuary in Rome,"—in which he compared the Laocoön with the Locomotive as symbols of two civilizations, the ancient and the modern.[1] But what lingered in his mind, most of all, from the visit to Rome was the portrait of Beatrice Cenci, "the sweetest, most touching but most awful of feminine heads," that appeared on a memorable page of his novel *Pierre*. At an exhibition in New York,—among those "wretched imported daubs" which the effrontery of the picture-dealers "christened by the loftiest names known to art," —Lucy was fascinated by a copy of this picture; and the vaguely incestuous relation of Pierre and Isabel, who were standing near, accounted for its presence in the story. For, to Melville, Beatrice was "double-hooded . . . by the black crêpe of the two most horrible crimes," parricide and incest; and for this reason Hawthorne was also obsessed with the portrait and what he called its "indefinable spell." Hawthorne had little feeling for art, and it was largely to please his wife that he dragged himself through miles of picture-galleries, but the portrait of Beatrice was a symbol for him of that "existence of evil in the world" of which he was to make so much in *The Marble Faun*. He had associated Italy with evil in *Rappacini's Daughter*, in which the old scientist cultivated poisonous herbs, so that his daughter's breath became poisonous also; and Miriam's connection with crime in his Italian novel was ambiguously involved with the crime of Beatrice Cenci. Hilda was making a copy of the portrait when Miriam came to see her, and Miriam's expression became "almost exactly that of the portrait" as she thought of the "something evil" in Beatrice's mind. It was, moreover, to the Palazzo Cenci that Miriam asked Hilda to deliver the mysterious packet. Hawthorne felt that the portrait of Beatrice Cenci was "the most profoundly wrought picture in the world."

[1] Melville seems to have had in mind some such comparison between the characters of two civilizations as Henry Adams later suggested in comparing the Virgin and the Dynamo.

Hawthorne and his family drove down from Civita Vecchia, after a sea voyage from France, in 1858, accompanied by Maria Mitchell, a countryfied, racy, childlike soul, the astronomer from Nantucket who had discovered a planet. All the way Miss Mitchell told the children about the stars, "she being as familiar with them as a gardener with flowers," Hawthorne wrote in his Italian notebook; and the family spent most of the winter in Rome before they went on to Florence, where Hawthorne wrote his first draught of *The Marble Faun*. He was surprised himself by the number of Roman objects and sights that found their way into the story when he came to write it, the Tarpeian Rock, among them, which he first saw by moonlight in the company of the Swedish novelist Frederica Bremer. For this lady with the prodigious nose who had written *Homes of the New World* was living near the rock when the Hawthornes went to see her, and, strolling out together, they visited the precipice that became the scene of the crime of Donatello.

Hawthorne had planned in England *The Ancestral Footstep*, a romance that he took up later when he returned to Concord, and he was at loose ends in Rome waiting to find an idea that would stir his active imagination. He began to think of those dryads and fauns, wild woodland creatures that were links between sentient humanity and animal existence, and the notion of a faun, any faun, took possession of him before the Faun in the Capitol brought it to a head. [2] It was

[2] One can follow in Hawthorne's notebooks the growth of this idea from his first mention of it after visiting the Villa Borghese. "I like these strange, sweet, playful rustic creatures. Their character has never, that I know of, been wrought out in literature; and something quite good, funny and philosophical, as well as poetic, might very likely be educed from them . . . The faun is a natural and delightful link between human and brute life, with something of a divine character intermingled."—Hawthorne, *Passages from the French and Italian Notebooks*, Vol. I, p. 175.

then he awoke to his surroundings as a possible setting for the romance that was growing in his mind, and, first of all, to the artist life that was to bring the characters together. He saw much of Story, whose work appealed to him, though he must have agreed with Miriam's comment in *The Marble Faun* that all these sculptors were plagiarists, Story among them. But Story's mind was full of suggestions for tales that Hawthorne would have told in his own fashion,—for instance, the tale of a ring worn by a widower who said, when he was asked what it was, "It is my wife," for he had caused her body to be chemically resolved into this stone, a theme that set Hawthorne's mind racing. If he had thought of the story, he would have made the ring a bridal gift of the widower to his second wife,—and Hawthorne began to imagine the consequences.

If not the sculptor himself, Story's statue of Cleopatra was to appear, with the studio, in Hawthorne's romance; so were Paul Akers's "Pearl-Diver" and bust of Milton; and so was John Gibson whose delicate power Hawthorne admired, though he too was a plagiarist without question. Gibson had spent forty years making his marble "dream-work, or rather frost-work, all a vapoury exhalation out of the Grecian mythology," as Hawthorne put it, "crystallized on the dull window-panes of today"; and Hawthorne was not surprised that the younger sculptors drank in his wisdom and listened deferentially to Gibson's quiet "Yes." The Greek myths were as popular as ever with the sculptors, and *The Age of Mythology* (1855) by Thomas Bulfinch, the son of the old Boston architect Charles Bulfinch, was useful to many of them who were looking for subjects. Harriet Hosmer was only one of the prototypes of Hilda, who was herself the prototype of several other innocents in Italy later,—Daisy Miller, in her way, and the Lady of the Aroostook; for Hilda might have been suggested by half a dozen others. Why not by Vinnie Ream, for one, who actually had some white doves that flew about her studio and perched on her shoulder, except that this American sculptor girl of whom Georg Brandes was to see so much actually came to Rome a little later? Vinnie Ream showed the Danish critic, a young man travelling to discover the world, "the spectacle of a human being entirely happy, and good because she was happy, . . . a breath of the independence of the great Republic"; and he enjoyed with her "a pleasure based only on good fellowship and with no erotic element about it." [3] Hilda was one of many examples of the "freedom of life" that, as Hawthorne said, a young girl artist was able to enjoy in Rome, though he drew Hilda's tower from an actual tower with battlements, just as he drew other Roman scenes. How many readers of *The Marble Faun* came to look, or half look, for the Spectre at a shadowy turning in the catacombs, and how many half expected to see in some sylvan glade a dance like that which Miriam and Donatello witnessed,—realizing one of those bas-reliefs in which nymphs and satyrs hand in hand frolic about the circle of an antique vase? Or how many tried to see the furry ears of the Faun in the Capitoline museum? Hawthorne observed that the Roman ruins, black or brown, remained hard and sharp, never again becoming a part of nature,—as stone walls were apt to do in England,—with dry and dusty grass sprouting from them but seldom the green mantle of ivy of the damper north.

As with many American husbands and wives, it was Mrs. Hawthorne who took the lead when it came to looking at pictures in churches and museums, where, like Hilda in the

---

[3] See Georg Brandes, *Reminiscences of my Childhood and Youth,* New York, pp. 316-324.

Vinnie Ream sculptured in Rome the statue of Lincoln, ordered by Congress for the rotunda of the Capitol in Washington.

end, Hawthorne knew so well "that icy demon of weariness who haunts great picture galleries." He never tired of studying people, and at Siena, as his son remembered, he was fascinated at the hotel window by the passers-by,—he jotted down notes about many of them,—just as in Paris he had been absorbed by the Sunday crowd at the Louvre while it was Sophia who studied the pictures. Sophia had been a teacher of drawing; she had been as faithful as Margaret Fuller at all the exhibitions in the Athenæum, and she had painted at the Manse a whole set of furniture with outlines after Flaxman on a dull gold background. Hawthorne felt that, by taking pains, he "might get up a taste," for he began to "prefer some pictures to others"; but he liked colours that were bright and fresh and he thought the mosaic of the "Transfiguration" must represent Raphael's idea better than the painting. He noted that a process was going on within him that made him "more fastidious" in looking at pictures,—"more sensible of beauty where I saw none before,"—though he felt to the end that he would never think of looking twice, "except as curiosities," at Botticelli or Giotto. His heart sank when he saw their poor faded relics clinging, forlorn as they were, to so many walls, as if they were symbols of the spirit that had once made Catholicism a living religion,—for, like Lowell, he supposed that Catholicism was on its death-bed. The "glory and beauty," he was convinced, had departed from both. It was the American "Mr. Brown" whose work gave Hawthorne more pleasure than "any of the landscapes of the old masters." While he was obliged to suppose that Claude was a greater landscape painter, for his own satisfaction he preferred Mr. Brown.

So Hawthorne was not surprised when Mrs. Jameson, coming to Rome, gave him "no credit for knowing one single simplest thing about art . . . Nor do I think she underrated me," he added. He, on his part, thinking her a "sensible old lady," doubted if she had "the highest and finest perceptions in the world." It was true that she knew every cypress on the Roman hills, every vine overhanging a garden, every picture and statue, and she knew the mystic symbolism of the early mosaics and the emblems and attributes of the saints and fathers. She took Hawthorne for a drive in her little carriage beyond the walls of Rome on the Appian Way, and they visited churches and galleries together; but, while he liked her books and she liked his, Hawthorne preferred his own elucidations. He was more responsive to the wonders of Rome than William Cullen Bryant, whose daughter, as Hawthorne recorded, dragged him out,—on his fifth visit to Europe,—and who, as Hawthorne said again, and as one felt in his poetry, had not sufficiently cultivated his emotional nature. Bryant, now an old man with a long white palmer's beard, had resumed the simpler ways of an early country breeding; but, with his old-fashioned dignity, his life struck Hawthorne as cool and calm like the days that end in pleasant sunsets. The old poet was baptised in Naples by a minister whom he met there,—and whom he reminded of one of the ancient prophets,—in his hotel bedroom overlooking the bay; and he remembered that the apostle Paul, on a ship from Alexandria, had once sailed past this window on his way to Rome. St. Paul had landed at Pozzuoli, bringing Christianity to Italy with him.

Meanwhile, more and more, in Rome, the visionary splendour of St. Peter's took possession of Hawthorne's imagination, —it was "the world's cathedral," as he called it, while he saw in the Borghese Gardens a woodland scene that seemed to have been projected from the mind of a poet. He was delighted with the sound of falling water, like that of a distant cascade in the forest, that one heard in so many of the Roman squares

and streets, filling the air when the tumult of the city was
hushed; and, commenting shrewdly upon Canova's statue of
Pauline Bonaparte, represented as Venus with an apple in her
hand,[4] he was not unresponsive to Bernini.[5] He was disgusted
with the "wicked filth of Rome," the rotten vegetables thrown
everywhere about, the rivulets of dissolved nastiness, the standing puddles, the women flinging slops into the street, the children every day more uncleanly, just as in all the Italian towns
cripples displayed their scars and sores and mothers held up
for charity their unwashed babies. He did not, like Matthias
Bruen, an earlier American traveller, visit on the Romish religion all the crimes,—the ignorance and the beggary and
thievery,—that degraded the country; but neither was he interested in the Risorgimento that hoped to put an end to all
these evils. No doubt, like Ruskin, he thought the Italians were
as indolent as lizards, by nature,—irremediably so,—though the
gentle courtesy of the Romans impressed him as well; and,
for all the sunless dreary alleys that were called streets in Rome,
he noted as very singular the sad embrace with which the city
took possession of the soul. "It may be," he said, "because the
intellect finds a home there more than in any other spot in the
world, and wins the heart to stay with it."

It was in Florence, however, that he began *The Marble
Faun*, the romance that he was to write mainly in England,
and there, like Fenimore Cooper, he enjoyed the happiest
moment of his life (if one could accept the statement of the

[4] "Very beautiful . . . but it is wonderful to see how the artificial elegance of the woman of this world makes itself perceptible in spite of
whatever simplicity she could find in almost utter nakedness."—Hawthorne, *Passages from the French and Italian Notebooks*, Vol. I, p. 176.
[5] "Bernini was a man of great ability . . . There are some works in
literature that bear an analogy to his works in sculpture,—where great
power is lavished a little outside nature, and therefore proves to be
only a fashion, and not permanently adapted to the tastes of mankind."
—Vol. I, p. 149.

families of both). He walked, as he said, "on the smooth flags of Florence for the mere pleasure of walking and lived in its atmosphere for the mere pleasure of living," and he added, "I hardly think there can be a place in the world where life is more delicious for its own simple sake." It was in Florence that he so enjoyed the conversation of Hiram Powers and Browning's talk that was so effervescent you could not recall it even if you recalled the words, as Hawthorne wrote in his Italian journal; and there was Mrs. Browning whom he described as "a pale small person," speaking "with a shrill, yet sweet tenuity of voice." Of Seymour Kirkup, the English necromancer with the voluminous beard and the glittering eye, Hawthorne was to write his impressions in three romances. He called one day on the patriarch in his disorderly den in the old hospice of the Templars, the withered old man with his sprite of a child,—the twelve-year-old daughter of mysterious birth,—who were to appear, transformed, in *Dr. Grimshawe's Secret*. It was Seymour Kirkup who suggested Dr. Dolliver in *The Dolliver Romance*, that "worthy personage of extreme antiquity" whose little grandchild Pansie remained with him sole amid a throng of circumambient ghosts; and, moreover, he evoked the figure of the antiquarian who had once come to the tower of Monte Beni,—as Donatello told Kenyon in *The Marble Faun*,—and who had known the traditions of the tower, the sieges it had withstood and the prisoners who had been confined in it. He had been able to give Donatello the story of his own family of Monte Beni.

It was the villa in which Hawthorne lived at Bellosguardo that he described as Monte Beni, a villa with forty rooms, a tower that was haunted and a view of Galileo's tower in the distance. There he placed part of the romance that was largely suggested by his memories of Rome, the story that resolved itself into a parable of the fall of man and the growth of a soul and intellect in consequence of this. Hawthorne had found in Italy a "sort of poetic and fairy precinct" where his imagination could have free play and where, as he said, actualities need not be so terribly insisted upon as they were, and had to be, at home. There he could indulge his taste for ambiguity and mystery, for the systole and diastole of the sad and the merry, for the sudden alternations of light and shade, for the dark element that he loved, side by side with the idyllic and the innocently gay.

CHAPTER XII

HOWELLS IN VENICE

IN ROME, in 1860, "the lights and shadows were still mediæval," Henry Adams was to write many years later, and "the shadows breathed and glowed, full of soft forms felt by lost senses. No sand-blast of science had yet skimmed off the epidermis of history, thought and feeling. The pictures were uncleaned, the churches unrestored, the ruins unexcavated. Mediæval Rome was sorcery"; while Rome itself was "the worst spot on earth to teach nineteenth-century youth what to do with a twentieth-century world." Adams, in search of education, had come down from Germany, and, sitting at sunset, remembering Gibbon, on the steps of the Aracoeli, he reflected that no law of progress applied to Rome. "Not even time-sequences," he felt, "had value for it. The Forum no more led to the Vatican than the Vatican to the Forum. Rienzi, Garibaldi, Tiberius Graccus, Aurelian might be mixed up in any relation of time." The great word Evolution had not yet filled the modern mind, but to this young man who was disposed to question all values the history of Rome was a flat contradiction of it. Rome seemed to him a bewildering complex of energies, ideas and ambitions, but for him it did nothing to solve the enigma of existence.

Nor did the sphinx Garibaldi whom he saw in Palermo, where he had himself been sent as a bearer of dispatches at a moment when the red-shirted hero and his famous thousand were about to attack the barricaded city. An American naval officer there took him, in the July heat,—amid the Sicilian dirt and revolutionary clamour,—to call on the great soldier at supper with his staff, all "picturesque and piratic," suggesting to Adams an Italian operatic Rossinian scene. Garibaldi left the table and sat down at the window for a word with the American captain and his young friend, and Adams never forgot the lesson that Garibaldi seemed to teach, how extremely complex extreme simplicity could be. But the simplicity alone impressed many sympathetic minds that were also less contemplative and less fatalistic, minds for whom this great man was the incarnation of a cause that was to triumph ultimately but not yet. One was the painter William J. Stillman,—the "American Pre-Raphaelite," as he was called because of his relation to the circle of Rossetti,—the consul at Rome from 1861–1865 who wrote a book on the union of Italy later. But at Rome this romantic lover of Garibaldi was less concerned with politics than with art, and, having time on his hands at the consul's office, he spent many days on the Campagna painting.

At the moment when Adams was in Rome, Stillman had been in Switzerland where Ruskin had invited him to spend the summer so that they might work together, Ruskin drawing mountain forms and Stillman making other Alpine sketches. Stillman, some years before, stirred by *Modern Painters,* had founded *The Crayon,* the first American art-journal, for an ever-increasing art-loving public at home that was full of Ruskinian enthusiasm and feeling for nature. He had broken with his first associates, painters of the Hudson River School, disliking as much as George Inness their insistence on "facts,"—the notorious "foreground plant," for one example,—and Ruskin had converted him to Turner whose favourite spots they looked for during their summer in Switzerland together. "I don't know what I should have done without him," Ruskin wrote to Norton, "for I couldn't work and yet moped when I did nothing." Every day they climbed some secondary peak, while they discussed in the evening art and religion, Ruskin still holding the literal beliefs of his evangelical childhood, insisting that on the Sabbath no one should work. At Chamonix he read to Stillman some of the chapters of *Unto This Last,* the great new conception of social science that aroused such a storm of disapproval when it appeared in England, but Stillman could not long endure the tutelage of Ruskin who even told great painters how to paint. He obliged Stillman to see everything through Ruskin's eyes,—Stillman was to hold the brush while he did the painting; and in the end Stillman could no longer bear Ruskin's peremptory ways and extravagant notions. Ruskin had been his "artistic ruin," he told a friend in Rome, and there were other painters, the American Hotchkiss, for one, who could not sufficiently express their indignation at Ruskin. Hotchkiss said he had lost years in "those Miss-Nancyish efforts" to follow the teacher, and another newcomer, Elihu Vedder, found, as he wrote, "how unsatisfactory this teaching turned out to be." He too had been deeply affected by it.

The restless Stillman, for many years, drifted back and forth between painting, writing and archæological ventures, in the Italian south and in Crete and Greece, and he found at the moment in Rome a sort of dreamland that was given over wholly to religion and art. It was a hugh cloister in which the processions of priests and theological students provided the only animation, and, besides art, the only industry was the production of jewelry and objects connected with the Church. Decaying, picturesque, pathetic, majestic, it was also full of lotus-eaters and people who believed that any picture painted in Rome was better than any picture painted elsewhere. Stillman had hoped for an appointment as consul in Venice, not in Rome, for he wished to write a history of Venetian art; but that appointment had gone to William Dean Howells. It was a reward to this young man from Ohio who had written a campaign biography of President Lincoln. Howells, twenty-four years old in 1861, was already known in literary Boston, where Lowell and Dr. Holmes had welcomed him and even begun to publish him in *The Atlantic*. He was a poet and student of literature whom the Venetian scene presently served as a setting for several novels. The consulship for Venice "and the ports of the Lombardo-Venetian kingdom," like the consulship at Rome, was given by custom either to an artist or a writer; but, in spite of the universal admiration for Venetian painting, the American artists were scarcely aware of Venice. The impressionist painters discovered it a few years later. Moreover, as Howells himself observed, Venice was not, like Florence and Rome, a place of residence for foreigners, Americans at least.

Howells and his wife established themselves in a palace on the Grand Canal, the birthplace of the great doge, Marino Falier, in which a descendant, a mild old priest, Canonico Falier, still lived, with a venerable white head and crimson stockings. There were other tenants from England, Dalmatia and France, and the Howellses' parlour, with its frescoed ceiling, looked out on the life of the canal, invariably stirring, lively and full of colour. The consul was expected to report on the commerce of the city and watch for Confederate privateers, —the "Alabama" was supposed to be in the offing,—and he was obliged to disabuse the exiles of all nations who were eager for places of honour in the Northern service. They flocked to the consulate, shabby, incapable, hungry. His only other duty was to look after the interests of American ladies who were travelling, often with daughters, a consul's only duty, as they frequently imagined, but one that brought before him a great variety of American types whom he could study at his leisure. They stood out in bold relief against this foreign background as if they existed to serve as a novelist's models, the bright brisk widows on errands of health and the sometimes charming daughters who were studying Italian, music and the history of art. Howells marvelled over what he called "the mystery of women's nerves,"—for these ladies constantly suffered from strategic headaches or had "an old attack," as they occasionally called it, competent and alert as they usually were,—while with the girls, who were apt to be perceptive, sympathetic, gay, every man fell in love at sight. At the consulate might have appeared Don Ippolito, the young priest, the inventor who had lost his faith and asked for a passport, hoping to start a new life in the country of inventors; while, sooner or later, in his four years there, Howells observed the all-European world. He was to be one of the creators of the "international" novel.

Keeping a diary all this time, he studied the animated scene that he was to picture in *Venetian Life,* bent on avoiding the wish-wash of the romantic travel-books, faithful to what he actually knew and saw. For he was as eager as Mark Twain to escape the sentimental, the tendency to accept for one's own the conventional impressions; and, freshly responsive to the brilliancy of Venice, he disliked the sham with which the romancers and poets so often brought it out. Nothing could have been more untrue to history and actuality than Byron's *Marino Faliero,* and the Bridge of Sighs had never been what the poems purported it to be,—it had been merely a passage for common malefactors. With his own concern for reality and truth, the note of all his later work, he felt he had to expose these foolish errors, and he found that Venice, like life, lost little when one removed the illusions, for it still retained all its uniqueness, mystery and charm. Why, moreover, perpetually talk about gondolas and bridges, about light, colour, palaces, canals? The artists who painted there thought that without these properties one could not produce a picture that represented Venice; yet where were the gondolas or the canals in *The Merchant of Venice* or in *Othello,* both of which fairly pulsated with the life of the city?

What was to make *Venetian Life* so unlike the usual travel-books was that Howells saw Venice as a student of people, as a householder, besides, who had encounters with chimney-sweeps, with glaziers, chair-menders, upholsterers, fishermen, milkmen. He liked to talk with the old peasant woman who brought her eggs to the door and the old man roasting coffee in the court at night who looked so venerable and grand in the red of the flame, while he delighted in the artistic perfection of a ragamuffin boy who sold baked cakes of meal in one of the piazzas. In short, in Venice, Howells saw what Walt Whitman would have seen, or, for that matter, Goldoni, if he had been still living, the eighteenth-century playwright, the kindly creature whose comedies were still regularly performed there. Many of Goldoni's characters had been gondoliers, servants, notaries, dancers, the sort of people one saw on the canals, in the streets, whom, with a light-hearted sweetness, he had portrayed eating and drinking, singing and making love on all possible occasions. Later, Howells edited the memoirs of Goldoni, one of the first books he had read in Venice, and the plays of Goldoni, who seemed to him a sort of Italian

Goldsmith, had humanized for Howells this wonderful city.[1] Howells marvelled at the cheerful prudence that he saw all about him, the temperance and frugality of the Italian people, in whom he found nothing of the laziness and sloth that Ruskin was always reprehending. "After all," said Colville, speaking for Howells in *Indian Summer,* "the Italians have only to make a real effort in any direction, and they go ahead of everybody else." *Venetian Life* paid its respects to Giorgione and Tintoretto, the Lido, the Spanish synagogue, the Rialto, St. Mark's, but its uniqueness rather consisted in a vivid picture of the popular life that one saw all abroad in the footways and squares. What Howells called his "mild domestic lay" was a counterpart of Story's *Roba di Roma.*

At that time Venice was a city in mourning. The Austrians were in occupation and the prouder Venetians avoided the opera and would not enter the square of St. Mark's when the imperial band was playing there. Priests were spied upon by priests, or they were shunned themselves as spies; and the young men who were Garibaldians especially recoiled from them as enemies of Victor Emmanuel, their "own king." [2] Venice had a "suppressed look," Howells recorded, and an American could not be seen talking with Austrian officers on pain of losing his Italian friends. But, for all the constraint, one still saw there the gorgeous Corpus Christi procession and

[1] The Chicago novelist, Henry B. Fuller, translated many of Goldoni's plays. He published his translation of one, *The Coffee-House.*

[2] Howells noted that the cause of united Italy raised the self-respect of many of Garibaldi's followers, "I lived in Italy," he wrote in a letter, "in the Garibaldi days, when he was still a god, and the gondoliers expected him as in a second coming. Once . . . in order to pay a boatman . . . I had to change a five-franc piece, which I did by grace of a kind fellow who went to get it done. When he came back I offered him half a franc for his trouble; but he drew back, hurt . . . A bystander whispered awe-strickenly 'E Garibaldino!' So the hero consecrated and ennobled his followers."—*Life in Letters of William Dean Howells,* Vol. II, pp. 243-244.

the great festa of gondolas on the Grand Canal when, at any moment, in one of these "coffins clapped on a canoe," the consul might observe some king in exile. For Venice was a perennial refuge of the undesired royal, perhaps some Duchess of Parma or Infanta of Spain. Polyglot Russians abounded there, with superb Levantine figures, Greek and Turk and Albanian, as the young girl noted in Howells's *No Love Lost*, the novel in verse the scene of which was laid in Venice; and there were still gondoliers who chanted the songs of Tasso, while the golden-billed blackbirds sang in the cages above them. Howells may have encountered the Englishman who liked to collect "Americanisms" and whose rowing was the wonder of all Venice, for he propelled his own gondola,—in *The Lady of the Aroostook*,—and somehow managed not to fall into the water. He saw the chapel where Staniford married the young New England girl who had come over as the only woman on the ship, a ship that had sailed from Boston chiefly for the return freight,—"statuary," perhaps, as Captain Jenner said. Howells was all eyes for the young girls and their mothers who seemed to have a passion for manœuvring and intrigue and who sometimes knew themselves too well "ever to unpack anything that would not spoil by remaining unpacked." For Venice was only a bivouac in their quest for a suitable husband, culture, bric-a-brac or what not. There they were always quoting "that line from Byron," as they had begun to quote Browning in Florence.

Like Elmore, the American consul in *A Fearful Responsibility,* Howells was hoping to write a history of Venice, and he too tried "to set the material in a new light before himself," an effort that he never quite relinquished.[3] Whether or not

[3] "So many literary Americans have projected such a work that it may now be called a national enterprise."—Howells, *A Fearful Responsibility.*

Howells's predecessor as consul at Venice, Donald G. Mitchell ("Ik

he found time to work in the Martian Library, he arranged to
get documents copied for John Lothrop Motley, the minister
to Austria, his own chief, who came to Venice in 1861 and
drifted about, as he put it, in a gondola with him. Motley, a
"figure of worldly splendour," as Howells recalled later, was at
work on his *History of the United Netherlands,* and he wished
to obtain transcripts of the relations of the Venetian ambassadors at the European courts of that epoch. Howells, before he
left Venice in 1864, made, first or last, the series of excursions
of which he wrote later in *Italian Journeys,* to Petrarch's
Arquà, Passagno, where Canova was born, Vicenza, the birthplace of Palladio, and other cities. He had for Canova a special
feeling because, he said characteristically, this great man
"rescued the world from swaggering in sculpture," for Howells,
who disliked Byron, disliked Bernini also,—for him the baroque
was the worst form of the romantic.[4] There, at Passagno, the
custodian of the Canova gallery was the old sculptor's body-
servant, who had survived his master by a good forty years
and who liked to talk, devotedly, about him. Howells went to
the Sette Commune where the Cimbri lived on their lonely
Alpine hills near Bassano on the Brenta, a remnant of the
ancient Cimbrians who had invaded Rome and were now
hunters, wood-cutters and charcoal-burners. Speaking their own

---

Marvel") planned in 1853–4 a history of the city; but although he
continued for some time "doggedly," he was finally obliged to give
it up.

Later William Roscoe Thayer and the novelist Marion Crawford
wrote histories of Venice. So, in her mid-twentieth-century way, did
Mary McCarthy in *Venice Observed.* Howells never did so, but as late
as 1900 he sent Henry M. Alden at *Harper's* a long and careful synopsis
of the work he had long wished to write.

[4] This was all part of Howells's preference of what he called the "low
tone." In a later book, *Tuscan Cities,* he expressed his distaste for the
"strutting and mincing allegories" in Santa Croce, the "pompous effi-
gies" that, as he said, made death ridiculous.

dialect, they were still isolated from the Italian people. In Rome he found Joseph Severn, the gentle old Englishman, still hovering fondly about the Piazza di Spagna;[5] and the sculptor Gibson, engaged upon a bas-relief, a "Visit of Psyche to the Zephers," talked with pleasure about his coloured marbles. Howells touched the right spring when he said how much he liked them, and the old man went on to speak of his favourite theory with visible delight.

[5] Joseph Severn was still living in 1879 when Richard Watson Gilder called upon him twice in his apartment near the Fountain of Trevi. Keats had remained for six decades the centre of his life. "He placed in my hands," Gilder wrote in a letter, "the original of his pathetic drawing of the dying boy."

CHAPTER XIII

HENRY JAMES AND OTHERS

Howells's great later friends, Mark Twain and Henry James, both appeared in Italy in the eighteen-sixties,—the two incompatibles whom Howells knew equally well, the *délicat* of Renan's phrase and the literary frontiersman. Between them these two were to divide the American literature of their time, Howells being the sympathetic mediator, as the "Europeanizer," Turgenev, and Dostoievsky, the Slavophile, divided the literature of Russia. No two men could have been more unlike than the lover of Europe, Henry James, and the pilgrim who arrived in Italy in 1867 on the first American pleasure-cruise the fruits of which he was to report in a hugely popular book, *The Innocents Abroad*.

Mark Twain had promised his shipmates to hide the "uncouth sentiments" that naturally expressed a mind devoid of the culture, congenital or aspirational, of earlier pilgrims, from Irving and Allston to Emerson, Hawthorne and Howells. But there was no concealing the fact that he thought "Renaissance" was a man and that Titian and Rubens were no better than Ferguson and Simpson, or that it made any difference if one felt so. In Italy, which he called "that vast museum of magnificence and misery," Mark Twain was often appreciative and very funny, as when he took the part of "Mr. Laura" and asked why poets never wrote of him. He admired the facility of

Lucretia Borgia in ordering a sextuple funeral and then getting the corpses ready for it, and he was amusing when he imagined a show at the Coliseum as Barnum of the modern circus would have advertised it. He had something to say, moreover, to the culture-seekers who were apt to gush and were sometimes given to pretension and who talked perhaps less glibly about "tone," "feeling" and "expression" after Mark Twain mildly rebuked them for showing off. It comforted many a travelling American when Mark Twain floored the guides by what he called "imbecility and idiotic questions," pretending that he had never heard of Columbus, and he dampened the emotion that delighted the guides when he said that at moments Venice suggested a half-submerged Arkansas town in a spring freshet.

All this seemed rather infantile to the cultivated traveller, but it pleased the famous average man, the so-called "new American" who had grown up far from the older centres of culture. This practical man of a new generation who lived in a business world, and who had long since been weaned away from Europe, shared Mark Twain's interest in numbers and sizes,—the length of the catacombs, the height of a church,—and his calm spreading of the wings of the American eagle. He shared Mark's breezy incredulity among the "bottled fragments of saints" in a world where the "relic matter" was a little overdone, and he too thought the snowy figures of the new cemetery sculpture were lovelier than the dingy wrecks of ancient art. Mark Twain himself was the original man from Missouri, and when he spoke of Missouri in two or three later books he expressed a whole civilization and a whole epoch. But when he spoke of Europe he seemed to say that America could get along very well without it. In short, in *The Innocents Abroad*, Mark Twain cut the umbilical cord that had bound colonial America to the mother-culture; and, both for good and for

evil,—largely for both,—this was to have momentous consequences.

*

* *

Henry James, arriving in Rome in 1869, reeled through the
streets, he wrote, in a fever of enjoyment. He had put up at
the Hotel Inghilterra, in the Via Bocca di Leone where the
Brownings had lived, and he hurried out, heedless of breakfast, after a night's journey on the train, open-mouthed, as
he added, only for visions. Within four or five hours, he had
traversed the whole of Rome, from the Lateran to the Tiber,
from the Tiber to the Vatican, treading the Forum, scaling the
Capitol and the Alpine chain of the Coliseum, visiting St.
Peter's, the Pantheon, and the Appian Way. Then walking
homeward, on the Via Condotti, he was rewarded with the
strangest vision of all. The street had been suddenly cleared
by mounted, galloping, hand-waving guards, and, while everyone uncovered and women dropped on their knees, the great
rumbling black-horsed coach of the Pope drove by. A large
handsome pale old face showed from within as from the dim
depths of a chapel like some dusky Hindu idol in its shrine.
"At last—for the first time—I live!" James wrote, summing up
the day. "For the first time I know what the picturesque is."

James had come down from Venice and Florence,—mere
"wholesome tapioca," he felt, beside the "great plum pudding"
that he found in Rome, as England, beside Italy, that "beautiful dishevelled nymph," had struck him simply as a "good
married matron." He had come in a spirit of fervent devotion
like so many others of every race who had dreamed of the
Italian journey since the days of Goethe, and although, for a
life-companion, he was to prefer the matron to the nymph, he

was to be a lover of Italy all his days. Meanwhile, he fell in at once with Story and his circle, about whom he was to write many years later, and he joined them in picnics on the Campagna where he went for long lonely horseback rides. He mounted his horse on the grassy terrace before San Giovanni in Laterano and rode away over the meadows that Claude had painted, where the great aqueduct dragged its slow length along, and sometimes on towards Albano. There one saw Soracte, rising from its blue horizon, as one so often saw it in Claude's mellow backgrounds, and there were the shaggy-legged shepherds leaning on their staves in motionless brotherhood with the heaps of ruins. Or one met some contadino in cloak and peaked hat jogging through the haunted vacancy on the back of an ass, and with some white village or grey tower in the distance, recalling the Italian landscape of the old-fashioned painters. What his Rowland Mallett felt James too felt in Rome, that "a passive life," thanks to the number and quality of one's impressions there, took on "a respectable likeness to an active pursuit."

Many of these impressions James was to include in time in his first novel *Roderick Hudson* and in the story of Daisy Miller, the "child of nature and freedom" who was buried near Shelley and Keats under the thick spring flowers. Meanwhile, on his earliest Italian journey, in this last year of papal Rome, James visited Verona and Mantua,[1] with Venice and Florence and the lakes Maggiore and Como where the pink

[1] "What words can reproduce the picture which the northern Italian towns project upon a sympathetic retina? They are shabby, deserted, dreary, decayed, unclean . . . But . . . I found in them an immeasurable instruction and charm. My perception seemed for the first time to live a sturdy creative life of its own. How it fed upon the mouldy crumbs of the festal past! . . . In these dead cities of Verona, Mantua, Padua, how life had revelled and postured in its strength! How sentiment and passion had blossomed and flowered!"—Henry James, *Travelling Companions*.

villas gleamed through the shrubberies of orange and oleander. He described himself no doubt in the hero of *Travelling Companions* who wandered about with Baedeker and the *Chartreuse de Parme,* looking at Palladio's palaces in Vicenza and "enjoying them in defiance of reason and of Ruskin." He was certainly the young man who sat outside the café in the Piazza dei Signori at Verona, delighting in the elegance and grace of the ancient palace of the Council with its image-bordered mass above the light arched loggia.[2] For what he called a deep delicious bath of mediævalism, Henry James went to Assisi, the greatest possible contrast to Rome where all things connected with the Church were so much of this world, so artful, so florid. As a boy at Newport, studying with William Morris Hunt, he had felt strongly the influence of Ruskin, thanks to whom he had made a conscientious copy of a leaf and the faithful drawing of a rock that stood by a pond. Now he was to find Ruskin's *Mornings in Florence* "invidious and insane,"—charming as the great man was when he spoke of Giotto,—for he insisted that Brunelleschi was stupid and he had come to regard Ghirlandajo as vulgar. But James carried in his pocket *The Stones of Venice* when he visited the city where his friend Howells had been consul and where, as he wrote, decay was golden and misery itself was *couleur de rose.* There Ruskin's narrow theological spirit and his moralism and prudery seemed "mere wild weeds in a mountain of flowers."

Meanwhile, in 1869, on his first visit to Rome, James must have encountered two boys who were there at the moment, John Singer Sargent, thirteen years old, and Francis Marion Crawford, the son of Thomas Crawford, who was two years older. The Sargents and the Crawfords had been friends when

[2] This was the Consiglio that later suggested to Stanford White his own design for the New York Herald Building, once so famous but, like everything else in New York, so soon torn down.

their children were babies, and Crawford's older sister re-
membered tumbling John Sargent over when, one day, he and
Marion came to blows. They all belonged to the circle of
Story, with whom James was constantly thrown, and Marion
Crawford had just come back from a three years' stay in
America, intended to "make a good American" of him. James
missed by three years a little girl, Edith Newbold Jones, whom
he was to know as Edith Wharton and who, in 1866, had
spent her liveliest hours in Rome on the Pincio with Marion
Crawford's small half-sister. They had dodged in and out
among the old stone benches there, rolling hoops, skipping rope
and pausing out of breath to watch the procession of riders
and stately barouches. Edith Wharton remembered later the
stone pines of the Villa Borghese and the Villa Doria Pamphili
with its springy turf where she had walked with her mother,
the long sunny wanderings there and the throngs of models on
the Spanish steps, heaped with early daffodils, violets and
tulips. She remembered the warm scent of the box hedges, the
texture of the sun-gilded stone and the heavy coaches of
cardinals in scarlet and gold flashing through the narrow
mottled streets. She had hunted on the slopes of the Palatine
for the bits of blue, green and rosy stone, fragments of lapis
lazuli, porphyry and verd antique that cropped up like ane-
mones through the wild grass. As a child, with her family, she
had spent six years in Europe.

As for Sargent, when James put up at the Hotel Inghilterra,
he was in temporary lodgings just round the corner, and
Vernon Lee, one of his playmates, remembered him as a boy
wearing a pepper-and-salt Eton jacket. She saw him bound
down the steps in the Piazza di Spagna, weaving his way
among the costumed models. Two of Sargent's own early
memories were of digging up fragments of ancient marbles in

the still unkempt region of the Esquiline hill and of bombarding with acorns and pebbles as he stood on the Pincian terrace
the pigs outside the Porta del Popolo below. In that very year,
1869, the Sargents had made up their minds that the boy was
to be a painter, but he was in Rome for a few months only
before he was taken back to Florence, where he had been
born in 1856. The family wandered like gypsies all over
Europe, from Biarritz to Venice, to Switzerland, to Paris,
"living one year like ambassadors and the next like paupers,"
as Henry James was to describe them in his story *The Pupil*;
for the tale of the Moreens was based on the tale of the
Sargents, as the painter was to relate it to the story-teller. Sargent had spoken with loathing of his nomad's childhood,
dragged as he was to and fro by parents who rushed about
Europe, trying to "get in with people who didn't want them."
Perhaps they were not the toadies and snobs that Henry James
pictured in the Moreens, with one fixed idea of "making an
appearance and passing for something or other," for James
wished to create his own effect. But certainly Sargent's childhood had been far from happy.

In one of his articles, in after years, James was to introduce
Sargent, who also settled in England, to the English-speaking
world, while Sargent himself retained to the end a special
feeling for Italy, the country of his early memories that had
been his birthplace. Marion Crawford was to spend his life in
Italy, and there could never have been a question that he knew
more about it than any other American story-teller. Fifteen
years old when James was in Rome,—James being twenty-six,—
he lived on the Corso with his mother, who had married,
years after the death of Thomas Crawford, an old family friend,
the painter Luther Terry. The family occupied a floor of the
Odescalchi palace with the great marble staircase and the

vaulted ceilings that were to appear in some of Crawford's novels, and two of their constant visitors were Augustus Hare and Edward Lear, who sang *The Owl and the Pussycat* to the Crawford children. When Daisy, Marion's half-sister,[3] said she would like him for an uncle, he called himself "Dopty Duncle" and wrote verses for her. Augustus Hare told tales of ghosts and vampire bats that might have been suggested by happenings in the rambling old palace or in the neighbouring palaces in one of which it was known that a man had been walled up alive. Later the author of *Walks in Rome* enabled Marion to visit India and gave him introductions to various friends there.

No other American, certainly, had ever possessed the knowledge of Rome that Marion Crawford drew in with his first breath, for the Forum, the Coliseum and the Palace of the Caesars had been the class-rooms of all the Crawford children. With their tutors and their governesses they had stood on the legendary spot where Mark Antony said, "Friends, Romans, countrymen," and they had lived as it were the stories of Tarpeia's Rock, Horatio at the bridge and the House of the Vestals. To Marion Crawford, Latin was a living language, for his tutor's lessons had been in Latin. In earlier years, at the Villa Negroni, near Thomas Crawford's studios, his playmates had been Prince Massimo's children, and the most intimate friends of Marion's sister were the nieces and nephews of Cardinal Antonelli. Marion Crawford had grown up in the shadow of this cardinal, the incarnate chief of reactionary politics in Rome in the last years of the temporal power when, riddled with conspiracies, the city was a hunting-ground for political spies. He had seen the antiquated vehicles of the Inquisition, different from all others, driving through the

[3] Afterwards Mrs. Winthrop Chanler, the author of *Roman Spring*.

streets, with the agents, in plain black, seated within, and he had known at first hand the life in some of the old palaces where the sombre magnificence of feudal times still went on. He had once witnessed the excavation, in one of these palaces, of a dry well that had been used as an oubliette, with skeletons in it, one with a knife driven through the skull, and fragments of sixteenth and seventeenth-century weapons. A passage ran from the cellars over to the Tiber. He knew another palace under which the "lost water" had been found, the water that ran, silent and black, beneath the city and suddenly appeared in unexpected places; and he had been present, as a ten-year-old boy, at the digging up of a gilt-bronze statue under the courtyard of the Palazzo Righetti. This was the colossal statue of the Vatican Museum that was presently set up in the Rotunda and that had been concealed in a vault under the theatre of Pompey,—why it had been so hidden no one could guess. The previous year he had been taken to see the great Vatican statue of Augustus on the spot where it came to light in a famous villa. He knew every landmark in the Alban hills where the family spent several summers and the children, riding on donkeys to the Lake of Nemi, saw the barges of Caligula far down in the water, and he had visited some of the castles of the great Roman families that were perched on every summit there. Well he knew also the dark streets of the city with their damp acrid air, laden with the odours of decaying vegetables, stables, cheese and mud, the fumes of roasting coffee and vapours from the wine-carts.

All these Roman scenes were to come alive, in later years, in Marion Crawford's novels,—the good and the bad,—years in which Henry James was to see more of this boy, grown up, one of his humbler rivals in the art of the novel.

CHAPTER XIV

THE JAMESES

MEANWHILE, Charles Eliot Norton had returned to Italy where he spent two years in Rome, Florence and Venice, settling for a long stay in an old-fashioned villa at Siena, with a chapel, a spacious hall and a terraced garden. There Ruskin joined him in 1870 with a mother and daughter who were friends of his, a cousin, a valet, a courier, a maid for the ladies and an English gardener to whom he was devoted, wandering with Norton through the mediæval town and drawing the lioness and her cubs at the base of the pillar of the pulpit in the Duomo.

Ruskin had written to Norton that he had been wholly insane only about Rose La Touche and Turner, although he was already subject to attacks of brain fever, and at times he felt "like a wrecked sailor, picking up pieces of his ship on the beach." He had lost his religious faith, but he was gradually recovering it in the pre-Reformation form of the mediæval Church,[1] and it pleased him to spend mornings with Norton in the Campo Santo at Pisa, at Lucca, at Prato and in Flor-

[1] But the volatile Ruskin passed through various phases. In 1858 he wrote to Norton, "I've found out . . . that, positively, to be a first-rate painter, you mustn't be pious, but rather a little wicked, and certainly a man of the world." He had visited a dreary Waldensian conventicle at Turin and then went to a picture gallery and fell in love with a Paolo Veronese. At that moment he questioned the connection between art and puritan Christianity.

ence. Thirty times he visited Lucca, sketching the tomb of
Ilaria by Jacopo della Quercia in the Duomo, where he had
just drawn one of Filippo Lippi's heads when Norton showed
him his own favourites in the Academy at Florence. Near by,
Ruskin found four frescoes by Giotto that nobody, he was
convinced, knew anything about, though he felt now that
Giotto, "a loving realist in little things," could not compare
with Cimabue in majesty of thought. Giotto was a "mere
domestic gossip," he wrote to Norton later. For the rest, the
two agreed about the nuisance of the railway whistle that
one heard behind Santa Maria Novella,—an unpleasant reminder for Norton of the Back Bay station,—and in general
every sign that Italy was not merely taking to trade but was
bent on remaining alive like other nations. If, as Henry Adams
said, the tourist is always a Tory, Ruskin himself was doubly
one. He had no sympathy with the Risorgimento. But Norton's
political conscience was at war with his mediæval tastes. He
could not assent to Ruskin's condemnation of every existing
arrangement of the modern world.

At intervals, during the following years, Norton, to please
Ruskin, sent him a few Greek vases that he had picked up,
fragments of Pisan sculpture of the thirteenth century and
bits of a mediæval font; while Ruskin wrote Norton about
his work on Angelico at Perugia or the "stupendous power" of
Botticelli. Once he suggested that they should give up their
"confounded countries" and travel away together and "live B.C.
or in the thirteenth century," drawing and writing, neither of
them to be "too merry for the other and both much stronger
for the other . . . We had better arrange that expatriation plan
at once." But that was after Norton had gone home from England, where he had spent three years, on intimate terms also
with Carlyle and Darwin, whose son married Mrs. Norton's

sister. He had returned to Harvard with a dedicated mind, bent on "fighting," as he said, "the devil and his allies," thanks to whom his own country was going to ruin; for so he saw the epoch of Reconstruction. He had planned for a while to write on the European power of Italy, which at one time had civilized all Europe; and he had prepared in Italy for the book that he actually wrote, *Historical Studies of Church-Building in the Middle Ages*. This consisted of essays on the cathedrals of Venice, Florence and Siena, where he had spent months working in the archives. He had lived, as he felt, on Italian chronicles and mediæval biographies, studying the political and social conditions of the period when the cathedrals were built till he felt at home with the builders and their character and life. He would have been content, he wrote, to spend his life in Siena "if the world were not so bad and if America were better," for to him Siena was "still Italian of the true stamp," of the days before America was discovered. The cathedral seemed to him the most picturesque building in Italy, and he delighted in watching the peasants cutting their grapes, loading their carts and beating out the grain on the threshing-floor. These scenes of real life seemed to him more beautiful even than Benozzo Gozzoli's painted scenes. While, moreover, Ruskin despised the Italians of this day,[2] Norton was deeply drawn to them. "If one knows how to live with them, they are the sweetest people on earth." He added, "If I ever come back, may I be born Italian."

* *

*

[2] "Take them all in all, I detest the Italians beyond measure . . . They are Yorick's skull with the worms in it, nothing of humanity left but the smell."—Ruskin, Letter to his father, 1845.

When, after his first visit to Italy, Henry James returned, —with "an absolute sense of need to see it again,"—he was already launched on the career as a writer that had begun, he felt, in Norton's study. This was the golden-brown study in the old house in Cambridge, and Norton had shown Ruskin a paper of James's on Tintoretto that pleased his great capricious English friend. Tintoretto's pictures seemed to James "less an operation of the mind then a kind of supplementary experience of life," for he had felt, pictorially, the beautiful terrible spectacle of life very much as Shakespeare poetically felt it.

For the winter of 1872 and 1873, William James joined his brother in Rome and Florence. After four years of invalidism, William had not yet begun his career, but one could see already how different in outlook the brothers were in a world in which William was troubled by the "weight of the past." They made together the moonlight visit to the Coliseum which was to be the death of Daisy Miller, and William recoiled from what he called its "damned blood-soaked soil", bent as he was on helping to build a new world. There was something in both Rome and Florence that seemed to him "fatal," as he wrote. "My very enjoyment of what belongs to hoary eld has done more to reconcile me to what belongs to the present hour . . . than anything I have experienced." But Henry felt, like his Theobald the painter, that only since he had come to Italy had he "really lived, intellectually and aesthetically speaking." For the rest, he did not agree, aesthetically, with Norton,—he regarded St. Peter's simply as "the builded sublime,"—though he and William shared Norton's distaste for the Church of Rome and the "crooked teachings" of the Jesuits, as Henry James called them. He disliked the "uncleanness of monachism" and the "brutish-looking monks," and he wrote, "I'm sick unto death of priests and churches . . . Their 'picturesqueness' ends by making me want to go strongly for political economy or the New England school system." William James, nearly thirty years later, put into words in a letter what he must always have felt on this general subject,[3] while he also said that Rome, with all its suggestions of "moral horror," [4] was simply the world's "most satisfactory lake of picturesqueness."

With his own passion for the picturesque, Henry James was startled by the change that had taken place since the new Italy had triumphed, since Rome had been suddenly secularized and the Vatican had gone into mourning and everything seemed remorselessly curtailed and clipped. The rust of centuries had been scraped off, ancient palaces were coated with white, the weeds had been scraped away from the Coliseum, the convents were being turned into offices, the barred windows had been opened and more windows broken in the walls. The new industry was death to the old idleness, the leisure of thought and the stillness of mind to which Rome had admitted the traveller. Absent were the monsignori, treading the streets in their purple stockings, followed by servants who returned for them the bows of the meaner sort, and black now were the cardinals' coaches that had formerly glittered with scarlet and swung with the weight of the footman clinging behind. Instead of the Pope, one met the King, in a low carriage with a single attendant, pocketing, like a good-natured man ac-

[3] "I dote on the fine equestrian statue of Garibaldi, on the Janiculum, quietly bending his head with a look half-meditative, half strategical, but wholly victorious, upon St. Peter's and the Vatican. What luck for a man and a party to have opposed to it an enemy that stood up for *nothing* that was ideal, for *everything* that was mean in life. Austria, Naples and the Mother of Harlots here were enough to deify anyone who defied them."—William James, Letter from Rome, 1900.

[4] "The things the eyes most gloat on, the inconceivably corrupted, besmeared and ulcerated surfaces, the black and cavernous glimpses of interiors, have no suggestions save of moral horror, and their tactile values, as Berenson would say, are pure gooseflesh. Nevertheless, the sight of them delights."—William James, Letter of 1900.

cepting circulars on the street, the petitions thrust into his hand by passers by. When James saw a newspaper-stand, he knew that something momentous had happened, something that was hostile indeed to picturesqueness, for the absence of any but the two papal newspapers had had much to do with the quietude of old. Rome reading unexpurgated news was altogether another Rome, and, for every subscriber to the "Libertà," James was inclined to think, there was an antique masker or reveller less. It seemed to him that the population had lost its relish for play without yet acquiring any marked relish for work.

James responded to the great old painters as Howells, a lover of architecture, and certainly Hawthorne, had largely failed to do, and his essays on the hours he spent with them,—"exquisite hours, enveloped in light and silence,"—were proofs of a rare talent for this kind of writing. He discussed, in Venice, Carpaccio, "the most personal and sociable of artists," along with Giovanni Bellini and Paolo Veronese,—feeling that Titian could be seen better elsewhere,—with Andrea del Sarto in Florence, "poor exploded Domenichino" [5] and Rubens's "great carnal cataracts." Then, just at the moment of Pater's essay, he found Botticelli, of all his group, "the one who detains and perplexes and fascinates you most" with his "illimitable grace" and "adventurous fancy." How perceptive, for the rest, were James's travel papers, soon to be collected in *Transatlantic Sketches,* some of them portraits of the little hill-towns that

[5] Domenichino's talent "went about trying this and that, concocting cold pictures after cold receipts, dealing in the second-hand and the ready-made, and putting into its performance a little of everything but itself."—*Transatlantic Sketches.*

 James marked here the change of feeling regarding the Bolognese school that had been universally admired for a century hitherto. The Brownings, he wrote, had "burned incense to Domenichino," and the Murray guide-book of the eighteen-seventies called "The Last Communion of St. Jerome" the "second finest picture in the world."

were miniature cities with ravines down which the houses scrambled and slid. Milan, so long under Austrian rule, seemed to him Germanized and rather the last of the northern capitals than the first of the southern, and there was Como that figured "so largely in novels with a tendency to immorality," Como, the operatic, that suggested a libretto. At Cortona, he had chosen a spot over the Etruscan ramparts, an empty crumbling citadel behind one of the churches, and there he had spent a good part of a day, stretched out, observing the view over the top of a novel of Balzac.

For, of course, fiction was Henry James's métier, and the first of his published stories had an Italian setting. He was never to reprint this himself, nor another called *Adina* in which a Roman rustic on the Campagna found in a broken old tree a great jewel in a box, a theme that vaguely suggested Hawthorne, as *The Last of the Valerii* brought back the Donatello of *The Marble Faun*. For James's young Roman count who reverts to the faith of his fathers, dormant for so many centuries, and secretly worships the marble figure of Juno dug up in his garden, was "fundamentally unfurnished with anything resembling an idea" and had nothing that one could properly call a "soul." All good nature and good health, he had only appetites and tastes like the Count of Monte Beni before he was awakened, and there was much of Hawthorne too in *The Madonna of the Future*, the story of the deluded American painter in Florence. Theobald's dream was to paint a picture that would sum up all the Italian madonnas, and "the noiseless years had ebbed away and left him brooding in charmed inaction, forever preparing for a work forever deferred." No doubt there was also in this a reminiscence of Washington Allston and the fate of his ever-unfinished "Belshazzar's Feast," from which James at home had taken warning, as in a way he warned himself in the long tale of *Roderick Hudson,* the story of an artist's failure and disintegration. "Can there be for a while a happier destiny than that of a young artist, conscious of talent, with no errand but to educate, polish and perfect it, transplanted to these sacred shades?" So, in *Transatlantic Sketches,* James wrote of one of the academies in Rome, where Roderick's first fortnight had been, like his own, a "high aesthetic revel." But Roderick, in the golden air, had gone to pieces.

James began this book in Florence in 1874, and five years later he was to begin *The Portrait of a Lady* also in Florence, for he returned to Italy again and again. It was, he wrote, "really so much the most beautiful country . . . that others must stand off and be hushed while she speaks," but he had found Paris, and presently London, where he settled in 1876, "more substantial to live upon . . . than the romance of Italy." In the circle of writers he met in Paris, he was intellectually more at home, just as he was more at home socially in England; and, as for the picturesque, he found this abundantly also in the setting of his *Little Tour in France.* It was true, as he wrote, that he never wearied of "feasting a foolish gaze" on Italian sun-cracked plaster and shadowed gateways or lingering by shabby half-barbaric farm-yards; but he was only the "sentimental tourist" there and he could not exist forever on the picturesque. Was he not speaking for himself when he quoted "my friend X" who said, "I prefer a good 'interior' to a good landscape"?—and it was he who replied to a lady's remark that the Roman villas would be a good subject for him: "A Roman villa . . . seems to me to have less of human and social suggestiveness, a shorter, lighter reverberation, than an old English country-house, round which experience seems piled so thick." It had more suggestiveness to James if only because the Italian palaces seemed, as it were, to "frown" on him; they looked, he wrote, "as if they were meant to keep people out" much more than they were meant to "let people in." James may have had small respect for Marion Crawford as a novelist, but he might well have envied Crawford's knowledge of the Italian world where he himself knew only "washerwomen and waiters." He could not penetrate behind the high walls of the still feudal nobility, though he kept wondering in Italian towns about the old-world social types who lingered and vegetated in the houses there. He could see only pictorially the young Venetians, splendid in dress, whom he surveyed one day at Florian's in Venice, and who needed only velvet, satin and plumes to be subjects of Paolo Veronese. Of the Italians, he complained, besides the washerwomen, he knew only servants in hotels and custodians in churches, and, being neither a Dickens nor a Howells, he had nothing to say about such humble types.

On the other hand, he found in Italy a legion of Americans, many of them with red books and opera-glasses, struggling artists in the galleries, in the streets, business men in the cafés and mothers who were anxious to give their daughters "all the advantages." What struck him in many of these travelling Americans was a lack of culture one could scarcely believe, so that one ceased to be surprised to hear someone say of the Coliseum that it would be a fine building when it was finished. There were girls like Daisy Miller, strikingly pretty with her flounces and frills, who cared for nothing so little as "pictures and things," so that any observation of the dreadful old men who talked about them went into one of her ears and out of the other. But there were other girls who were travelling, as they said, "for general culture, to acquire the languages and to see Europe for myself," and there were older ladies who were "studying European society" and whose daughters were "receiving the education of a princess." (Meaning that they read hundreds of French novels, while learning to speak at least Italian and French.) So said the mother of Christina Light, a consul's daughter, born in Rome, who was to become in time the Princess Casamassima. There were the retired proprietors of borax mines in the West who were "eager to patronize our indigenous talent," and there were artists like Sam Singleton whose family wrote him peremptory letters appealing to him as an American to hurry home. Then there were lady journalists like Henrietta Stackpole who were studying the position of Italian women. James encountered scores of types of which he made the portraits that appeared in so many of his earlier novels and stories and that summed up an aspect of the *zeitgeist* and a whole phase of the history of American culture. Only at that moment could Winterbourne have murmured Byron's lines from *Manfred* in the Coliseum, and only then could Miss Blanchard have quoted, among the ruins of Veii, the poems of Mrs. Sigourney and N. P. Willis.

In his extraordinary portrait-gallery of Americans in Italy,—when they were not in Switzerland, France or England,—James rearranged traits he observed, sometimes drawing from actual characters and sometimes embroidering characters of whom he had heard. In the Moreens of *The Pupil*, for instance, no one would have recognized Sargent's family, nor would anyone have recognized Sargent himself in the little cosmopolite Morgan Moreen, so pale, lean, acute and undeveloped. And who would have known that Gilbert Osmond and his daughter Pansy, the small, unobtrusive, submissive, infantine Pansy, "the ideal *jeune fille* of foreign fiction," had been suggested by Francis Boott and his daughter Elizabeth,—Lizzie Boott,—who lived in the Villa Castellani at Bellosguardo? Lizzie Boott painted there, and Henry James did all he could to dispose of her pictures in London before she married Frank Duveneck, who had come to Florence. It was her father, the composer of songs, whom William James described, in *Memories and Studies,* as honest and sturdy, tender-hearted, modest and faithful in friendship, the liberal in politics who spent eighteen years abroad, drifting back and forth between Italy and Newport. Yet he was the "original" of the sadistic Osmond, who looked "rather like a demoralized prince in exile," one "who had abdicated in a fit of fastidiousness and had been in a state of disgust ever since." But no one was more a type of the moment than this sterile dilettante for whom Isabel Archer was another collector's piece and who, in his sorted, sifted world, caused everything to wither that he touched. Types too were Madame Merle, who had "the note of rarity" with her world-wide smile that over-reached frontiers, and Henrietta who had so many clear-cut views and who was unquestionably in the van of progress. The events of Gilbert Osmond's life were finding an old silver crucifix or discovering on a daubed-over panel a Correggio sketch, and he was more "disAmericanized" than any of the Touchetts, who were assimilated in Europe but unconverted.

In Florence, later, Eugene Lee-Hamilton told Henry James the story which he was to recompose in *The Aspern Papers,* for there, although Venice appeared as the scene, had lived Jane Clairmont, the original of old Miss Bordereau. Sargent is said to have told James the same story, and his account was at least more circumstantial. When Sargent was thirteen, in 1869, the old lady lived in the house where his dancing-class was held, and one day, when the regular pianist had been unable to attend, she had been persuaded to come down and play for the class. Sargent remembered her, handsome still, in a black silk dress, the former mistress of Byron and the mother of Allegra who had later been a governess and continued to live on a legacy that had been left her by Shelley with many of his papers. A lodger in her house in the Via Romana was a friend of the Sargents, Captain Silsbee, an old seadog who worshipped the memory of Shelley and who dug himself in to acquire the manuscripts in case Miss Clairmont died, as she finally did in 1879. Silsbee, at that moment, was absent, and, rushing back to obtain the papers, which the spinster niece inherited, he was told he could have the papers if he took her too. At this point the Captain ran away.[6]

Every detail was changed in the story that James himself eventually wrote about the American Miss Bordereau in her decayed old palace on one of the more sequestered Venetian canals, the "Juliana" of the famous poems that Jeffrey Aspern composed when he had been her lover sixty years before. The tone of the old lady, once renowned but unapproachable and unvisited now, almost carried the narrator back to Casanova and Guardi in their rococo eighteenth-century Venice, while Jeffrey Aspern, who had since become the property of the human race, suggested another Edgar Allan Poe. For he too, almost uniquely, when so much of America was crude and provincial, had found means to live and write like one of the first, to be "free and general and not at all afraid." Henry James, who had known so many of his countrymen in Europe and the strange ways they sometimes took up there, had found or invented in this old lady a new romantic type of the American adventure.

[6] So Evan Charteris relates the story in his life of Sargent. Lee-Hamilton, the poet, who certainly told James the story, was Vernon Lee's brother. A similar true story is that of Constance Fletcher and her Byron papers in Venice.

The Aspern Papers no doubt suggested the somewhat similar stories of Henry B. Fuller (A Coal from the Embers) and Edith Wharton (The Angel at the Grave).

CHAPTER XV

FRANCESCA

For forty years the American painters had been gathering in Italy,—ever since the death of Benjamin West, the master, in his London studio, of a whole generation,—but they began to leave Rome and Florence at the end of the Civil War at home, often resorting to Paris, Düsseldorf or Munich. While many remained and others came, drawn sometimes by Rome-sickness, George Inness, who returned in 1870 to paint the Tiburtine olive-trees, was a type of the new time in preferring Barbizon and Paris. That Rome was eternally sketchable every-body said, and the number of studios there was always in-creasing, outnumbering four times over, as one of the painters presently remarked, the three hundred and sixty Roman churches. But the fall of papal Rome and the unification of Italy were the death-blow of mediævalism, together with roman-tic Italy and the picturesque, or at least much of the picturesque that enchanted the painters of "drawing-room art" who were to disappear with the costumes that pleased them. One seldom saw any longer the classic head-cloth or the famous crimson bodice of the contadina.

Modernity, in short, was at variance with the poetry of the old Italian life, although young Italy was naturally tired, as Henry James remarked, of being admired for its eyelashes and its pose. Every town soon had a Corso Vittorio Emanuele, a Via Garibaldi, a Via Cavour, and a statue of Mazzini too, though the science and prose of Cavour had replaced the heroic idealism of the earlier prophet. In Rome especially the cosmopolitan was taking the place of the old traditions; the young were concerned with the political and economic future; and, with the railroads bringing security, one could not very well repine if they had put an end to the reign of the bandit.[1] The aroma of the bandit had lingered romantically over the country, but only artists and writers could regret its passing, just as they only could regret the embanking of the Tiber that was to put an end, largely, to Roman fever. To them, it somehow seemed of the essence of Rome that Daisy Miller should have died of this, while Hawthorne's daughter Una almost died, after staying out late sketching in the Palace of the Caesars.

These notes of the new age, however, were relative and gradual, and, as for the aroma of the bandit, it lingered on for many years in the presence of the dandified American, Augustus Hayter.[2] Who did not know the story of this dapper little man, mysteriously rich, in his flat in the Piazza di Spagna, a friend of all the musicians in Rome and himself a clarinetist whose wife had been the daughter of a well-known brigand? As a young man, on a lark, walking to Naples with a group of musicians, he had been kidnapped with his friends by a party of banditti and carried off, blindfolded, into the mountains where the chief bandit apologized for discommoding them,— but how could his daughter be married without music at the

[1] "The last bandit of any note flourished for a few months in 1868 and 1869, a boy of Ravenna called Gagino, a good-natured youth . . . always polite and civil, as I was assured by one of his victims . . . Since he was shot, brigandage has ceased [not in Sicily, of course]; and the roads here are safer by night or by day than in the vicinity of most of our large towns."—Eugene Schuyler, *Italian Influences*, p. 60.

[2] The pseudonym given this American by Daniele Vare, who tells the story in *Ghosts of the Spanish Steps*, pp. 73-84.

wedding? A friar had also been kidnapped to perform the ceremony at which the musicians played a quartette of Haydn, while they spent a jovial week, learning to dance the tarantella, in a real brigands' cave under an old ruined castle. It was a promising young robber who married the older daughter, while Hayter at the marriage feast fell in love with the younger, an all but incredibly beautiful mountain girl; so the friar had on his hands a double wedding. Hayter took the girl to Rome, but there, obliged to wear boots and gloves and drive on the Pincian hill like any lady, she rapidly wilted away and presently died. Such was the true Washington Irving story of the red-coated little man who was still hunting on the Campagna thirty years later.

The unification of Italy was a sacred cause to Longfellow, who returned to Rome in 1868, shortly after the publication of the translation of Dante on which he had worked off and on since the eighteen-forties. Norton, who was to follow him with a prose translation, and Lowell, who was lecturing at Harvard and writing on Dante, had formed with him in Cambridge a Dante Club, later the Dante Society, to read the poet and discuss problems of translation. An Italianate circle joined them, Christopher Cranch, who had lived in Rome, Dana of *Two Years Before the Mast* who was to die there,[3] Howells and the old consul at Rome, George W. Greene, whose bust by Thomas

[3] In January, 1882, after he had retired as a lawyer and while he was writing in Rome a work on international law. He caught pneumonia driving home after dark from St. Paul's-outside-the-walls. Shortly before this, he and his wife had visited the Protestant cemetery. "As they stood there under the tall cypress-trees by the ruins of the old walls, looking across them to the city beyond, the air filled with the fragrance of flowers and resounding with the song of nightingales, Mrs. Dana said to her husband, 'Is not this the spot where one would wish to lie forever?' and he answered, 'Yes, it is indeed!' And this spot his wife now selected for her husband's grave."—Charles Francis Adams, *Richard Henry Dana*, Vol. II, p. 386.

Crawford stood in Longfellow's study. Greene, the poet's ancient friend who came up from Rhode Island, was rather like an old Italian house-priest, gentle and suave, as Howells remembered, quoting, with an exquisite Roman accent, the poets, especially Giusti, whom he had known. Then, occasionally bringing out some faded Italian anecdote, threadbare in its antiquated texture, with a scent of civet, he would speak of the writers whom Howells was discussing in lectures and in essays, Goldoni, Manzoni, Leopardi, Niccolini, Monti. While Lorenzo da Ponte in New York, Mozart's librettist, had been the first in America to expound Dante, Ticknor's interest had been linguistic mainly. Longfellow, Lowell and Norton popularized the study of the poet and deepened this study also in the academic world.

In the winter snows of Cambridge, all books on Italy made Longfellow restless, and, reading Norton's *Cathedral-building*, he had dreamed of villas by the margin of lakes, walks in chestnut groves and sunny piazzas. Now, on his return, he spent a night in Monte Cassino and made the visit to Amalfi he recorded in a poem; then he became a shepherd of Arcadia when the secretary of the arch-flock bestowed on him great possessions in that dreamland. Franz Liszt, the "piano-centaur," as Gregorovius called him, inasmuch as he and the instrument seemed to be one, played for Longfellow in the convent where the composer was living,—Mephistopheles, as someone said, "disguised as an abbé." Then Liszt set to music the introduction of Longfellow's long poem, *The Golden Legend*. The so-called "painter of princely sitters," G. P. A. Healy, the pictorial head-hunter who had come from Boston, painted Liszt for Longfellow and the poet with his daughter standing, in a well-known picture, under the arch of Titus.

Just at that moment, Augustus Saint-Gaudens who, in 1870,

had witnessed Victor Emmanuel's triumphal entry and his progress from the railway station to the Quirinal palace, was modelling his first statue "Hiawatha" and cutting cameos for a dealer in the Via Margutta. Saint-Gaudens, the young sculptor from New York who had gone to the Beaux-Arts in Paris, where he had earned his way as a cameo-cutter, was symptomatic of the new age in breaking away from the classical tradition that all the sculptors had followed since the time of Canova. The themes of the earlier sculptors, vaguely Greek or Roman,—Captive Slaves and Graces,—bored Saint-Gaudens, who had no interest, for example, in Story as an artist and respected him only as a cultivated man of the world. The new ideas and feelings that had come in with the Civil War were putting an end to Story's kind of sculpture, and many of the sculptors were working at subjects,—statues of statesmen and soldiers,—which the war suggested. Randolph Rogers, for one, in Rome, was representing in bronze, for Madison Square in New York, Secretary Seward. For several years Saint-Gaudens devoted himself to cameo-cutting in amethyst or malachite or onyx, cutting portraits in pink shells but mainly making brooches and seals, earrings and scarf-pins with heads of dogs and lions. He became known as the most skilful cameo-cutter in Rome or Paris. Tourists were buying these objects by thousands, with contadina corals, jet chains with gold clasps and Roman scarves. The cameo-cutters vied with the makers of inlaid paper-weights and inkstands modelled on the Pantheon and the so-called Temple of Vesta.

*

*   *

Among the Americans living in Florence during all these years were the family of Francis Alexander, the portrait-painter, who had arrived from Boston in 1853 when Fanny, his only child, was in her teens. The father had died some years before, but the mother and daughter continued to live in their spacious rooms at the top of an ancient palazzo, with their old servant Edwige and with clothes of an old Boston cut, copied year after year by a Florentine seamstress. They both spoke Italian with a Yankee accent, and Mrs. Alexander for sixty years kept up with the gossip of Boston while she maintained her accounts in Boston stores. Except for the tables and chairs and the pictures on their walls,—a Ghirlandajo, two Giottos and a Perugino triptych, more and more precious, these, as the years went on,—they might have been living still in Louisburg Square, and their dining-room was filled with East Indian china which had been brought over from Massachusetts. Mother and daughter went to church at a Lutheran conventicle where all the other parishioners were humble and poor. The pastor of the brethren there was T. P. Rossetti, a cousin of the now famous English painter and poet.

Fanny, who was docile and childlike and who liked to paint and write, had her own workroom on the upper story, opening on a terrace garden set about with flower-pots and with neat little beds of New England flowers. There one saw mignonette, sweet alyssum and lemon verbena, with larkspur, pinks, nasturtiums and "my wild olive," a small tree which the great John Ruskin had dug up for her in order that she might watch its beautiful unfolding. He had helped her to place the tree in its wooden tub. Fanny always wore a basque, buttoned down the front, modelled on one that she had brought from Boston, and, obedient to "Mammina," who crocheted her hairnets, she closed her eyes when anyone spoke of sin. As an artist, she was not permitted to study anatomy, for it did not please the Alexanders to think of men and women without their clothes on, and when she went through picture galleries Mammina would admonish her, "We are coming to a nude. Cast down your eyes." When, many years later, she broke her hip, she forbade the doctor to set the bone until he had first covered the hip with a blanket. She wrote and drew with the naivety of a mediæval nun.

For many years the Alexanders spent summers in the Apennines, among the Tuscan peasants, at Abetone. They had a cottage there at the head of the valley. To reach the mountains behind Pistoia they drove through the Val d'Arno, winding up among chestnut groves till they came to a region of upland streams, woods of fir and beech and pastures full of flowers. Fanny loved the farms there, the olive-trees and cypresses and the little green foot-paths sprinkled with red-tipped daisies, and she had been struck at once by the beauty of the mountain girls, who looked as if they had stepped out of old altar-pieces. They had charmingly formed oval faces, with large soft eyes and sunburnt cheeks and the air of a Tuscan madonna of the *cinquecento*.[4] In these mountains everyone sang, the farmers, the shepherds and the charcoal-burners who, as they watched their fires at night, kept one another company by singing together and improvising verses. Fanny began to record their stories and their songs. Sometimes two lovers on adjoining farms sang to one another, the boy singing one verse and the girl responding in a sort of metrical musical conversation, and Fanny made friends with these mountain singers, men and

[4] Hawthorne might have been thinking of Francesca's subjects when he wrote (in *The Marble Faun*): "A Pre-Raphaelite artist . . . might find an admirable subject in one of these Tuscan girls, stepping with a free, erect, and graceful carriage. The miscellaneous herbage and tangled twigs and blossoms of her bundle, crowning her head (while her ruddy, comely face looks out between the hanging side festoons like a larger flower), would give the painter boundless scope for the minute delineation which he loves." Hawthorne might have been describing here one of Francesca's drawings.

women, old and young, among them Beatrice de Pian degli Ontani. Beatrice, a stonemason's daughter, sixty years old at the time, was the most famous poetess of this part of the country. As a girl, following sheep, she had sung ballads to pass the time, "The Battle of St. Michael and the Dragon" or "The Fall of Man," and she was making hay out in the meadow when Fanny first approached her on the high ridge. She threw down her rake and ran to meet the stranger, wearing her old-fashioned red bodice and with eyes full of fire, and she stood quite still, looking down, before her face lighted up again and she sang a song of eight lines with an "Adio" after. She improvised as she spoke the lines, and later, unable to write herself, for all her skill in composing the songs, she dictated a number to the foreigner from Florence.

As the years continued, Fanny collected hundreds of songs, together with many stories of the lives of the peasants, from the singer Faustina Petrucci, for one, or the rough loud-voiced Assunta, a neighbour with a donkey that was called Garibaldi. They were mostly stories of poverty, grief and the simple religion of the mountaineers, "people of pure Etruscan descent, quietly laborious and honest," said Fanny, "keeping the happiness of their earliest Christian faith." There were tales of household life that were often heroic, and Fanny, who drew every day in the cloisters and churches roundabout, gradually became known also as a miracle-worker. She nursed the invalids whom the peasants brought to her, made herb-tea and broths and often cured them, and she sent to the seashore their scrofulous children, bought mattresses, dresses and shoes for them and paid their rent when it was overdue. She redeemed the pawned farming tools of many of them, while in Florence she maintained a soup-kitchen for the poor and employed women to make clothes for them. She worked at her drawings and sold them to help the peasants. Meanwhile, she collected her *Roadside Songs of Tuscany,* with drawings of flowers, rustic scenes and portraits, and she wrote a little book called *The Story of Ida.* This was the tale of a Florentine girl who had died some years before, a seamstress, devoted and gentle, whom the Alexanders had long known and who had lived in a dismal old house in the slums.

Then it happened that in 1882, when Ruskin was in Florence, he heard of the *Roadside Songs* from Henry Newman, an American painter who was living there and whose water-colours pleased him so much that he bought a number for his St. George Museum. Ruskin also bought for his house in the country in England several of Newman's pictures of Florentine buildings; and, hearing now of Fanny's work, he asked to be taken to see it and straightway formed an alliance with both mother and daughter. Ruskin was already an old man, bent, with a patriarch's beard, recovering from his second attack of delirious brain-fever, and Fanny had been breathless at the thought of meeting the art-dictator of the English-speaking world. Mrs. Alexander demurred at the suggestion that Fanny might go for a walk with Ruskin, but she finally agreed to let them go, taking Edwige along to chaperon them; and they strolled out far beyond the Porta Romana. There, beside a vineyard, they found the wild olive tree that presently grew in its tub on Fanny's terrace. Ruskin was delighted with Fanny's stories and pictures, and he examined her drawing minutely, remarking that no modern drawing was in any way comparable to it. He said he could recall no drawings of flowers since Leonardo da Vinci that matched hers for strength and delicacy, reverence and truth; and he bought the illuminated manu-scripts of the *Roadside Songs* and *The Story of Ida,* paying a large price for the benefit of her contadini. He forbade her to sell her drawings until he had put a price on them,—they must never go for less than forty guineas,—for otherwise Fanny might be made "a prey, and savoury morsel, and marrow-bone of, by the wolfy multitude." He had always said that missal-writing was the best thing in mediæval art, and here it was again in Fanny's pages. Or, no, not Fanny's,—she should be called Francesca, and henceforth Francesca she became.

Returning to Oxford as professor of art, Ruskin lectured about Francesca, astounding his audience as he had already done by his extravagant praise of Kate Greenaway's "girlies." He published, with his own prefaces, *The Story of Ida* and the *Roadside Songs,* and presently *Christ's Folk in the Apennine,* another of her books, distributing drawings of hers among various museums; and, because Ruskin had praised them, Francesca's drawings soon appeared, appropriately framed, in many an Oxford bedroom. Founding at Sheffield a school of art, he lectured on her work again, her drawings of mountains, trees and Tuscan peasants, and Watts soon joined him in praising her, saying of Francesca's "Madonnina" that he would rather have made it than almost anything he had done. Francesca was suddenly famous, for the followers of the prophet in England formed virtually a religious sect, and for Ruskin's adorers she was one of the adored. Flocking to her workroom, they asked her where the great man had stood and then they went and stood in the same spot, and, watching Francesca as she drew flowers and portraits of her peasant friends, they carried off her pens as souvenirs. In short, she became one of the sights of Florence. Charles Perkins came to see her and told her about the Tuscan sculptors, Lowell and Whittier wrote sonnets on *The Story of Ida* and clergymen preached sermons on it in America and England. The little book, said Cardinal Manning, was "as simply beautiful as the *Fioretti* of St. Francis."

After this, for several years, the trio corresponded, Ruskin and his "darling Sorella,"—or "darlingest Sorel,"—and his beloved Mammina or "sweetest Mammie"; for Mrs. Alexander almost replaced the grim old mother, recently dead, who had never relaxed her control of this emotional genius. Francesca was one of the "mouse-pets" who had succeeded Rose La Touche and who was to be succeeded by another young girl whom he found copying in the National Gallery in London and whom he presently asked to marry him; for Francesca, not so young, was undoubtedly a child, though he did not like to look at her because she was so plain. (As he told Mrs. Newman, the wife of the painter.) He wrote to Mrs. Alexander, "I have taken you so faithfully and truly for Mammina that I would never do anything you forbade, any more than I would go against my dead mother's will"; and to Francesca he wrote, "I am as a vine torn by a wild boar out of the wood and you like the grass of Parnassus by its native stream."

In short, he felt as if his life "had been given back" to him "as it was before any of the delirious illness," and, as he worked on *Præterita*, he found himself writing "with my old decision and pleasure." All thanks to his dearest Sorel and the "new and powerful stimulus" that she had given to his life, while he in turn counselled her to draw old ornamental forms that would make her see beautiful things she might otherwise miss. She should also make pencil notes of skies, outlining the clouds, and she should copy Lippi and Botticelli flowers and leaves to feel rightly conventional grace in all its strength. She wrote to tell him the news of Florence,—how Rossini had just returned,—there had been an immense procession with his own music; and in that same year, 1887, the façade of the Duomo was unveiled, finishing at last the work of six hundred years. Then someone had given her a flower that had touched

Dante's bones, recently discovered at Ravenna, a most precious relic. Ruskin was so famous in Illinois that, when he was ill, bulletins were posted out there every day to give the latest report of his condition, while Ruskin clubs were rising all over the West,—so said a lady who had come to see her; and it happened that, when she herself had prayed for his recovery, Ruskin felt better at once, or so he said. Instantly, on her terrace, three lilies blossomed that had never had a flower before or since.

There were other notes in this idyll of the half-mad old prophet who had been wholly mad not long before and who soon entered the final stage of madness. Francesca restored for him his lost religious faith, and he too found harbour for a while in the poor Lutheran meeting-house that brought back the biblical atmosphere he had known as a child. It was so much like his mother's chapel in the Walworth Road, attended by small shop-keepers in their Sunday trimmings. Then, "out of conceit," as he wrote, with his "plans for endless books," he wanted to write "dame school" books that would be like Francesca's, nursery tales with innocent nursery pictures; and he liked to think of the "fine gold" that had been entrusted to him, previously "a treasure hid in a mountain field of Tuscany." He thought of the peasant world that Francesca wrote about just as Tolstoy thought of it in Russia, Tolstoy who shared the bad conscience of Ruskin about his self-indulgent life and the wealth that he should have devoted to the welfare of the poor. Formerly, in more savage moods, he had spoken of the peasants with contempt, calling them "foul wretches" and "ape-faced children," behaving "like flies and dogs" among their tombs and churches, but now they seemed to him "gracious and blessed . . . God's own poor . . . living in the presence of Christ and His saints and apostles." It was they who were doing most of the world's work, and one might learn from them how it should be done, while nothing could so counter-act the "fury and vice" of the writers of the day as candid stories of these heroes of everyday life. So felt Ruskin, thinking of Francesca. This was just what Tolstoy thought when, in his later years, he rejected the great art of his own novels, praising an art without artifice that appealed to the feelings, reflecting sincere and simple Christian minds.

CHAPTER XVI

FLORENCE:
CONSTANCE FENIMORE WOOLSON

FOR AMERICANS, during these decades, Florence was haunted by three or four English writers who had lived and worked there, the author of *Romola*, Ruskin and especially the Brownings of whom everyone seemed to have an anecdote. With his odd rhymes and his actuality, Robert Browning, in a score of poems, had brought, as he said, "the days of Orcagna hither," or the days of Fra Lippo Lippi, that "poor monk out of bounds," or Andrea del Sarto whose house one could still see. In his dramatic monologues, these artists of the Renaissance moved and spoke as if one had met them in the street or like the characters in *The Ring and the Book,* the story of which Browning found in a yellow parchment record he picked up in a bookstall. Not even George Eliot in her picture of Bardo dei Bardi brought back the revival of learning better than Browning in *A Grammarian's Funeral;* and at many spots in Florence one thought of this poet. At a corner of the Via dei Servi stood the palace that he had made the scene of *The Statue and the Bust.*

For countless travellers who ignored Ruskin's dispraise of it, the Renaissance had become the most golden of ages, and, more than any other book, *Romola* led them to feel that they were living in that splendid epoch. This was in part because

Florence itself had changed so little and one could still go to San Lorenzo by the same turnings and the same streets or follow the crowds that had trooped to hear Savonarola. One could still stand at the same street-corner shrines and pass the self-same shops where the great artists had laboured. George Eliot, moreover, who introduced some of these artists in her book, Botticelli, Fra Bartolommeo, Albertinelli,—and Piero di Cosimo, carefully studied in Vasari,—brought them close to the reader's eye by surrounding them with the humbler sort, Bratti, the iron-monger, and Nello, the barber. All the men came to be shaved at the sign of Apollo and the Razor, the "focus of Florentine intellect," as Nello called it,—Machiavelli, the lover of delicate shaving, and Poliziano, relaxing after his lectures. The Puritan Savonarola was a type that Americans understood, and they were not unwilling to witness the "bonfire of vanities" that consumed Madonnas with the features of notorious hussies. Or other works sanctioned by a Pope who described the Virgin as a goddess and burned a never-dying lamp before a bust of Plato. Romola herself suggested the kind of superior New England girl whom Abbott Thayer was to paint a few years later, and the villainous young Greek Tito, arriving in Florence for the first time and seeing the Campanile and the doors of Ghiberti, shared all the excitement of discovery of the Americans themselves.

Romola's own house was a place of pilgrimage, and then there were Ghirlandajo's frescoes that brought back for many the Florentine faces and figures of which they had read. In fact, one met every day on the street some familiar face that had its counterpart in Ghirlandajo, the painter whom Ruskin, in Mornings in Florence, now called "good for nothing," or a maker, at the best, of "plated goods." The sacristans told tales of Ruskin and the huge fees he had paid them when he had been preparing to write this book, and flocks of schoolgirls, reading it, were told what they might not have guessed, that the Duomo, for instance, was a blunder. Ruskin's constant "Do what I tell you" filled their minds with notions that to others seemed preposterous and even crazy, charming as he was when he spoke of Cimabue, of Giotto, the Shepherd's Tower and the Golden Gate. It was this, and the drill-master's explicitness, that made him so compelling.[1] But Charles Godfrey Leland, who was to settle in Florence soon, was right when he said that Ruskin was one of those minds whom one was obliged to "accept as it was and be thankful." He was "one of those dwellers in cloudland whose thoughts were streamed and dashed with startling hues . . . magnificently illogical, splendidly rhapsodical, sublimely egotistical," of whom one could say that he "poured forth showers of stars."

One visitor who came to Florence to stay, and who took Ruskin for her guide, was a grand-niece of Fenimore Cooper,— Constance Fenimore Woolson, the novelist, forty years old in 1880, who "patiently went at it" in churches and museums. She took "Cimabue, Giotto and the rest, one by one and in due order," and Henry James said to her, "Some day you will see it," when she remarked at first that Giotto was beyond her.

[1] " 'You admire him, then—Ruskin?' said the lady [in Constance Fenimore Woolson's *A Front Yard*].

" 'Admire? That is not the word; he is the divinest madman. Ah, but he makes us work! In some always inaccessible spot he discovers an inscrutably beautiful thing, and then he goes to work and writes about it fiercely, with all his nouns in capitals and his adjectives after the nouns instead of before them—which naturally awes us.' "

When one of the characters in the same story remarks that the sword on a certain statue "looks like the hammer of a sewing-machine," another says, "You will destroy all our carefully prepared mediæval atmosphere . . . Here we have all been reading up for this expedition, and we know just what Ruskin thinks . . . Wait a bit, and you will hear us talk! And not one will be so rude as to recognize a single adjective."

James, who was in Florence at the time, took her to San Marco, to the Uffizi, the Pitti and the Boboli Gardens, and through tangled corners of the green Cascine,—to witness the festa of Ascension Day,—while she learned the alphabet of Florentine history and art.

Miss Woolson was to spend fourteen years in Italy and England before she died, in 1894, in Venice; and she wrote in Florence some of the novels that Henry James praised highly in an essay that he reprinted in *Partial Portraits*. "She has a remarkable faculty," he said, "of making the New World seem old," especially in her stories of the American South, the best of which, *East Angels,* was a novel about Saint Augustine in the years that followed the Civil War. It was a subtle study of the relations between the old Southern families there and the Northerners who had come down for business or for health. Presently Miss Woolson began to write stories, like some of James's own, about Americans in Italy, colonists and tourists, and their relations with these exotic surroundings.

Along with the Brownings and *Romola,* she had read the impressions of Florence that James had published in *Transatlantic Sketches,* James who, with his brown beard and large light grey eyes, struck her as "quiet, almost cold in manner." She shared his curiosity about their countrypeople and the effect on them of the continental setting, and there is no doubt that all this time Henry James was studying her as a striking case of the sensitive American in Europe. It is also certain that Miss Woolson studied James. For did he not appear in *A Florentine Experiment* as the cultivated expatriate Trafford Morgan who had "several theories" about Miss Stowe for whom he acted as a cicerone and who told her that "art" was so much better than "nature." For him, Giotto and Botticelli were the best things in Florence, and he explained to Miss Stowe why she should like them, while "he invented as he went along and amused himself not a little with his own unusual flow of language." They strolled together through dim cool churches, and, sitting on a bench overlooking the town, they talked about *Romola* together. Miss Stowe felt that Romola was not a natural character because her love for Tito came to an end, while the unnatural thing for Trafford Morgan was that she should have loved Tito at all.

There was obviously much of Henry James, who knew "all about pictures" and tried to make Miss Stowe admire the Duomo, the bleak interior that she could not like, in this art-loving countryman who was always going somewhere else, at one time to Tarascon, at another to Trieste. "He grew didactic and mystic over the round Botticelli of the Uffizi and the one in the Prometheus room at the Pitti." Meanwhile, Miss Woolson experienced in Florence "that old-world feeling" which, as she said, "I used to dream about, a sort of enthusiasm made up of history, mythology, old churches, pictures, statues, vineyards, the Italian sky, peasants" and what not; and this continued long after she had ceased to go about with a Baedeker at nine o'clock in the morning. She was especially struck by the ringing of the church-bells, swinging far out of the campaniles, into the air, back and forth, as they swung in the pictures on Christmas cards at home.[2] Well she knew the pensions, in some old palace on the Lungarno, with battered marble gods adorning the court, with tattered furniture and a slipshod air, steps that rambled up and down, labyrinthine corridors and rags of carpets. One always found English curates there, four or five blooming English girls who were taking lessons in Italian and music, and various detached American ladies whom

[2] Cf. Hawthorne's remark in his *Notebooks* on the sweetness of the bells of Florence, "as if the bells were full of liquid melody, and shed it through the air on being upturned."

her Mrs. Tracy called "the cultivated superfluous and the intelligent remainders." Many of these had been taught by Ruskin to raise their eyebrows and turn their backs in the presence of anything created since the *quattrocento*.

It was somewhat later that Miss Woolson took the villa at Bellosguardo,—not far from the villas in which Fenimore Cooper had lived and Hawthorne had first sketched *The Marble Faun*,—with the view that Mrs. Browning had seen one afternoon and presently described in *Aurora Leigh*. It was a great ancient structure of pale yellow hue, with vineyards and olive trees and a farm below, and one looked from the terrace over river and hills, the city, old bell-towers and castles and with olive groves and the Apennines beyond. Ruskin's Francesca had lived there for seventeen years, and there was the desk that Henry James had used when he too occupied the villa, where he put on a crimson *lucco* and a beautiful black velvet cap to celebrate the completion of the façade of the Duomo. Everything in Florence reminded one of something else, or of somebody else, like Mrs. Browning, whose favourite chair Frank Duveneck gave Miss Woolson; and one day she went to a party at the William J. Stillmans',[3] who were also spending five years there. The former American consul in Rome had married the famous Pre-Raphaelite beauty, the Greek lady who appeared in Disraeli's *Lothair*, the tall, thin hostess who drifted dreamily through the rooms, among the aesthetic bluestockings, her guests at the party. In pale yellows and paler greens, they stood about gazing into space, for they

[3] In the late eighties and early nineties, serially in the *Century Magazine*, appeared Stillman's *Old Italian Masters* with the wood-cut reproductions of Timothy Cole in which "line could go no further." So said the painter A. A. E. Hébert, the director of the French Academy in Rome, of these extremely skilful and sympathetic woodcuts. Both Stillman and Cole were especially drawn to the Florentine and Sienese primitive painters.

had nothing to say on ordinary topics, mysterious, mystic and wan, as they seemed to Miss Woolson, whose own mind was astute, realistic and witty. They harmonized with the pictures of the aesthetic painters, Burne-Jones, Holman Hunt and Rossetti, that hung on the walls.

In Florence, or at Sorrento, or Rome,—or in Switzerland or England,—where Henry James took her one day to Stonehenge,—Miss Woolson wrote the stories, too good to be forgotten, about the Americans in Italy whom she had observed. There were those who came, and remained, "for art" or to educate their children but who never admitted they had come to "live" there, patriotic as they were in a post-mortem fashion, —they were at least determined to go home to be buried. There were students from the Beaux-Arts in Paris who were making architectural tours and others who were exploring "Titian's country," bent on catching a glimpse of the reputed Titians supposedly existing in that unvisited region. Sometimes their hearts were set on finding the master's early drawings of which they had unearthed dim legends in monasteries. There were scholars who for fifty years had been planning a book on Columbus that was to supersede all other lives and who were always expecting to go home "next summer"; and there were the mothers who hoped to secure for their daughters a count with a castle, perhaps, and certainly a name. One young man was making a collection of Renaissance cloak-clasps, another was studying the history of the Malatestas, a third was supposed to look like Raphael's St. John in modern dress, and there was the girl who looked like a Bonifazio. (When she wore green velvet with big sleeves and appeared with her hair braided close to the head.) Most of them were happier if their villas were haunted, whether the ghost in question clanked its chains or glided noiselessly at midnight up the great stairway.

In a few cases Miss Woolson's stories rivalled Henry James's, and two or three were memorably comic or tragic, especially when they concerned the "unadjusted" Americans or a revolt against the search for culture. There was *A Transplanted Boy*, about the son of Mrs. Coe, who lived for seven years in a pension at Pisa. Mrs. Coe hated the Leaning Tower and "that everlasting old sarcophagus,"—her one undying hope was to live in Paris,—she only stayed in Pisa because it was cheaper; and, with results that one could imagine, her room was the only home that her small solitary son had ever had. In another tragedy of the transplanted, an old New Hampshire farm-woman found herself stranded in Assisi, the drudge of a rapacious peasant family there. What for others was picturesque was, for her, merely the filth in the streets, she never saw the view over the Umbrian plain, and her only dream was a "front yard" with currant bushes and a white fence in place of the malodorous pigsty that she saw there. She was rescued, too late, by three fellow-countrywomen who had come to sketch the Giotto frescoes.

In other tales, *A Pink Villa* and *The Street of the Hyacinth*, nature asserted itself against the dream of culture, or perhaps the dream of a title that filled many minds. In one, a young girl whose ambitious mother expects her to marry a Belgian count falls in love with an American farmer who is moneyless and cultureless but who seems to her a "man" instead of a "puppet"; in the other, the great art-critic marries the art student from "somewhere out West" because she has none of the traits that he usually admires. Thirty years later the revolt against culture was to become a common theme. Miss Woolson was one of the first to understand it.

CHAPTER XVII

HOWELLS IN FLORENCE

HOWELLS RETURNED to Italy for a year in 1882. A good part of this he spent in Florence, in a lodging on the Piazza Santa Maria Novella about which alone, he said, he could have written a book.

During the intermediate years, he had been living in Cambridge and Boston, forming a friendship with Henry James, whom he had seen every day at first, while they read to one another whatever they wrote. Howells, who was seven years older than James, had thought of himself as a traveller and poet,—"I did not yet feel my fiction definitely in me," he was to write later in reminiscence,—but he had been studying the American life which he had begun to present in *Suburban Sketches* and *Their Wedding Journey*. These preceded the novels that had Venice as a mise-en-scène, *A Foregone Conclusion*, *A Fearful Responsibility* and *The Lady of the Aroostook;* and meanwhile some of James's writings appeared in *The Atlantic*, with which Howells was connected.

For all of Henry James's delight in the picturesque in Italy, his literary sympathies were intensely French, while Howells's own were Italian; and Howells had been present at meetings of the Dante Club in Cambridge, first at Longfellow's house, later at Norton's. Already in Venice he had felt that "there is no life in the whole world so cheerful, so social, so beautiful as the

American," so that, with all his affection for the Italians, his allegiance as a writer was never divided.[1] But the humanity of the Italians deeply touched him. He marvelled over their temperance—they were "greedy in nothing," and the "union of grace with sympathy," as he put it, was the "true expression of Italian civilization." The Italians had "not learned bad manners from the rest of us," he remarked in *A Florentine Mosaic*, and, as he presently wrote in *Tuscan Cities*, "It was their lovely ways, far more than their monuments of history and art, that made return to the Florentines delightful. I would rather have had a perpetuity of the *cameriere's* smile when he came up with our coffee in the morning than Donatello's San Georgio, if either were purchasable; and the face of the old chambermaid, full of motherly affection, was better than the façade of Santa Maria Novella."

In keeping with this, it was the human side that Howells saw best in the Florentine life, "the delightfully natural human beings one could always be sure of . . . in this land of human nature unabashed." He relished the domestication of Italians in the open-every-day churches where they were always at their ease, in any rags they happened to have on, unlike the dressed up church-goers one saw at home; and, for that matter, it pleased him that the Florentine crowd was so well-dressed, so much better dressed than the average in Boston. He was happy to be able to say again that "in quality of courtesy the Italians" were "still easily the first of all men," while he enjoyed all the signs of active life in the streets, from the dying zouave in wax in a booth in the Mercato Vecchio to the circus in the Via Nazionale. He witnessed a wedding in the office of the syndic, who tied a tricolour sash about his waist as he did when he

[1] Howells had noted, on a previous visit, that all intelligent Italians knew four American writers, in this order—Cooper, Mrs. Stowe, Longfellow and Washington Irving.

married Colville and Mrs. Bowen. (For Howells recalled the scene when he wrote *Indian Summer*.) He visited the police court and the hospital for paupers, airy and sunny, to which everyone was sent who was found begging in the streets. Howells was amused by the sentimentalists who were abundant in Italy and who regretted the good old days when the streets were unsafe after nightfall and nothing seemed to matter but the picturesque: they were incensed by the restorations that were necessary to keep buildings up, and they had no language for the American horse-cars which the Florentines themselves found so convenient. It shocked them to see the wash stretched over the front of a white old palace and fluttering across the rear of Dante's house. But Howells rejoiced in all these signs of life, for to him, at least, Italy was never a museum.

It is true that he had much to say of Ghirlandajo's frescoes, along with Benozzo Gozzoli's in the Riccardi chapel, "perhaps the most simply and satisfyingly lovely little space that ever four walls enclosed." But he did not speak at greater length of statues or of pictures because others, he said, had spoken more than enough, which meant perhaps that, as Joseph Pennell remarked, Howells, comparatively speaking, was indifferent to painting. Something in him sympathized with many another American male confronted with "that dreary farce of old-master-doing." He shared at moments the dull vague rage of those who had to go through it again, that slavery to the guide-book asterisks which had reduced many a man to the last extremity of weariness and degradation. Remote from him was the drawing-room rapture over works of art that had irritated Margaret Fuller years before, and, visiting museums and churches, he never dreamed, like George Sand, that he had turned into a mosaic. But nothing could have been more sensitive than the notes he wrote for *A Little Girl Among the*

Old Masters, a collection of drawings by his ten-year-old daughter whom the galleries and churches enraptured with the poetry
of mediæval art. She had begun to sketch martyrs, saints and
heroes after reading Mrs. Jameson's *Sacred and Legendary Art,*
with angels, suggested by frescoes, blowing long slender
trumpets like those which the boys at Epiphany still blew in
the streets. The first to please her fancy had been Fra Angelico,
who was followed by Botticelli and Filippo Lippi, and in one
drawing she introduced cat-tails from a remembered American
swamp as unconsciously as the old masters in their sacred
stories introduced the Italian flowers in biblical scenes. She
drew many pictures from the life of the Madonna before
Catherine of Siena became her favourite saint.

For the Howellses had moved on for a while to "fair and
soft Siena" on a new tour of Tuscan cities. In Siena, mediæval
to the marrow of its bones,—and so lately moribund,[2]—Howells
could imagine a little Italian republic of the days of which
Norton had written so capably, though he was more careful
than ever himself to avoid fine rhetoric in writing about this
ancient Ghibelline city. For him the cathedral was "second in
splendour and surprise" only to the San Marco he had known
in Venice, and the exquisite walled up Gothic arches in the
wandering, narrow, darkling streets brought out his special
feeling for architecture. He was impressed by the red brick-
work of some of the smaller palaces that warmed the cold grey
general tone of the town, while he could not forget the sounds
that had once assailed the Seigniory when it met in the
Palazzo Communale. The councillors had had to put up with

---

[2] In *Italy: Florence and Venice,* Taine quotes a priest who said to him
that "the lifelessness and ignorance" . . . of Siena in 1821 "were complete . . . There was not a library, not a book." A friend, another priest,
told this one that he had subscribed to two French newspapers . . .
"The report spread instantaneously like a ray of light in a chamber
closed for a century."

the screams of the victims who had been mutilated behind the building, the blasphemers who had their tongues torn out, the perjurors who had their hands struck off and the highwaymen whose right feet were cut off with the axe. As one might have expected, Howells made much of the gentle old priest and his niece who rented him lodgings in Siena, and he found much to interest him in the registers of the hotels everywhere.

At Pistoia, Howells visited one of the bronze foundries, the oldest of several that were maintained in the town, on an errand for a sculptor whom he knew and who had dispatched there a number of medallions to be cast. This was no doubt his brother-in-law, Larkin G. Mead, who had been living in Florence since the early sixties and who was now a professor in the Florentine academy in which Horatio Greenough,—and Michelangelo,—had taught. A few years before this, Larkin Mead's brother, the architect, of the later firm of McKim, Mead and White, had spent a year and a half in Florence, soon to be followed by Stanford White, who was planning at the time to become a painter. Touring northern Italy in 1878, this great friend of Saint-Gaudens who was famous later for his "Italian Renaissance" American buildings,—the most versatile of men,— was known already as a Benvenuto Cellini in modern dress. With his prodigious vitality, he poured out drawings and water-colours and was soon producing in New York the picture-frames, book-covers, jewelry that anticipated his festive architecture.

The veteran American artists in Florence had fallen, if not on evil times, at least on times that were less propitious than of old, for American travellers seldom went in for their statues and their pictures now, preferring old chests and chairs, carpets and hangings. Howells was touched by these old-timers, most of them simple and innocent, still using the American slang of pre-Civil War days, dim and vague about their country yet with a fervent patriotism that was overlaid with patches of something alien. Among them was Thomas Ball, whose statue of Washington had been modelled in Florence and who had made a bust of Liszt in Rome, and there was the Kentucky sculptor Joel T. Hart, one of whose statues had been lost at sea. For thirty years Joel Hart laboured in Florence on a group that was to be called "Woman Triumphant," but, like Allston with his "Belshazzar's Feast," unwilling or unable to complete it, he dreamed away his life, leaving it unfinished. How many justified Hawthorne's feeling about that "emptiness" of the years when one spends too many on a foreign shore, the feeling that sent Hilda and Kenyon home even when they were obliged to return to Hawthorne's own "dry and dusty New England"! [3] The new artists seldom came to spend their lives in Italy and usually stayed only at most for two or three years.

One exception whom Howells knew was Elihu Vedder, who was to spend much of his own life in Rome but who had been in Florence when, for a few years at least, it became the capital of the new Italian kingdom. He had watched the Grand Duke leave the city, going into exile with a great quantity of luggage, while the crowd in the streets stood perfectly silent as the grand-ducal carriages rolled out of the gates. Vedder was drawn to the little forgotten towns that were still off the track of travel, Orte, for one, with its church and castle and a fine old

[3] "The years, after all, have a kind of emptiness, when we spend too many of them on a foreign shore. We defer the reality of life, in such cases, until a future moment, when we shall again breathe our native air; but, by and by, there are no future moments; or, if we do return, we find that the native air has lost its invigorating quality, and that life has shifted its reality to the spot where we have deemed ourselves only temporary residents. Thus, between two countries, we have none at all, or only that little space of either in which we finally lay down our discontented bones. It is wise, therefore, to come back betimes, or never."—Hawthorne, *The Marble Faun.*

campanile that was curiously lost among the closely packed
houses. He loved Perugia, especially, where he sketched the
mountains of Gubbio and where his villa looked off towards
Assisi, and there E. J. Ellis, who edited Blake with the poet
W. B. Yeats, first showed him FitzGerald's translation of Omar
Khayyám. For this, Vedder was to make his well-known drawings in the studio outside the Porta del Popolo in Rome.

The "Duveneck boys" had recently appeared in Florence,—
in fact, they were just disbanding when Howells arrived,—the
class that Frank Duveneck, the painter from Kentucky, had
brought down from Munich where he carried on, for some
years, a popular school. It was these English and American
students whom Howells described as the "Inglehart boys" when
he wrote *Indian Summer,* the novel about Florence, where
Duveneck married Elizabeth Boott,—Henry James's "Patsy,"—
and made the bronze figure of her after she died there. Joseph
Pennell and Whistler, when they came to Florence, found
Duveneck hiding in out-of-the-way cafés, for "the greatest talent
of the brush of our generation,"—Sargent's phrase,—was so
much in demand that he could not work. Pennell, who had
travelled with *Italian Journeys* and *Venetian Life,* was to illustrate presently Howells's *Tuscan Cities,*—together with Henry
James's *Italian Hours,*—and he went with Howells to Lucca,
Siena and Pisa, drawing along the roads and etching in the
streets. A year or two later, with his wife, he returned to Italy
on the first tandem tricycle that had ever been seen there,
riding from Florence to Rome through Tuscany and Umbria
by way of Cortona, Perugia and Assisi. The two spent several
days in the monastery of Monte Oliveto, which the government had turned into a pension for artists, and their *Italian
Pilgrimage* bristled with almost as many adventures as Robert
Louis Stevenson's *Travels with a Donkey.* The "Philadelphia

Méryon" had spent a week with Vernon Lee,—whose work he was also illustrating,—and another "good and proper English girl," acting as "chaperon, knight or encumbrance" through untouched and primitive Italy on a drive from Siena to Urbino.

Meanwhile, Howells continued to study the poets of modern Italy, about whom he had lectured in Boston a few years before, poets, beginning with Alfieri, after the French Revolution, who had been devoted to the freedom of their country. It was they who had put an end to the ancient mechanical literary dogmas that had frozen the minds of the eighteenth-century poets, and their poems had been "not productions but deeds," as one Italian writer said,—"When we have not the sword, we must take the pen." A single tendency had run through their work for the greater part of a hundred years. Alfieri, violent and harsh, had aroused the Italians from slumber and all but suggested the idea of an Italian nation, united against foreign invaders and local tyrants, while Ugo Foscolo and Silvio Pellico, Niccolini, Giusti and others had helped to destroy the old regime. Parini had ridiculed the folly of the nobles, and one and all had laboured to elevate the national mind and create a political sense in the minds of the people.

Howells's *Modern Italian Poets,* published in 1887, consisted of sensitive essays and his own translations. He had published in the previous year *Indian Summer,* perhaps the most perfect of all his novels, a fruit of his long stay in Florence and the last in which he used an Italian setting. Coming from Boston, he had found, in this cosmopolitan world, Americans of all the regions mingling freely, and this contributed to detach him from the New England world to which for so long he had been devoted. With his own all-American mind, he was to write in future only of his countrymen at home, and he felt, like Colville, his hero, the editor, that what concerned him deeply were "the problems of the vast tumultuous American life." Colville, once an architect, had returned to Florence in his early forties planning to write about Florentine architecture, which, with Ruskin always in mind, he had studied in his youth, full of scorn for every modern motive. Then, on the Ponte Vecchio, he had met Mrs. Bowen, whom he had known there seventeen years before, and "life, the life of his own day," called to him again,—"Could he turn his back upon it, for any charm there was in the past?" Howells was not tempted to do so, for all the attraction of Italy, and much as he delighted to write about it; while he conveyed admirably the feelings of early middle age in characters who had known the scene before. "Certain emotions, certain sensations failed to repeat themselves to Colville" in a Florence, resembling "a collection of views of itself," that he had examined many times before. He could not warm over the old mood in which he had treasured his impressions of the town, the men with cloaks draped over their shoulders, the shopmen's pathos, the customers' scorn, the handsome heavy-eyed women who thronged the streets. This was part of the note of Indian summer that marked the leading characters, Mrs. Bowen, thirty-eight, and Colville, forty-one, who were suspended as it were between youth and age, between the old New England minister who was writing a life of Savonarola and the radiantly youthful Imogene who was also in the picture.

CHAPTER XVIII

MARION CRAWFORD

ARION CRAWFORD installed himself in 1887 in a large villa at Sorrento overhanging the cliffs, with spacious courts and several buildings, a Moorish fountain in the garden and a long illuminated terrace over the sea. He faced the cliffs with a buttress of hewn lava and a flight of steps that led down to a pier, where he kept the yacht, a converted felucca, that was manned by a smartly accoutred crew whom he maintained along with a retinue of servants. For Crawford, ascetic in his personal tastes, preferring a hard monastic life, liked grandeur for his family and his surroundings. Standing about in the garden were sculptures by his father, and for his parties on the terrace, with professional dancers and Bengal lights, there were tents for the guests covered with Oriental draperies. "A magnificent giant who lived up to his magnificence," as Joseph Pennell said a few years later, Crawford, still in his early thirties, was already at the height of his career, successful, industrious, popular and rich. He wrote in one of the sea-bird caves that honeycombed the cliffs, where he set up a table looking off towards Capri.

In the years before and after 1882, when Crawford had published his first book, he had lived the lives of a dozen ordinary people, and *Mr. Isaacs,* the story of a diamond-merchant at Simla, had placed him far beyond the reverses of

fortune. The book was acclaimed by Gladstone in England as
well as by the Boston illuminati, and Crawford, in Boston himself for a while with his aunt Julia Ward Howe, had made a
great sensation with two other novels. He had lived for a while
in India as editor of a paper at Allahabad, and his picture of
the British raj anticipated Kipling, while he had an astonishing
faculty of creating exotic atmospheres and he seemed to be at
home in every country. He had studied at Harvard, at Cambridge in England and at Karlsruhe in Germany, as well as at
the university of Rome, where he had learned Sanskrit, one of
the seventeen languages he spoke or read. In India he had kept
his diary in Urdu,—it was there he joined the Roman Catholic
church,—and he had married soon after in Constantinople,
about which he also wrote a novel. He was to write novels
sooner or later about Arabia, Bohemia and Spain, and he had
the air of a native when he pictured German student life,
Prague, Newport in season or a village in England.

But Crawford knew Italy best of all,—Rome, Venice and the
South, at least,—as a man knows the rooms in his own house.
As a boy, with his tutor on a walking tour, he had seen every
inch of the region where he was to place the castle of Saracinesca, and later, one autumn, he had walked again through
the wild parts of Calabria where it was not safe to go alone. At
another time he had spent a month in the Abruzzi mountains,
working with the peasants in the vineyards to study their
ways; then, dressed as a peasant himself, he had led a mule
with sacks of beans and sold them in the villages through
which he passed. He had seen in the mountains the grand old
castles with their grey round keeps, their dungeons, vaults,
dark cellars and trap-doors, and their vast halls and guard-
rooms as large as churches, dreadful old places with chambers
where they used to chop off heads or tumble prisoners into

oubliettes. He saw one of these rooms that had four seats, two for the executioners and the others for the confessor and the victim. He had visited gloomy monasteries, many of them still active, where life had scarcely changed in a thousand years, and he was familiar with Sicily where many things were possible that had not been possible for two centuries elsewhere in Europe. Crawford was convinced that only those knew Italy who had trudged on foot, and ridden by mountain paths through hill and valley, gorge and plain, where there were no highways and no inns.[1] He had himself a passion for investigating byways, philological, historical,[2] ethnographic.

Now, settled in Sorrento, where he was to live for the rest of his life when he was not out in his yacht exploring the coast,— cruising in search of adventures and new scenes,—he turned out novels at such a rate that critics lost account of them and failed to say how good they sometimes were. Or they praised him indiscriminately when a few of his novels were enduringly good while most of them were mechanical and shallow. In two or three he pictured the spectacular life that he carried on with his guests and with his costumed boatmen, who told one another fairy-tales that were actually those of the "Arabian Nights" with the Oriental characters and places transfigured as Italian. For in most of the Sorrentine sailors there were visible traces of Saracen forbears, and they had been brought up on these Italianized stories. One shared, in *To Leeward*,

[1] "I do not hesitate to say that, without a single exception, every foreigner, poet or prose-writer, who has treated of these people, has more or less grossly misunderstood them . . . To understand Italians a man must have been born and bred among them."—F. Marion Crawford, *Sant' Ilario*.

[2] In the preface to his play *Francesca da Rimini* (written in French and produced by Sarah Bernhardt in 1902), Crawford related how he discovered the room in the fortress of Verrocchio where Giovanni Malatesta killed his wife Francesca and his brother Paolo. There Crawford found the trap-door that figured in the last act of the play.

the picnics for which he and his guests sailed over to Capri
with quails stuffed with truffles, boxes of sweetmeats and
champagne, well iced, stored away in the boat; and the hero of
the book, the English novelist who had lived in all sorts of
places and ways, resembled Crawford himself in his masculine
charm. Ravello was the scene of another book, *With the Im-
mortals,* in which a scientist created a storm that revived some
of the great men who had "passed from the condition of life
to the condition of existence." Leonardo,[3] Pascal, Francis the
First, Chopin and Heine were a few of these spirits who
seemed well suited to appear in the old palace grounds in
which Wagner said he found Klingsor's garden. Crawford,
who knew so well the Sorrentine peninsula, "all orange-scented,
sweet with gardens and soft sea-breath," and the coasts of
Campania and Calabria that lay southward,—with their tiers of
white and brown houses on the mountain slopes,—knew well
also the history of this region, as of Sicily and Malta, from the
days of the Phœnicians and the Greeks to his own time. This
he related presently in *The Rulers of the South.*

Later, in America, Crawford bought a Brooklyn-built pilot-
boat, schooner-rigged, without steam, which he turned into a
yacht, and on this, after he had received a master mariner's
certificate, he made longer voyages and crossed the Atlantic.
On the "Alda," as he called her, he took Norman Douglas on
a cruise, touching at Corsica, Elba and some of the smaller
Tyrrhenian islands, landing at Baiae and going on to Rome.
An old priest had shown Norman Douglas the parochial
archives from which he wrote his first story, *A Tale of Elba,*

[3] Saying that his own age had been "an age of individuals" and that
"*this* is the age of the millions," the shade of Leonardo utters a pro-
phetic remark. When the young girl asks, "And what will the next
age be?" he replies, "The age of collapse and of barbarian domination,
I suppose."

and Douglas left a record of Crawford's fine presence, his intelligence and his aggressive Catholicism,—as a convert, he was "more Catholic than any Italian." At about this time, for greater seclusion, Crawford leased a tower, a mediæval stronghold on the Calabrian coast, a refuge from the Saracen invasions, called San Niccola, on a lofty cliff overlooking a wild little bay. There, in this high stone dungeon-like building, he wrote more of the romances in which he assumed the colour of every setting, while he revealed a remarkable range of knowledge; for he seemed to know everything one could know about a dozen forms of life that he had either minutely observed or shared. He had been his own architect, he had been a singer, an editor and a clerk in a bank in Rome who knew the world of finance inside and out, he had made a fine repoussé cup after working with a silversmith and had taken a turn also in a Venetian glass-works. He had fought duels in Germany and described them in such a way that the reader almost felt he was a duellist himself, and he knew how a forger manufactures antiquated documents with bread, molten lead and plaster of Paris. He remembered the atmosphere of a metal-worker's shop, pervaded by the smell of wax and pitch, mingled with the odour of steel tools in constant use, and he knew not only all the details of the trade of a cigarette-maker but how a tiger's claws differ from a cat's. He knew how church-organs are made, and he knew the feelings of a Cossack at night driving sheep over the steppes and how his horse feels at the end of the day, how the woolly coats of the sheep redden in the evening sun and how soft is the sound of the sheep huddling together.

That Crawford was a capital story-teller no one denied in the days when the "fable" was all-important in a work of fiction. He was, besides, the most varied of romancers, prone as he may have been to the "lapses of literary conscience" to which he referred in a book on his own craft, a book in which, calling novelists "public amusers," he did not enhance his reputation. Some of his tales abounded in the absurd coincidences that readers in his time were more willing to accept, for he did not hesitate to wreck many probabilities in order to keep the story going. Sometimes he forced his characters to fit the story. In short, he created thrillers for the English-speaking public of the great days of Baedeker and Tauchnitz, novels, read in hotels and on trains, which gave the reader a pleasant sense that he was in the presence of a travelled and cultivated author. But he was never melodramatic, he only used violent incidents when they were characteristic of the world he wrote of, and, while he had no particular distinction of style, a few of his novels were almost as good as the best. This was true, certainly, of the so-called *Saracinesca* series, with *Pietro Ghisleri*, *Corleone* and *Taquisara*, in which he pictured the great world of Rome he had witnessed as a boy and which he had followed in its later evolution. The author of *Ave Roma Immortalis* undoubtedly knew the Rome of the past [4] and the present, the Rome of antiquity in which he had lived as a schoolboy and the Rome he had seen developing under his eyes.

For in Sorrento his mind went back to the old-fashioned ceremonious life of the last years of the temporal power in Rome, when twenty nobles still owned a great part of the Papal States and lived with a pomp and magnificence one seldom saw elsewhere. They continued to possess hereditary traits that were fostered by ages of absolutism and that survived the decay of the feudal regime, with a right of life and death

[4] Crawford left incomplete at his death a series of archæological studies that were intended to form a history of mediæval Rome.

over their retainers that had not yet been abolished in 1867. Fierce, unforgiving, frank, direct, stately, frugal, rigid, they lived behind the grey walls of their grand old palaces with huge stone coats of arms glaring down from above. Grim and proud, some of these palaces stood in old and narrow streets, while the great families maintained their strongholds in the country, the vast and gloomy fortresses that Crawford had seen. The Romans knew their features, owing to countless pictures of them, as they knew the stones of the city itself, and, except for a few details of dress, they might have been living in the thirteenth century still. Some of the women were like the paintings in their own galleries, and among the men there were heads and faces that recalled Caesar Borgia and certain of the great Renaissance popes and captains. They had a suave gravity, Crawford remembered, that was in itself a charm, with a self-possession that had nothing of arrogance in it. Crawford had seen some of them at close quarters, with the secondary luminaries who revolved about them and reflected their light.

For in the days when the studios of artists were visited by princes and travelling kings and the Crawfords themselves lived with a certain splendour, Marion Crawford had known this world as tourists never knew it, or even old sojourners from other countries. He had had playmates in the princely families, and he had often seen Cardinal Antonelli, the uncle of his sister's most intimate friends; moreover, in 1869, the general in command of the papal forces, when Garibaldi was skirmishing near Arezzo, had been married to an American friend of Crawford's mother. The nephew of this general was one of Crawford's cronies. So he had seen almost from the inside the old traditional, serious, gloomy and sometimes dramatic life of the patriarchal system, while he had known well the excitement in the streets when the shouts went up, "Viva Pio Nono!" or "Viva Garibaldi!" He remembered the cry "The Italians are coming!" when no Roman gentleman ever spoke of himself as an Italian and when the Blacks looked with contempt on the Whites who whispered across a glass of champagne, "Viva Vittorio Emanuele!" But he also knew of those who kept both Italian and papal flags, ready to thrust either of them out of the window. He had witnessed the clashes between the parties as early as 1865, the moment when his finest novel, *Saracinesca,* opened, and when the temporal power had been assured by Napoleon III and the city, still all but mediæval, had been held by the French. On every hand there one had seen French dragoons and French hussars, side by side with the papal zouaves in their grey Turko uniforms with bright red facings, sashes and yellow gaiters. He had seen the gorgeous equipages and the gorgeous costumes and decorations when cardinals, great nobles and ambassadors drove up to a church for a wedding performed by the cardinal archpriest of St. Peter's; and, if he had not been present at a great Frangipani ball, he had heard it described by people who had been there. He had heard of the torchbearers on the grand staircase, the long files of lackeys, the vast suites of apartments that had been thrown open, the supper that suggested a mediæval banquet and the appearance of Antonelli, with gracious nods and winning looks, his flowing robes falling back from his courtly figure. With his red hat in his hand, he bowed his way through the assembly, departing so that the dancing might begin.

In the series of Saracinesca novels, the history of a family, Crawford followed the course of modern Rome from the end of the mediæval world and the temporal power to the period of unification and the decades that came after. With old

Prince Leone Saracinesca, with his son Giovanni and finally with his grandson Don Orsino, one lived through three generations of a Rome that was gradually transformed, ending as a modern cosmopolitan city. To the grandfather, who clung to the ancient political mythology and the most old-fashioned social code in Europe, there were few things baser than earning money, nor could Giovanni adjust himself to the new regime in which the grandson was able to swim so freely. Giovanni, the son of the old prince, had grown up in a time of confusion when the ancient social life was falling to pieces, when many of the old families were ruined and their palaces fell into the hands of self-made financiers and speculators. One of these was the distant cousin who had grown up as an innkeeper, the Saracinesca, born in a village, who understood the new regime, made a fortune and acquired a new title of his own. Don Orsino, the grandson of the old prince, was more or less at home in this world of the future, the world of applied science, railroads and money, when buildings were going up and there were bank panics. He was accustomed to hearing newsboys shouting in the streets the bankruptcy, perhaps, of some great contractor in a Rome in which many old palaces now were used for public offices or rented out as apartments. One might find there, on one floor, a cardinal or a Russian count and on others an insurance company or a widow from Chicago.

The ingenious Crawford introduced many other characters along with the three protagonists and the women who lived with them,—chief among these Donna Corona, Giovanni's wife, the perfection of a modern Roman matron. There were the nobles who stood firmly united with Prince Leone for the old order of things when it was threatened, and there was Count Spicca, the melancholy duellist who had played with the best swordsmen of Europe as a cat plays with a mouse. There were the intransigent clericals and the other nobles who, disliking idleness, went in for study, writing perhaps an exhaustive work on the mythology of Pindar's odes or committing to memory the verses of Petrarch and Tasso. There was Anastase Gouache, the fashionable painter, at first a French revolutionary who talked about stringing up the priests and who became in the end a papal zouave, putting away "childish things" and defending the Pope, evidently with the approval of his creator; for Crawford's heart was always with the Blacks. Crawford no doubt wished to be fair to what he called "the great party of Massimo d'Azeglio, Cavour and Mazzini," but the only Liberals he presented at length were the depraved Del Ferice and the scheming Donna Tullia who became his wife.

Another character one could not forget was Monsignor Saracinesca, the brother of Don Orsino and the fine priest who appeared in certain novels that were outside the series. In some of these Crawford conveyed a sense of the wonder and mystery of Rome. But whenever he introduced one of the Saracinescas, he seemed to rise at once to a superior level, and one could not but feel that in a few of these books at least he produced a historical record that was lastingly living.

CHAPTER XIX

PAINTERS AND SCHOLARS:
HENRY B. FULLER

"A RHAPSODY OF Venice is always in order," Henry James once remarked, and more and more the painters felt as he did, Whistler, for instance, who had long wished to visit the beautiful city, "most beautiful," as he wrote to his mother, "after rain." Arriving for a year in 1880, Whistler avoided the monuments, the subjects of the eighteenth-century painters, the themes of Canaletto and of Guardi, sketching the smaller canals, the doorways and the gardens in preference to the palaces and the churches. He found motives for some of his pastels in drawings of Titian and Tintoretto, but there was always, as he said, "something still better round the corner" that made it almost impossible to sit down and paint. There were altogether too many "bits" in Venice. But he fancied that the ceiling of his own Peacock Room was actually more splendid than the dome of St. Mark's. It was in Venice that Whistler fell in with Browning, who had returned to Italy in 1878, avoiding both Florence and Rome where he had lived with his wife. Browning was to spend eight autumns in or near Venice before he died there in 1889.

In Venice, Frank Duveneck had made his well-known etchings two or three years before Whistler's visit there, and William M. Chase had also spent nine months there, painting his "Venetian Fish Market" and copying Giorgione. But all kinds of painters of all kinds of subjects gathered in Venice during these years, and every morning, all over the canals, one found a new growth of white umbrellas that seemed to have sprung up, like mushrooms, during the night. For generations they had painted, and repainted, the same scenes, the same stretches of water, palace and sky, and they were to seek out in days to come "the landing that interested Ziem" or the curious "arch that Whistler etched." A few years before, another artist had copied Carpaccio's "Dream of St. Ursula," working side by side with his master Ruskin, who associated the young saint with Rose La Touche. This was Charles Herbert Moore, who spent four months in Venice in 1876. Perhaps the most promising of all the younger American painters, Moore had become a Pre-Raphaelite disciple of Ruskin; then, virtually ceasing to paint, he accepted, at Norton's suggestion, a professorship of fine arts at Harvard. He was well-known later as the author of books on Gothic architecture. As Ruskin's companion in Venice, however, he returned to painting and made many water-colours there.[1]

Of Venice, it was "never too late for a glorification," as Henry James remarked again; but James himself, who was often there, found it, in fair weather at least, "not a place for concentration of mind." [2] Florence was much better for his own writing. But the surprising gardens nestling on the small

---

[1] "I am very much delighted at having Moore for a companion," Ruskin wrote to Norton (October 5th, 1876). "We have perfect sympathy in all art matters and are not in dissonance in any others."

Ruskin offered Moore a salary to teach at Sheffield, in St. George's Guild, but Moore felt that his duty lay at Harvard.—See *Charles Herbert Moore,* by Frank Jewett Mather, Jr.

[2] "The effort required for sitting down to a writing-table is heroic, and the brightest page of manuscript looks dull beside the brilliancy of your milieu . . . Afterwards, in ugly places, at unprivileged times, you can convert your impressions into prose."—Henry James, *Portraits of Places.*

canals, crowding over the walls with their tangles of flowers, struck him as they struck many of the painters, their greenness making an arrangement with the rosy brick, while Venice itself seemed to him somehow like a theatre and the people like "members of an endless dramatic troupe." As they clicked over the bridges and tripped along the footways, they suggested actors moving to and fro against the battered scenery of their little houses. It was there, on one of the obscure canals, in a shabby old palace, that James placed Miss Bordereau, the heroine of *The Aspern Papers,* who had come to Europe with her father, a painter, early in the century, and lived in a queer old-fashioned Bohemia as a child. In Venice, Densher, in *The Wings of the Dove,* finding Milly Theale's door closed to him, repaired to the drenched piazza which the first sea-storm of autumn had chilled and douched and covered with salt spray. The piazza seemed to Densher then "like a great drawing-room, the drawing-room of Europe, profaned and bewildered by some reverse of fortune."

The old Italo-Yankee school, the painters and sculptors of an earlier time, the innocents who had come over in the thirties and forties, were beginning to fade away in dark back hallways or in auction-rooms or the corridors of hospitals at home. Their pictures and sculptures were soon to slip into the basements of museums, though sometimes they were to be remembered as Americana, and many a bust retained its place in a parlour in Boston, perhaps, commemorating a departed Cabot or Thayer. The art-loving public was losing its interest in Campagna sunsets and in painted contadini and pifferari, while the art-students multiplied year by year on every hand,[3]

[3] To such an extent that May Alcott, the sister of Louisa M. Alcott, wrote for the women students alone a handbook called *Studying Art Abroad* (1879). This contained information on expenses, the renting of studios, etc., recommending Rome for the study of sculpture, Paris for

and even the American students of the history of art. These young men might be planning a book on Etruscan influences in Italian art or an essay on the Bronze Age in southern Europe, and cases were not unknown in which they named their children Filippo, Sandro, Duccio and Donatello. Sometimes, like one of Howells's characters, they talked Ruskin so incessantly that they spoiled all their chances with the girl of their choice, and occasionally they suggested the "connoisseurs and coxcombs" whom Smollett had encountered in his travels.[4] Eugene Schuyler, the diplomat, convinced that one might trace every topographical and historical allusion in Dante, spent a summer on the slopes of the Apennines visiting obscure castles and towns that the poet mentioned in his writings. Schuyler examined manuscripts connected with Dante in the libraries of Faenza, Ravenna and Forlì.

Two other American scholars in Italy were George Perkins Marsh, the first United States minister to the Italian kingdom, and the young William Roscoe Thayer, who was to write in time *The Dawn of Italian Independence* and the life of Cavour. George P. Marsh, who was to spend twenty years in Italy, where he died in 1882, was often consulted by those who were framing the new Italian constitution, to which he made many contributions. Then he influenced the Italian government in matters of reforestation when his *Man and Nature* had been translated. He showed how calamitous was the denuda-

---

oil-painting and London for painting in water-colours. May Alcott noted that the "tearful face" of Beatrice Cenci still "universally interests and absorbs," and she especially recommended as subjects for painters in Rome the Ghetto bazaars and Hilda's Tower.

[4] "They are seized with the ambition of becoming connoisseurs in painting, music, statuary and architecture . . . Raw boys . . . all of them talk familiarly of the arts and return, finished connoisseurs and coxcombs, to their own country."—Smollett, *Travels through France and Italy.*

tion of mountains, the destruction of forests that caused both floods and drought, and the efforts the Italians presently made to reforest their mountainsides was largely a result of Marsh's writings. He died at Vallombrosa, where he was spending the summer in the school of forestry established in the monastery there; and the body of the old diplomat and scholar was borne down the mountain to the railway below on the shoulders of some of the young students.[5] William Roscoe Thayer had first thought of writing a life of Cavour while spending on Capri the winter of 1876, learning Italian with a priest and preparing for Harvard, where he was to study Dante with Charles Eliot Norton. Fifteen years old, he fell in love with the country and the people, and Italy for him was always to be a homeland,— "not so much a temporal and local home as the country beyond time, where one roams the immense and majestic past." The thirteenth century had come alive for him in poetry, theology, painting and architecture, but for nearly thirty years the nineteenth-century Cavour was to be his main preoccupation. His *Dawn of Italian Independence* (1893) began as an expansion of the opening chapters of his first draught of a life of the statesman, who loomed up in the background of his mind. Thayer had been deeply impressed by the fact that Mazzini as a young man had been imprisoned quite simply for being "a thinker," and this had aroused in him a passionate sympathy for the Risorgimento.[6]

[5] George P. Marsh was buried in the Protestant Cemetery in Rome near Constance Fenimore Woolson and Richard Henry Dana.

Lewis Mumford has called Marsh "the fountainhead of the conservation movement."

[6] Thayer was working on his *Cavour* while Trevelyan was writing his *Garibaldi*. The two historians exchanged chapters as the work of each progressed, discussed problems as they arose and asked questions of each other.

Thayer was named William Roscoe after the Liverpool merchant who had written about the Italian Renaissance.

A friend of Thayer's, the author of *The Mediæval Mind,* was to visit Italy often in the nineties and after,—Henry Osborn Taylor who, at Harvard, had also imbibed the "melancholy preciosity" of Charles Eliot Norton. But he had been a pupil, too, of Henry Adams, the robust, who was also engaged later in mediæval studies at a time when, in Assisi, Taylor joined Paul Sabatier in visiting some of the Franciscan holy places. On his first long stay in Rome, preparing to write *Ancient Ideals,* studying the pagan statuary and ruins, he had avoided the Sistine Chapel; then, hearing that the Pope might die and fearing that the Vatican might be closed for a while, he rushed in to see Michelangelo's ceiling. For weeks he steeped himself in its prodigiousness and in the other canvasses and frescoes in Rome, finding it difficult after that to restore his interest in the older marbles and ruins of the Forum. He was attempting to formulate the fundamental laws of the various arts, unable to agree with his mentor John La Farge that the principles of art are the practice of the best artists. This pragmatic notion ignored, he felt, the real problems of literature and art. At this time, in the Vatican gallery, a certain Faun made real to him the old story of falling in love with a statue, and it came over him that Italy and Rome were a great continuation of the antique. For the real mediæval break with the antique and the creation of something new, one had to go north, he was convinced.

Meanwhile, a young man from Chicago, Henry Blake Fuller, who had first appeared in Italy in 1879,—and who visited the "inexhaustible" peninsula many times later,—presently produced a charming Italian travel book, *The Chevalier of Pensieri-Vani.* Inscribed to Charles Eliot Norton, it was written in a business office, where "little business was done," remarked the author, who regarded Chicago, he said to a friend, as "a pestilential slough," adding, "I would live in Italy if I could." A distant cousin of Margaret Fuller and always a solitary man, Fuller described himself in one of his characters: "Birth and habit drew him in one direction; culture and aspiration in another. But he had never been a good American and he feared he would never make a good European. He was between two fires, both of which scorched him; between two stools, neither of which offered him a comfortable seat; between the two horns of a dilemma, each of which seemed more cruelly sharp than the other." These two horns were Italy and America, in neither of which he ever felt really at home; and in this respect, in his own time at least, Fuller was one of the great American types.

However, this dichotomy, which did not make for happiness, served Fuller as a writer very well; for, seeing Chicago all the more vividly because of his passion for Italy, he appreciated Italy more keenly because of Chicago. Fuller's realistic Chicago novels were, in their way, quite as good as his romantic writings about the land of gardens whose walls "shut out . . . the wide wastes of horror" elsewhere; but he was closer in feeling to the cavaliere than he was to any of his own countrypeople. For this "poor gentleman" in his travelling-carriage who loved the Tuscan postroads and every tree and stone in the Italian land, lived, with his few kindred spirits, wandering with maps and sketching-blocks, the life that Fuller himself always longed for. He too loved music, like the cavaliere who had won his title on a certain famous occasion in Orvieto, playing the organ in the cathedral there. Fuller had first come abroad as a student of music who was to write many scores for voice and piano, and he too had wandered through central Italy like the cavaliere and like the Prorege of Arcopia who travelled with him. The object of the Prorege's quest was mainly architectural. He was in search of models for the town-hall he hoped to build with a Roman frieze and neo-Ionic columns, while the cavaliere, planning a great work on unknown Tuscan masters, was also looking for a rumoured Perugino. But on their way the two savoured as well the great illuminations at Siena, the ruinous Tuscan abbeys, the village campaniles, the vine-covered pergolas on the slopes, the bustle at the inns, the oxcarts on the roads, the flowers and the sunshine.

The cavaliere's idle thoughts, or *pensieri vani*, were, like his fund of knowledge, Fuller's own, and he too, like the Prorege and like Fuller himself, was a bachelor, living, and glad to live, alone. The cavaliere had lodgings in Florence and in Pisa, where a walk through the streets wrapped him in measureless content, a tranquil reposeful pleasure, at the hour before sunset; and for possessions he cared only for a few bits of mosaic, a few shells from Amalfi and the Perugino (which turned out to be a Sodoma, his favourite painter). Fuller would also have felt at home with the other friends of the cavaliere, the Seigneur of Hors-Concours who lived in Savoy and who joined him, with the Prorege, at Viterbo,—where the three unearthed an Etruscan tomb,—and the Duke of Avon and Severn, a book-collector who was on the track of a number of rare Aldines. The duke fell in with the others at Ravenna, a "petrified phantasmagoria of long cold altars and episcopal thrones" which was to Pisa "as the dead is to the sleeping," a town whose monuments seemed to the cavaliere greyer and hoarier by far than the oldest in Rome. At Padua, the young George Occident joined the others,—the American whom the Prorege regarded as a promising young barbarian of whom something might be made. George Occident had fled from Shelby County where "the bare figure of leisure," as he said, was "expected to be draped in the garment of strenuous endeavour," and the

Prorege, lecturing him on the difference between leisure and idleness, laboured to improve his untutored mind.

In *Gardens of This World,* many years later, Fuller returned to the cavaliere, and to the Seigneur who had travelled with him, both old now and, like himself, unreconciled to a modern world in which they counted for as little as they had counted in the past. In this world motor-cars took the place of diligences, there were palace hotels instead of the *osterie* of old and thousands of tourists where there had once been dozens, but the two friends were indifferent to its tumult and exactions: all they cared for was to perceive, to understand what they perceived and extract the full measure of enjoyment from so understanding. By this time Fuller had written some of his best stories,—for one, the tale of the lady from the West who had seen so many historical things that she was tired of the past and even of grammar. There was too much civilization from her point of view: she had heard so many good orchestras that she preferred hand-organs, and, tired of good art, she was "reverting," as she said, to the carved walnut of the fifties and hair-cloth sofas. Beside the girl who could not wait to see the Fra Angelicos, Mrs. Pritchard was on her way to Milan for a glimpse of the latest thing in French automobiles. Then there was the tale of Waldo Trench, the young man from Nebraska who regarded his trip to Europe as a "sacramental matter" and who was first impressed, in New York, before he sailed, by the "ancient edifice" of St. Paul's chapel. Beginning at the end and working backwards, he went from Copley and Stuart to Van Dyck, then Raphael, then Fra Angelico and the Middle Ages, then Rome, then the Etruscans and the Pelasgians at last,—until he heard of the work of the Sicilian rock-dwellers. Arriving at each phase, he denounced, as not old enough, the phase he had abandoned, and finally gave them all up for his

ranch in Oklahoma, resolved to return to the present and
determined to stay there.

Many of Fuller's characters, and perhaps the most amusing,
were connoisseurs,—mostly Americans,—collectors and what
not, like the young man who dropped carved ceilings and took
up terra-cottas, hunting down *bimbi* and the like as a dog scents
out truffles. There were innocents poking about the peninsula,
turning up fragments of columns or bits of a sculptured cornice
half-buried in the ground, or searching for Roman sanctuaries
made over into chapels, or reading the *Vita Nuova* and taking
it hard; and there was the young Chicagoan who collected
books on architecture for an alcove in the museum that was to
bear his name. This Raymond Prince, of *On the Stairs,*—a
more or less familiar type in all the American cities of the
eighties and after,—was filled with a vision of other young
men studying Byzantine building there and all the varieties
of Renaissance architecture. Then there was the Freiherr, of
The Last Refuge, who was looking for rose-windows and lion-
portals, ambones, tombs and candelabra near Taranto and
Bari, on his way to Sicily where, with the lady who was hoping
to lose her sense of time, he hoped to recapture his lost youth.
One of the best bits of *The Chevalier of Pensieri-Vani* dealt
with the "theme of the hour,"—the Iron Pot,—to whom the
pot belonged and what it was, Etruscan, Roman or a relic of
the age of Garibaldi.

To Fuller the subject of Italy was "everlasting,"—Italy was
the reverse of everything he hated at home,—just as it was
to Eliza Hepburn, his old maid who lived in Chicago and who
had really stopped living about 1855. Eliza, who had lived in
Florence as a girl, still cherished her Sassoferrato Madonna, she
was still deep in Byron and Shelley, and her house was full of
scenes from the Campagna and pictures of Roman peasants of

the eighteen-fifties. To Eliza, who might have appeared in one of the stories of Henry James, romance was always "about so many miles away and about so many years behind"; while no doubt James's *The Aspern Papers* suggested *A Coal from the Embers,* perhaps the finest story that Fuller wrote. This also dealt with an American poet, a former Confederate cavalry officer who had come to Italy after the Civil War, who had written most of his poems in Florence and Lucca and who died "in circumstances dimly tragic." With time the fame of John Edgar Haynes had risen, but there seemed to be no trace left of him when his biographer arrived, hoping to reconstruct the great poet's career. Then all too many relics came to light, involving not only two old ladies who were still living in Florence but "a flaunting wayside blossom called Teresina." The romantic Fuller was at his best when, with his usual tranquillity of style, irony came into play as a part of this repose.

CHAPTER XX

THE REVENANTS:
CHARLES GODFREY LELAND

A<small>S THE</small> century waned, the old sojourners in Florence, Rome and Venice revisited, one by one, the Italian scene, Howells, William and Henry James, Mark Twain, Henry Adams,— "old-time victims of Italy," generally speaking. The phrase was Henry James's, and he described them all; for the time came when even the author of *Huckleberry Finn* confessed his infatuation with the land of magic. Henry James had himself returned again and again, and he wrote to Charles Eliot Norton, "As I grow older, many things come and go, but Italy remains."

Henry James and William James were both there in 1892, when Mark Twain was living and writing at Settignano, and William James went to Padua to receive an honorary degree at a celebration in memory of Galileo. He found Florence as delicious as ever, though its "general debility" and "sweet decay" soon led him to crave for a change to robuster air, to the "thickness" of the atmosphere at home and the "vitality" of Cambridge, even while the sunny manners there and the magnificent remains of art redeemed it all and spread a charm around him. "When Gemütlichkeit is banished from the world," he wrote, "it will still survive in this dear and shabby old country." Henry James was at Siena during the same year, visiting Paul Bourget and his wife who were living there, witnessing the Palio, driving to San Gimignano, and finding that for him "the magic" was "still in the air." It was true that modern crudity ran riot over the relics of the past and ancient wayside shrines emitted the odour of petroleum, "the votive taper" being "nourished with the national fluid of Pennsylvania," as Henry James wrote in *Portraits of Places*. He who had first described himself as the "sentimental tourist" had called himself later the "analytic" tourist, but he was the "brooding" tourist nowadays. He had first met Fanny Kemble in Rome and later spent a week with her, an old lady now, at Lago Maggiore,—a "very extinct volcano" but "easy to dwell with in her aged adoucissement and resignation."

Many years later, Owen Wister, this great old lady's grandson, remembered from his childhood a certain occasion: somewhere in Italy, he had heard the old sculptor Story read his *Nero* to Henry James and Fanny Kemble. James saw Story many times during these end-of-the-century years when the sculptor and poet spent summers at Vallombrosa, near the old mountain monastery, surrounded by beech and chestnut woods, with its Etrurian shades and enchanting views. Story wrote about it a little book called *Vallombrosa*, a charming historical sketch of this shadowy domain where the leaves strewed the winding paths as thickly as when Milton, a student in the library of the monastery, strolled along them. There too Story wrote his summer idyll *Fiammetta*, about the young Roman artist, an impoverished count, who hoped to paint a naiad and, returning to his villa in the Abruzzi, actually found one. This moving and pathetic little tale was one of the notes of the Italian scene that presently led Bernard Berenson to settle there,—the critic who in years to come also spent summers at Vallombrosa, where Story died in 1895. Story, the ever-lively author of *Conversations in a Studio*, sprightly dialogues on

sculpture, poetry, law, the classics, Roman history, Goethe and
what not, appeared, not long before his death, as Cimabue at
a costume party with Marion Crawford as Mephistopheles. It
was at about this time that, at Sorrento, Marion Crawford
made the chief address at the celebration of the three-hun-
dredth anniversary of the death of Tasso.

Howells did not actually reappear until the new century
had well begun, but then he came twice and wrote another
book, finding the new and very different Rome as much to his
taste as the old Rome and picturing it in *Roman Holidays*.
Revising *Venetian Life* for a new edition, he had begun to
dream of Italy again,—the old wine, he said, got into his brain,
—and he wrote to Norton wishing that they could creep together among the busts of the poets in the Borghese Gardens.
Niccolini and Giusti said to him, in friendly recognition, "Oh,
yes," and they seemed to like having been written about.
Howells only regretted the long tables of the old table d'hôte,
—replaced now by small tables everywhere,—with Danes, Norwegians, Germans and Finns carrying on what Howells enjoyed, the old-fashioned American neighbourly talk. One usually also encountered there the inevitable "adventuress," the
famous "fast woman" of the time, and perhaps a Dutch baron
and a French marquis amiably conversing on the basis of the
Almanach de Gotha. Henry Adams had returned to Naples
in 1899, finding the lazzaroni poorer than ever but more like
poor people everywhere else. The general taste was "flat," said
Henry Adams, for whom the world was always going to the
dogs; and Naples, a trifle less filthy, was very much less
Neapolitan,—in fact, this ancient city had lost its soul. Even
the fleas had virtually ceased to bite him. The tourists came
in crusading hordes, howling mobs of Cookies; and what had
become of the corals and the macaroni? Perhaps they were

there, but one did not see them. Even in 1873 Adams had found good Greek vases, but now he searched the antiquity shops in vain.

Mark Twain had settled in 1892 in the Villa Viviani at Settignano, and there he finished *Pudd'nhead Wilson* and almost brought to an end his *Joan of Arc*. The big square villa with its orchards and gardens belonged to an old Florentine family whose portraits were there, and Mark Twain "adopted" himself into this, "on account of its antiquity, my origin having been heretofore too recent to suit me." As hostile as ever to drawing-room rapture, Mark Twain had grown aesthetically during the years, and he felt that the view from this villa, the view that Boccaccio had known, was "the most enchanting . . . picture on our planet." The terrace overlooked the city and the hills beyond, strewn with white villas clear to the summits. "Sometimes Florence ceases to be substantial," Mark Twain wrote, "and becomes just a faint soft dream, with domes and towers of air."

William James, who saw him and took to him at once,—"a fine soft-fibred little fellow . . . very human and good,"—said that Mark Twain told him he had written more in four months there than he could have written in two years at home. James wished that he would come and live in Cambridge.[1] Then one day Charles Godfrey Leland had a long call from Mark Twain, "a regular spree and convivium of fun," said Leland, who had come to live in Florence in 1890. The old American "Rye," the adventurous Philadelphian who had spent so many years studying the gypsies, found among the Tuscan peasants

[1] "Mark Twain is here for the winter in a villa outside the town, hard at work writing something or other. I have seen him a couple of times, —a fine, soft-fibred little fellow with the perversest twang and drawl, but very human and good. I should think that one might grow very fond of him and wish he'd come and live in Cambridge."—William James, Letter from Florence, 1892.

something Francesca never saw and something that would never have pleased the Christian Ruskin. He found in the descendants of an Etruscan-Roman race the pagan religion of witchcraft still actively practised, a faith, carefully concealed from the priests, of which the cultured were as little aware as the old Philadelphians of his childhood had been of Voodoo. How unsuspecting they had been of the sorcerers, silent and unseen, who conjured and worked in darkness among the Negroes of the city! After the gypsies, nothing had ever enthralled Leland more than this unexplored world of the Tuscan wizards and witches.

Charles Godfrey Leland had visited Florence many years before in the days of Hiram Powers, whom he had known there,—Leland, with his white flowing beard and his velveteen jacket and skull-cap who was to live there now for thirteen years. His rooms in one of the old hotels were cluttered with gold-background Madonnas, parchment-bound books and crucifixes, Roman lamps, picture-frames, cracked violins and what not, objects he had picked up in hand-carts and from second-hand dealers. It was as cheap, he said, to burn Virgins as firewood, and he had bought a carved Pietà of the sixteenth century for only five times as much as a basket of kindling. He liked to restore and patch these objects, practising the so-called minor arts of which, in several cases, he had written handbooks, while, establishing a folk-lore society in Italy, like one he had started in Hungary, he carried on a separate occult life there. "Real folklorists," he wrote to a friend, "live in a hidden fairyland. We see elves and hear voices in the wind," and elsewhere he spoke of "the difference between collecting folk-lore . . . and *living* it in truth . . . I do not believe that in all the Folk-lore Societies there is one person who lives in it in reality as I do": and before he had spent a year in Florence he had entered this Tuscan underworld with the aid of the *stréga* Maddaléna.

Prowling about the town, he had ferreted Maddaléna out in her great grim apartment in a decayed old palace, with only a small table and two chairs and with tattered scenes from Tasso frescoed on the walls. This young woman had a gypsy look, with her antique Etruscan face and what Leland called "the indefinable glance of a witch," and she came from a family of witches who had told fortunes for centuries and prepared enchanted medicines, philtres and spells. She was a child of the Romagna Toscana, a land of wild scenery, torrents, cliffs, forests and legendary castles, and her witch grandmother had brought her up to believe in her fate as a sorceress and had taught her how to evoke the ancient gods. There was nothing she did not know about the magical incantations with which the household goblins of the old Etruscans were still addressed in many a Florentine cellar; and, while Leland saw her constantly, it was she who introduced him to Marietta and many another witch. His mind, before long, was full of their shadowy legends.

This towering old man with his Viking air had lived for years like the Wandering Jew, engaged in adventures in a dozen countries, always drawn to tinkers and tramps, fakirs, card-slingers and all who form "the outside class of creation," as he once called it. For he liked to say that he had a proclivity for low society and ways that are dark, for whatever gave him a sense of mystery and strangeness, for anything "to take one out of this neat-handed five o'clock tea Philistia of a common *comm'on dit* world." As a student at Princeton, Heidelberg, Munich, Leland had revelled in curious learning, old French poets, occulta, Paracelsus, magical and mystical writings of the Middle Ages; and he had fought in Paris on the barricades, in 1848, with a dirk and a pistol, a monocle and a red sash. In London he had founded a Rabelais Society; he had studied black African magic on a visit to Cairo; and, returning to America, he had lived with Indians, the Kaws in the far West and the northeastern Algonquins on the coast of Maine. He had recorded their legends, as much at home in their native tongues as he was in Hindustani, Persian, Turkish or in the tinker's talk that he called Shelta; while he had translated all of Heine and seemed unable to live down the fame of the *Hans Breitmann* ballads he had written in his youth. But he was known the world over as a gypsy scholar, second only to George Borrow, whom he had met often. He had first learned Romany in 1870 from old Matty Cooper in England, where he had seen much of the Windsor Froggie, and Matty had proposed that they should set out on the drum together,— "over the hills,"—with a nut-brown maid to support them by fortune-telling. Leland had actually followed the gypsies on Welsh roads, on English lanes, in Hungary, Russia, Egypt, at Bagni di Lucca, loving their free out-of-door life, in tawny tents, among rocks and trees, by hedge-rows, on river-sides, in forests. He had felt that he was one of them; they had told him their secrets; about them he had written his most interesting books. The pockets of his old coat were stuffed with amulets and charms, stones with holes in them, fetishes in little red bags. He owned the Black Stone of the Voodoos, and now Maddaléna found for him the Tuscan Salagrana Stone and put it in a bag for him with incantations.

Leland always wondered how he happened upon such characters, who came to him, he said, as in a dream, for he was scarcely conscious of seeking them out; and presently in Florence he fell in with another old witch in a room that was full of herbs and bottles. She had a great cat that sat on a chair and, after Leland mewed to her, never took her eyes off the stranger. "Ah, you know me!" said Leland to the cat. When he left, the old dame said, "You come to see me to learn, but I am the one who needs a lesson from you"; and he gave her the wizard's blessing, which she had earnestly asked for. Florence, so unlike Geneva, had the "witch aura," Leland remarked; and he collected legends of the town, stories of Galileo's tower, the red pillars of the Baptistry, Boccaccio's Fiesole, the fountains. Then he also collected unpublished legends of Virgil, whose fame as a magician had spread all over Europe, especially after his appearance in Dante's poem. Tales that had been told previously of other magicians and wizards were now attributed to the Roman poet "when things were so different, when blue was bluer and red was redder, when the grains of maize were as big as grapes and grapes were as big as pomegranates." Any and every sorcerer was called a "Virgil," and the poet survived as a wonder-worker, benevolent and genial, a friend of the poor who was always doing good. Leland collected a hundred stories in Florence, Arezzo, Siena, and he said there were many more that had never been collected. This Virgil had brought dead oxen to life, he had driven the flies out of Rome and he had made statues dance and sing.

Meanwhile, from Maddaléna and other witches roundabout, Leland had assembled tales of the "gods in exile," stories of Jupiter, Mercury, Bacchus, still worshipped under other names, with ancient rural deities, Silvanus and the fauns. Heine had perhaps never dreamed how far the old faith still survived in the secret rites carried on by the Tuscan peasants, evoking house-brownies, frolicking sprites, the spirits of river, rock, cave and spring that had lived on from early Etruscan times. There were the gentle creatures who guarded trees, mountains and brooks, the Oreads, Dryads and Naiads whom Fiammetta, in W. W. Story's tale, heard in the mountains, or thought she heard and saw when she wandered in the forest, and the pretty damsels in *The Marble Faun* whom Donatello's grandsire had called out of the fountains and the trunks of the old trees. There was a goblin for every plant, and red-caps and three-inch mannikins haunted the woods and ruined towers, along with the familiar spirits of fireside and kitchen. In times of trouble many a peasant appealed with equal confidence alike to Christian saint and heathen god, feeling that if one of them failed the other would be helpful, just as the young count in Henry James's *The Last of the Valerii* worshipped, with blood-sacrifices, the Juno in his garden. For, as James said, "the old gods still have their worshippers. The old spirit still throbs here and there." Leland discovered a vast number of magical cures with appropriate spells, that stood for a primeval shamanism. He recorded ceremonies and incantations that were supposed to attract love or insure good crops or a traveller's safe return,—a dark world of sorcery that was veiled from the Church as the gypsy traditions were veiled from everyone who was not "on the road." [2] With hymns that were still sung to the gods of Rome, Leland presented all this lore in his great book, *Etruscan Roman Remains*.

He had related what he was told, taking careful and accurate notes, but he had, as he said, to feel his way in a sort of lurid fog, a bewildering, strangely scented sorcerers' Sabbath,

[2] The novelist John W. De Forest, who was in Florence in 1854, collected there "a small museum of ghost frights and witch adventures." These were related to him by a young girl from Siena, a seamstress who was lodging in the same house. One was the story of a poor woman who fell into the power of Satan and was carried off by a goat over the treetops, who was then transformed into a toad and was ultimately restored to herself by the sacred words pronounced over her by a priest. De Forest recounted in *European Acquaintance* other stories of "Maria" that would have interested Leland.

"misled ever and anon by goblins' mocking cries, the cheep-ing of bats on the wing, the hoot of owls." He groped from the corner of one ruined conjecture to another, ever appre-rending that he had found a mare's nest or a nightmare of the most evasive kind. For he had to deal with the memories and minds of ignorant old people who were often dealing them-selves with dim traditions, or with more ignorant younger people who had only half learned them and who recited or sang them sometimes in fragments. Such, he said, was the ungrateful task of the pioneer in folk-lore whose work could be utterly condemned for small errors or faults that even the feeblest critics could find in it, critics who had none of the curiosity or the gusto or vitality of this old-fashioned romantic collector and student.

CHAPTER XXI

THE COLLECTORS: EDITH WHARTON

JUST WHEN did the great epoch of American collecting
begin, the period that reached its apogee in the years
before the first World War and that might have been called
the age of the millionaires? In those days the magnates of
steel and oil, of railroads, department stores and banks, erect-
ing their Renaissance palaces and Loire châteaux, sometimes
measured their success in terms of the pictures they were able
to buy, the well-authenticated Raphaels, Botticellis and Titians.
They went in for that new kind of big-game hunting which
Lewis Mumford was to call "the pillage of the past," seeking
with all the acquisitive instinct of the time for "the epidermis
and entrails of palaces and churches." But, as a result of
this, and whatever their motives may have been, their countrymen were to inherit great museums.

Perhaps one might say that this epoch began when, in 1875,
Mrs. Jack Gardner bought her first small landscape. Countless
travellers long before this had brought back copies of Italian
paintings and sometimes original pictures of the old masters,—
an Andrea del Sarto, perhaps, or a Perugino,—along with the
usual objets d'art, majolicas, bronzes, mosaics, Della Robbia
reproductions and alabaster cupids. Others besides James Jackson Jarves brought even Italian primitives, triptychs with
angular saints and gilded backgrounds, or manuscripts with

rare illuminations, and there were a hundred forerunners of the clever architect Stanford White who literally raided Italy in the eighteen-eighties. It was only a question of degree, and the time was coming when millionaires like Henry B. Fuller's Mr. de Munn were to send home castles in fragments, lettered and numbered. Mr. de Munn fixed his eye on the Coliseum and on the amphitheatres at Arles and Verona, but, finding these too securely anchored, he looked for a small Roman theatre that he could send to New York in a flotilla. Stanford White kept a sailing ship at anchor near Leghorn while he travelled through Italy buying, right and left, frescoed ceilings, panelled walls, mantelpieces, marbles, brocades for the city and country houses that he was designing. Before he sailed homeward he crammed with these objects a ship that might well have been thought a symbol of this age that was just beginning.

Indeed, the architectural firm that was known as McKim, Mead and White created an appropriate background for the great new collections with Italian buildings in American cities that might have been designed expressly to receive Italian pictures. The architects themselves were even rechristened with Italian names,—Charles McKim was called an American Bramante and Stanford White an American Benvenuto Cellini, who preached Italian Renaissance as better suited to American needs than Gothic or the classical style that his partner favoured. The architectural goldsmith Stanford White sometimes used Pompeian terracotta, while McKim borrowed many of his themes from ancient Rome, where he was to establish the American Academy in 1894.[1] He adapted his buildings from

[1] "As between Rome and all other Italian cities, give me Rome—not that I care less for Florence or Venice, but more for Rome. Rome contains for the architect the greatest number of typical examples."— Charles F. McKim, Letter to a student, 1894.

the Baths of Diocletian, the Villa Medici, the Pantheon, or Bernini's colonnade in front of St. Peter's, a model for his Pennsylvania Station in New York, as he also used as a model for this one room in the Baths of Caracalla and followed, for the Harvard Stadium, the Coliseum. McKim conceived that the problems of Washington should be "worked out along Roman lines." The Boston Public Library, with bronze doors suggested by Ghiberti's in Florence, the Pierpont Morgan Library, clubs and museums, had, thanks to McKim, Mead and White, in dozens of cases,—in structure and decorations,— Italian themes. They often included Italian faience, Renaissance enamels, ceilings from Venetian palaces and what not.

All this was quite in harmony with Mrs. Jack Gardner's mind and style when the "Serpent of the Charles,"—Bernard Berenson's phrase,—formed the great collection that was opened in 1903 at Fenway Court. Mrs. Gardner bought capitals and columns, choir-stalls, fountains and balconies, importing Italian workmen to erect her palace, and Berenson, beginning with a Botticelli in 1894, was to choose her most important pictures. Henry Adams acquired for her a great stained-glass window, and Charles Eliot Norton, from the first, had been her adviser,—especially in the purchase of rare editions of Dante: she had attended Norton's lectures in 1878 and later his Dante readings at Shady Hill. Marion Crawford, in Boston in 1881–1883, had read the *Divine Comedy* with Mrs. Gardner and afterwards had the two copies they used bound by Louis Tiffany, following Marion Crawford's own design. In Boston, Dante sometimes brought lovers together, John Jay Chapman, for one example, in 1885, and the half-Italian lady who became his wife. They read together in a large airy room, where no one ever came, at the top of the Boston Athenæum, and the Dante readings, as Chapman said, "moved gradually like a cloud between me and the law, between me and the rest of life." Chapman, a student at the Harvard Law School, was to write a book on Dante, with his own translations in *terza rima*.

The dashing Mrs. Gardner surrounded herself with musicians and artists whom she sometimes "took by the hand and marshalled to the front,"—as Bernard Berenson said, with some reason to know it,—and in this she was quite unlike most of the other collectors who were concerned only with artists of the past. Even Pierpont Morgan, a cultivated man, had no interest in living artists or writers, while he might have been taken for the final type of this neo-Renaissance epoch that Edith Wharton suggested in certain ways. For she too began as a sort of collector of Italian villas and Italian gardens, with a taste in decoration that was in harmony with this time of Stanford White, Isabella Gardner and Pierpont Morgan. Of American writers, perhaps only the novelist Catharine M. Sedgwick had examined Italian villas with any great care. She had studied, near Milan and Como, three generations before, "those gardens to which nature, climate, art and wealth have given the last touch of perfection," as Miss Sedgwick said; while Edith Wharton set out to examine the villas of Florence, Siena and Rome as well as of Genoa, Lombardy and Venice. She remarked that little had ever been written about them or about Italian garden architecture, and she wrote for a time when, following the cult of the Renaissance in building, the cult of the Italian garden had spread to her country. She herself preferred only marble, perennial verdure and water, clipped green and stonework,—without flowers,—the great garden art of the Renaissance with its water-organs, grottoes and fountains, its box-parterres, terraces, loggias and colonnades.

If, in *Italian Villas and Their Gardens*, Edith Wharton

struck one of the notes of this expansive age of American collecting, she was concerned with an earlier age in the story,—
False Dawn,—which might almost have been the story of James
Jackson Jarves. But Lewis Raycie, the hero of the tale, was
actually suggested by the character of another young man,
Thomas Jefferson Bryan, a contemporary of Jarves who brought
back a few Italian primitives and tried to establish a Museum
of Christian Art.[2] Lewis Raycie's father, a solid New Yorker,
had sent him to Europe to acquire a "gentleman's gallery"
with the correct pictures,—a Guercino, a Sassoferrato, a Carlo
Dolci, a Guido, a Domenichino and so on; but, falling in with
a young Englishman who turned out to be Ruskin, he forgot
the artists whom he was expected to admire. The young Englishman pointed out to him, in a small Venetian church,
frescoes "with a certain stiffness in the attitudes of the people,"
a "childish elaboration of their dress," an "innocent inexpres-
sive look in their young faces," and thus, in the presence of
Carpaccio, his eyes were opened to an altogether new world of
art. He shuddered to think of the languishing madonnas and
the pink-rumped amorini of the painters who seemed to his
father all-important, and he felt he was destined to go home
and preach the new gospel that Ruskin had unfolded for him,
as for so many others. But when, in New York, he tried to
dethrone the old powers and principalities in favour of Giotto

[2] Bryan's collection, brought back in 1853, was rejected by the collector's native Philadelphia as "unworthy of house-room." Although the
collection was greatly inferior to Jarves's, it was finally accepted by
the New York Historical Society. Bernard Berenson gave the story to
Mrs. Wharton. In *A Small Boy and Others* (p. 268), Henry James
recalled a New York evening at "Bryan's Gallery of Christian Art,"
that "collection of worm-eaten diptychs and triptychs, of angular saints
and seraphs, of black Madonnas and obscure Bambinos, of such marked
and approved 'primitives' as had never yet been shipped to our shores.
Mr. Bryan's shipment was presently to fall, I believe, under grave
suspicion, was to undergo in fact fatal exposure."

and Piero della Francesca, his father disinherited him, denouncing this "pack of bores" with "not a full-blooded female among them." Lewis set up, nevertheless, his gallery of Christian art, in the name of Ruskin and Lord Lindsay, hoping to find someone who would understand the pictures; but his missionary efforts went for nothing. Long after his death the pictures were found in an attic and then the collection was sold for five million dollars. It was one of the finest collections of primitives in the world.

Edith Wharton was herself, in a sense, a discoverer, one of the first modern writers to bring to the front certain unappreciated phases of Italian culture,—for one, the Venetian eighteenth century which nobody seemed to know anything about, or care anything about, when she began to write. Only Vernon Lee, whom Edith Wharton knew, was interested in it. The general assumption seemed to be that Italy, or Italian art, had ceased to exist at the end of the Renaissance, and it was assumed as well that the eighteenth century belonged to France when she began to prepare *Italian Backgrounds*. Canaletto was widely known, but no one knew Longhi,—a pictorial equivalent of Goldoni, as Edith Wharton called him,—and Guardi was known only to dilettanti, while the guide-books said nothing about Tiepolo, the "great scene-painter," or referred to him only in condemnation. Edith Wharton, who had known Italy ever since her childhood and who revisited it later year after year,—she spoke Italian as naturally as she breathed,—had steeped herself in Goldoni and Gozzi who lived when the bravo was active still in the country roundabout and even in Venice. She loved to follow in their pages the picturesque wanderings of the figures of the *commedia dell' arte*, and this enabled her to reconstruct the scene she brought vividly to life in her story *A Venetian Night's Entertainment*.

There one saw the senators in their short cloaks and feathered hats and the prodigious striped trousers one found in Longhi, the black velvet tunics slashed with rose-colour, the noblemen in ruffs, the masqueraders who beguiled the boy from Salem. This all seemed quite new when the story appeared, just as *The Valley of Decision*,—Edith Wharton's first novel,—revealed a scene that few readers knew in the Italian past, and just as her *Italian Villas and Their Gardens* was one of the first serious works that had been written on the subject. This book, as she said, became a working manual for landscape gardeners and architectural students.

In one case Edith Wharton actually discovered an important work that all the histories of art had overlooked, a work she found in the very heart of the most carefully explored artistic hunting-ground in Europe. It was one of those nameless uncatalogued treasures that still abounded in Italy, but this remarkable example of fifteenth-century art had remained unknown within a few hours of Florence. Edith Wharton had heard rumours of an obscure monastery, somewhere among the hills between Volterra and the Arno, containing a series of terracotta groups representing scenes of the Passion that had never been classified or studied. She presently convinced the authorities that they were superb, but because they had been restored by a later inferior artist, and ascribed to him, they had been overlooked. No piece of sculpture executed in the seventeenth century could have received, at that time, expert attention; and no one had taken the trouble to ascertain that these terracottas were fifteenth-century work. Edith Wharton found them on one of the journeys that she constantly made in Italy during these years, sometimes with the Paul Bourgets, when her husband bicycled ahead, engaging rooms and ordering dinner for them all. In this way she explored the

Bergamesque Alps and the scenes that presently appeared in *The Valley of Decision*. Her first Italian motor-drive was to the Villa Caprarola, in those days visible to the privileged only.

One of Edith Wharton's pleasures was to circumvent the far from alert compiler of her guide-book, finding rare spots that he had missed and little known objects in villages that sometimes hung aloft among the beech-groves. Occasionally she travelled alone, delighting in the patina of Italy, the bloom of weather-beaten marble, the soft texture of old stucco; and once she walked through the romantic passes connecting Valtellina with the Lake of Iseo. This was the country she later described in a story in *Crucial Instances,* the country from which Don Igidio had originally come; and she visited many an old villa on its cypress-hooded hill that was to appear in another story. She had certainly entered some such house as the one she pictured in *The Duchess at Prayer* with its long shuttered front, that equivocal mask, with the mutilated vases at the gate, the loggia with vanishing frescoes, the avenue barred by a ladder of cypress-shadows. Well she knew those vestigial remains of fantastic horticulture, the maimed statues stretching out their arms, the faun-eared termini grinning in thickets, the mock ruin of a temple in the blinding glare. She, best of all, could imagine the duchess laying out the garden, planting the groves, designing the water-jets and grottoes, surrounded meanwhile with her pet dogs, with blackamoors and mountebanks, and with travelling astrologers and strolling players. All these figures appeared in *The Valley of Decision,* for which she had studied so carefully the history of the Jesuits, the theatre, the music, the costumes and the thought of the time.

Preparing this great historical pageant, she had had the advice of Charles Eliot Norton, who lived in the summer in the Berkshires, a few miles from Lenox,—where she built her own Italian villa and garden,—and whom she visited often, driving through the hill-villages that gave her the idea and the setting of *Ethan Frome*. Norton lent her many books and followed the development of her tale, but her sympathies, like Berenson's, reached out far beyond Norton's own Ruskin-haunted mind. He had been open, imaginatively, only to the pre-Raphaelite world while she was drawn to the high Renaissance, to the Baroque as well and especially to the epoch of her first novel. Later, when she had begun to write of the New York of her own day, she sometimes returned, in her characters and settings, to the garden of the Villa d'Este, Lake Como or Venice, and Italy always retained for her, as it retained for Henry James, a golden aura that she found in no other country.

CHAPTER XXII

BERNARD BERENSON

IN LATER years, Edith Wharton came to know Berenson very well. She made an annual pilgrimage to his villa, I Tatti, on the hills of Settignano, overlooking Florence, setting out thence on garden hunts and architectural excursions to Siena and other Tuscan and Umbrian towns. Once, with Berenson himself, she motored to Weimar and Berlin, visiting various museums with this learned companion whose work as a trained scholar was rapidly replacing the writings of the gifted amateurs of old. "Literary appreciations" were being smiled away, she said,—the prose meditations of the followers of Ruskin and Pater,—and she herself was on the side of those who wished to banish sentiment from the study of art. In Berenson one found scholarly standards and scientific accuracy, while his sensibility and zest were as "life-enhancing" as some of the pictures in which he found this virtue. There were paintings, buildings and works of sculpture in the presence of which he said he felt "as if born to a new kingdom, to an enlarged life"; and he often enabled his readers to share this feeling.[1]

Berenson, too, like Edith Wharton, had been one of Charles

---

[1] "My husband has a special deep voice with which he says, 'How beautiful!' I tell him I shall have these two words carved on his gravestone or inscribed on his urn."—Mary Berenson, *Across the Mediterranean.*

Eliot Norton's pupils. He had first studied Dante with Norton at Harvard; but in all matters of art he had ranged far beyond the limits of this embattled disciple of Ruskin. Although he always refused to write or play expert, as he said, on any question outside his own parish,—Italian art of the Renaissance and the period in painting that later came to interest him, the pre-Giottesque,—he annoyed his teacher by opening his mind, with boundless curiosity, to regions where Norton could not follow him. For Norton was at home only in the age of Giotto. Ernest Fenollosa, in Boston, in 1894, showed Berenson the marvellous collection of Chinese paintings that he had not yet shown to the public; and Norton protested when Berenson gave naturalization papers as it were to the Japanese art that he had also studied. Berenson ranked Carlo Crivelli with the Japanese lacquers rather than with European painting, a heresy to Norton; while in his *Word for Renaissance Churches* he defended the pagan and classical style that, in these churches, both Ruskin and Norton detested. It was true that the churches did not evoke that sense of awe and mystery which the mediæval Christian felt in his places of worship, but they expressed the real Italian genius and its love of space effects, proportion and order. There were various other ways in which this young man broke the spell that Norton and Ruskin's teaching had cast over Boston.

Berenson had first visited Italy in 1888, and he had lived since 1900 on the Tuscan hillside near the villa where Mark Twain had written his *Joan of Arc*. Berenson, already an expert,—a role that he later regretted,—who had bought many of her pictures for Mrs. Jack Gardner ("Boston's precinema star," as he was to call her), had written, along with his masterly handbooks and his *Lorenzo Lotto,* an essay called *The Rudiments of Connoisseurship.* In this he more or less followed the

method of the great critic Morelli,—"my revered master," as
Berenson called him,—describing the tests by which one could
establish the provenance and authenticity of works of art.
There were the tests of costume, architectural backgrounds,
the dressing of women's hair, horses and what not, showing
when and where works were produced, as well as the other
measurable elements in pictures, especially the characteristics
of the various masters. (The deep-set eyes of Leonardo, Giorgione's eyes,—wide apart,—the bony lobes in the ears of a
Perugino, the bulb-shaped upper curve in Botticelli's ears.) By
means of this "science" of connoisseurship,—so different from
the "art" of connoisseurship, which was based on certain im-
ponderables, such as the "sense of quality," [2]—Berenson was
able to perform prodigies of judgment that gave him the un-
welcome name of a kind of wizard.[3] But this connoisseurship
proved to be immensely useful, especially in rectifying the
questionable attributions that were still common even in the
greatest museums. Countless pictures passed under the most
imposing names that were actually the work of forgotten
painters, whom Berenson sometimes resuscitated and "recon-
structed," as, in the case of Lorenzo Lotto, from a few pictures
he evoked the history of an artist's youth and education. Yet

[2] Or the "all-overishness" (William James's phrase) "which determines
our decisions more than all the detailed analyses that can be brought
in proof,"—Berenson, *Essays in the Study of Sienese Painting*, p. 27.
"How is it that I often get the full quality of a work of art at the
instant of infinitesimal duration between my seeing it and becoming
aware of looking at it?"—Berenson, *Sketch for a Self-Portrait*, p. 82.

[3] Among his feats was the invention of two Italian painters, the existence
of one of whom was ultimately proved. He isolated a group of pictures
that passed under various famous names and that gave him the sense
of a distinct artistic personality. He called this hypothetical artist Alunno
di Domenico, and presently documents came to light that confirmed his
inference. "Alunno" came into existence again as Bartolommeo di
Giovanni, who had painted all the pictures that Berenson had attributed
to him.

when he looked back on this phase of his life a sense of failure haunted him, as if, in his early days, he had taken the wrong turning.

What had he wished to do and be before he devoted so much time to the archæological study of art, as he called it? Something he largely achieved, both early and late, for, if he was not a novelist and poet, he was a thinker in the world of art who combined a poet's feeling with a novelist's concreteness. An "aesthetic spectator," as he called himself, for whom all the arts existed, he had wandered throughout Italy as a young man, and he knew the peculiar aroma of every one of its hundred cities as one perceives the scent of a nasturtium or a rose. Finding in out-of-the-way hill-towns this masterpiece or that, he had been filled with the ardour of discovery, especially after the sense of colour first really dawned upon him in the upper church of St. Francis at Assisi. It was a morning in summer, and, stepping suddenly into the nave, he found himself immersed in an atmosphere of disembodied colour. This colour was in the air, produced by reflections from the stained glass and the frescoed walls and ceiling, so that he seemed to bathe in it, he seemed to breathe it, just as he had first become aware of aesthetic form and movement facing the façade of a church at Spoleto. As he gazed at the leafy scrolls carved on the doorjambs, stem, tendril and foliage suddenly became alive, and, becoming alive, made him feel as if he had emerged into the light after long groping in the darkness of an initiation. He felt as one illumined, beholding a world where every outline, edge and surface was in a living relation to him, no longer in a merely cognitive relation. Then, spending days and sometimes weeks in Tuscan pothouses and Umbrian inns, he devoted himself in the evenings to study and reflection; and, carrying with him always Burckhardt's *Cicerone,* he organized and wrote out his impressions. The result was the series of handbooks that were collected in the end as *The Italian Painters of the Renaissance.*

Ever since Berenson's boyhood, Walter Pater had fed his mind, so that, first of all, he had to wrestle with Pater in order to establish his own point of view. In one of his books,[4] he related how he tried to find in the Mona Lisa what his delightful master found in this picture. Brought up as he had been on words, easily yielding to incantations, he was eager to be hypnotized as he stood before it, spending hours day after day trying to match what he saw and felt with Pater's famous passage on Leonardo's portrait. Berenson, however, brought up also in an age of science, could not see works of art in any such fashion, especially as they gave him physical sensations, appealing to his senses, muscles, viscera and nerves; and he felt the need of escaping from this literary method to the fruitful fields of fact and calculation. His own method began to appear in *Venetian Painters* and *Florentine Painters* in which one also discovered reflections of Nietzsche, the thinker who turned against Wagner as no longer life-giving but impoverishing life, exalting in his "Parsifalism" the weaknesses of men. Nietzsche, who also felt art in his nerves and his blood, had filled Berenson's mind for a while completely; and one of this young man's chief criteria was that great art is "life-enhancing," [5] as "life-diminishing" art is inferior art.

[4] *The Study and Criticism of Italian Art,* Vol. III, pp. 2-3.
[5] "Let me say then that by 'life-enhancement' I mean the ideated identification of ourselves with a person, the ideated participation in an action, the ideated plunging into a state of being, or state of mind, that makes one feel more hopefully, more zestfully alive; living more intense, more radiant a life not only physically but morally and spiritually as well; reaching out to the topmost peak of our capacities, contented with no satisfaction lower than the highest."—Berenson, *Aesthetics and History,* pp. 136-137.

His other chief criterion, besides space-composition and movement, was the supreme test of "tactile values,"—that one must
feel pictures physically if they have real merit, one must feel
the weight of the hand or the brocade. A painter's first business,
he observed, was to rouse the tactile sense, so that one had the
illusion of touching a figure, so that one felt in one's own legs
and feet "those ideated sensations of movement and pressure."
From them one derived the pleasure of activity with none of
its drawbacks or fatigues, as the forms of Michelangelo in-
creased one's own sense of capacity, so life-communicating they
were and so life-enhancing.

One felt in Berenson's writing how definite were these
effects in him, how often pictures set his pulses dancing, how
Giotto contrived to make life leap out and increase the life in
his own veins, how Pollaiuolo's David communicated buoy-
ancy as he realized the movement of this wonderful youth. Of
Masaccio's figures Berenson wrote that, feeling their muscular
pressure, one also felt as if the elixir of life, not one's own
sluggish blood, coursed through one's veins; and he caused
the reader to share this illusion, this hyperæsthesia not bought
by drugs nor paid for with cheques drawn on his own vitality.
It was no wonder that Berenson's handbooks were destined for
so long a life,—for how many writings on art had ever been
so quickening?—while he regretted later that his phrase "tactile
values" had, as he said, attracted all the attention. The phrase
was so mysterious, so promising, so new! He had taken it for
granted that the "human interest and ethical appeal" called
for no further discussion, for they had been discussed constantly already, so that he had felt free to devote his zeal to
the part of his theory that required exposition and defence.
But from the first he was deeply concerned with the spiritual
significance of art, with Raphael as embodying ideals and

expressing aspirations, with Michelangelo's "vision of a glorious but possible humanity," with Mantegna's vision of a "perfected" one. The great artists were greater than others, he said, not merely because they painted better but "because they created greater visual myths." In short, they were masters of illustration also, and from Berenson's point of view art was great only when the decorative and illustrative elements worked together.

Soon, in fact, in *A Sienese Painter of the Franciscan Legend*, Berenson dealt with spiritual significance alone, for he was not discussing works of art as such when he said that "Sassetta succeeds where Giotto fails." Giotto and his followers at Assisi had produced grand frescoes, but did they embody the spirit and the teaching of the saint? This was the only question in Berenson's mind when he said that the Sienese painting of Sassetta did so, the Sienese being the most mystically inclined of peoples, nurturing saints as others fostered statesmen. It was Berenson's belief that Chinese painters conveyed a sense of spiritual things that one scarcely ever found in European art, and the Sienese of Sassetta's time came closer to the schools of the Far East than any other school of design. They too avoided modelling in the round, procuring their effects by pure line, while Sassetta himself was supremely mythopoetic. Long before this, in his *Lorenzo Lotto*, Berenson had been concerned again with an artist mainly as an illustrator, as a pictorial psychologist, "the first Italian painter who was sensitive to the varying states of the human soul . . . He seems always to have been able to define his feelings, emotions and ideals, instead of being a mere highway for them; always to recognize at the moment the value of an impression and to enjoy it to the full before it gives place to another." Berenson added that Lorenzo Lotto's spirit was much like our own, and that "it has all the appeal and fascination of a kindred soul in another age."

This was rather in Pater's vein, and Berenson longed for many years to write an "imaginary portrait" of a certain young American who was buried in Ferrara. There on a lawn in front of a church he had found a sarcophagus, in the style of Canova, containing the body of a young Bostonian who had died in the eighteen-twenties. As a Protestant, the young man could not be buried in holy ground and had to be left outside the cemetery; and this youthful pilgrim to the land of his spiritual forbears deeply appealed to the Pater in Berenson's mind. Here again he ranged as far from aesthetic criticism in the narrower sense as in his portraits of Rabelais and Vasari,—Rabelais, "an artist glowing with the purifying fires of health . . . the last re-incarnation of Dionysus," and Vasari, whom Berenson loved and placed on a level with Boccaccio and the best raconteurs of all times. This "singularly warm, generous and appreciative critic . . . one of the great prose-writers of Italy," was, Berenson said, primarily a talker and in this respect much like himself, "born to talk and not to write," as he remarked in his *Sketch for a Self-Portrait*. "I was born for conversation and not for writing books," he said, resembling some of the humanists of the time of Vasari, admirably as, in fact, he wrote and although he continued to write, along with these books and essays, more technical papers. For instance, after the first world war, he brought out *Studies in Mediæval Painting*, regarding himself as a neophyte in this field, having only "certain intuitions." He had been led to a deeper study of the monuments in all fields of art in the centuries before the period of the Renaissance, and he even began to think that the late mediæval centuries were, after the Greeks, the greatest of all periods of art. As, twenty years before, the supreme Renaissance names had been sprinkled over paintings of a later style, so the great *dugento* and *trecento* names had been misapplied to many hieratic madonnas that had recently arrived. The pre-Giottesque epoch was still as uncharted as the pre-Raphaelite epoch had been once; and he expounded this on its pictorial side.

Berenson was a humanist in the true sense of the word, with an energy and curiosity that were all but Goethean, a spacious, catholic, zestful mind, interested in all human things, possessing a rare gift for "living" the work of art. Although he restricted himself in writing to three or four centuries of Italian art, he ranged in thought over all epochs and races, from the ruined city of Timgad, with its forest of grey columns, to China, Guatemala and the France of Picasso and Matisse. Growing up when only a few epochs and schools were known to our little Western world, he had seen the art of the whole planet thrown open, with artifacts brought in by explorers and dealers from Central Africa, from Polynesia, from the cave, the jungle and the krall. The material and the spiritual significance of art concerned him equally, perhaps, but the last word in his mind was that the task of art is to "humanize that monstrous polyp, 'man in the lump,'" and with this task of humanization he connected the canons of the classical art in which he found "so much of paradise." For "classical art is what it is," he said in *Aesthetics and History*, "because after thousands of years of groping, mankind, headed by the Hellenes, succeeded in discovering what channels of expression, what moulds of form corresponded best with our anatomical, physiological and psychological make-up." The art that is life-intensifying, life-expanding, life-enhancing tends to refine, he thought, and perfect us as instruments, created to shape the world into a cosmos, the humanized House of Life we hope to attain.

CHAPTER XXIII

THE PRE-WAR YEARS

LEO STEIN came to Fiesole, for the summer, in 1902. He had spent, some years before, two winters in Florence, planning, more or less vaguely, a study of Mantegna, but during this visit he was concerned rather with Cézanne than with the pictures in the Florentine galleries. "Do you know Cézanne?" Berenson had said to him when he had been struck by the dearth of art in Paris; and Berenson then told him about a collection of Cézannes that a friend of his owned in Florence. Leo Stein had bought a picture by the still obscure great man, and this became the nucleus of the renowned collection at 27 rue de Fleurus in Paris. Explaining these pictures to visitors, Leo Stein felt "like a Columbus setting sail for a world beyond the world."

So, in a sense, Berenson was the prime mover of the little show at which so many discovered "modern art," though he refused to abandon his own parish in order to expound the merits of newness in painting. He had published, in New York, an appreciative article on Matisse, but Leo and Gertrude Stein "sadly put me down," he said, "as having made the great refusal" when he would not turn aside from his chosen life-work. Gertrude Stein herself came to Florence presently, dressed in brown corduroy and walking as it were roughshod over the aesthetic interests that were in vogue there. She was determined, like Emerson, "not to be pleased except by that which ought to please *me*," and she cared nothing for "good taste," for the *trecento* or the *quattrocento*, or whether a person or thing was picturesque. With her "laugh like a beefsteak," —Mabel Dodge's phrase,—she ridiculed the Anglo-American worship of the past; and what pleased her were the forget-me-not brooches and the mosaic lockets that she found on the Ponte Vecchio in the little shops there. She liked the miniature alabaster fonts with doves poised on the brink, and she did not care whether they were "good" or not.

Thus, already with Gertrude Stein, "kulchur,"—Ezra Pound's word,—began to fade out and vanish with the new generation, just as it vanished with Mabel Dodge who had set out to conquer Florence as later she set out to conquer New York. It was Mabel Dodge with whom Gertrude Stein stayed at the Villa Curonia, and she too was equally indifferent or hostile to the Anglo-American "ohs" and "ahs" over the past. Florence, she thought, was a costume party in which everyone tried to "revert," to look like someone in the past or in some picture of the past,—Savonarola, or a figure in the "Primavera," or a Bronzino portrait, or a Veronese,—dressing to combine, if possible, picturesqueness and chic; while her own taste was for grandeur and for "a royal residence for the kind of queen I wanted to be." She found this in the villa on the hilltop above San Miniato where Raphael was supposed to have lived for a while, a villa with a courtyard of the best Brunelleschi type and great whitewashed rooms with vaulted ceilings. Edith Wharton might have been happy in the ninety-foot-long drawing-room with its "soft mediæval hush" and "soothing magic,"—as Mabel Dodge described it in her memoirs,—with its high French windows and dark oak floor, wax tapers, golden red curtains and the firelight that flickered over

silver and bronze. Mabel Dodge motored to San Gimignano
and various other towns, but in a sense she was never in Italy,
—she was only in a few people and "things,"—unlike her other
visitor Constance Fletcher. This author of popular novels and
plays, the "George Fleming" of *The Yellow Book,* originally
a child of New England, had lived in Venice, in a beautiful
old palazzo, most of her days,[1] pursued by "my story" wherever
she went. She had been engaged to marry Lord Lovelace, the
grandson of Byron, and, breaking away, he had left with her
some of his grandfather's letters, with a miniature of the poet.
She had been besieged by collectors ever since. This was the
"story" that followed Constance Fletcher and that might have
been the story of *The Aspern Papers.*

As for Leo Stein, "disaggregating" himself from the sister
who claimed the glory of discovering modern art, he returned
to Florence to live through the second World War and publish
a remarkable book called *Appreciation.* With his air of an old
ram,—another phrase of Mabel Dodge,—he had spent many
years sealed up in a neurosis; then, finally escaping and growing more plastic every day, he had worked out his own philosophy of art. He attacked the "cant of unreal appreciation,"
the "secondary appreciation" that characterized "kulchur,"—in
short, that variety of art-expression which is merely the running of water down hill, in poetry, in prose, in painting, in
writing about art. He denounced the music that sings itself
and the poets whose words slip into place as though they were
greased when they ought to go into place as though they were
jewelled. The prerequisite of living art, he said, was tension,
and the lack of this was precisely the matter with "culture,"
as the word had come to be understood. There was no longer
any tension in the piled-up knowledge that so many modern

[1] With her stepfather, the American painter Eugene Benson.

readers and travellers shared, any more than in most of the current poetry and art, or in the lectures in hotels on Florentine Society in Dante's Day or in so many books on Etrurian Byways and what not. Italy had become a paradise of the sentimental. In the interest of vital feeling and fresh thought, Leo Stein made war on the mildewed and flabby.

There were, to be sure, good books that might have been confused with the otiose and flaccid creations that passed for culture,—for one, the *Italian Cities* of the Blashfields, a mediocre painter and his wife who were, as it happened, excellent writers. This was the product of long and frequent visits to Florence, Perugia, Assisi, Spoleto, Cortona, in many of which there had been no building since the sixteenth century or any reason to build, only to patch. In Florence, the Blashfields had witnessed the "demolition of the centre," opening new vistas through the heaps of rubbish, a necessary measure for a living population; and, copying in Santa Maria Novella, they had made friends with the friars, one of whom had sat for a study of his head. They had traced the wanderings of the old painters through a landscape thickly set with the Umbrian and Tuscan hill-towns where some of them had lived and where the peasants still talked of "our Pinturicchio," or of "our Luca" or "our Gentile." The Blashfields had published in 1896 their learned American edition of Vasari's Lives.

Meanwhile, Henry James reappeared in Italy. He visited Marion Crawford in his villa at Sorrento where, on the terrace, after dinner, the local tailor, barber, saddler and joiner performed with violins, guitar and flute. Later, revisiting Capri, he stayed with Axel Munthe at San Michele, that "wondrous cluster and dispersal," as he called it, "of chambers, corners, courts, galleries, arbours, arcades, long white ambulatories and points of view. . . How [Munthe] understood the effect and the value of whiteness!" The singular Swedish physician had built this partly with his own hands, bringing to light under the vines many of the fragments of marbles that were strewn through the garden. Henry James had prompted the book about his island home that Munthe called *The Story of San Michele,*—James who liked to remember there the good old Capri of artistic legend and the days of the contadina and the pifferaro. There still lived, in his white Capri woollens, the painter Charles Coleman, in the villa that Elihu Vedder painted, where his guests drank wine out of silver goblets and watched the tarantella in the garden in the moonlight. In Rome, Sir Moses Ezekiel, the last of the old-time expatriate sculptors, the Virginian who had once been a protégé of Robert E. Lee, still carried on his work in the Baths of Diocletian where he had made statues of Poe and Stonewall Jackson. It was in Rome in 1905, at a Philosophical Congress, that William James met Papini and his friends who were carrying on in Florence a "pragmatic" movement that was inspired partly by himself. They did so with "a literary swing and activity" that William James never saw at home and that "probably our damned academic technics and Ph.D.-machinery," he said, "prevents from ever coming to birth." It all gave James "a queer sense of the grey-plaster temperament of our baldheaded young Ph.D's, boring each other at seminars, writing those direful reports . . . fed on 'books of reference' . . . Can't you and I," he wrote to Santayana, "start a systematic movement at Harvard against the desiccating and pedantifying process?"

Santayana, who had written from Rome in 1904 that "one gets so dry in America with no food for the senses," was to return to Rome at the end of the first World War and spend there the last thirty years of his life. In Florence, despite Berenson's *esprit,* he found too many "soulful tourists and weary dilettanti," and Rome was far more to his liking, "larger, nobler, more genuinely alive and more appealing to wide reflection." Before he moved into the nursing home of the Blue Sisters on the Caelian hill, he lived in the Piazza Barberini for several years, overlooking Bernini's Fountain of the Triton. Berenson said, "I am a stranger everywhere," and Santayana said, "I like to be a stranger. . . It was my destiny," he added; while Italy and Rome were, as he wrote, "My ideal point of vantage in thought, the one anthropological centre where nature and art were most beautiful and mankind least distorted from their complete character." Here, "as if I were the oldest inhabitant of the village, strangers," he said, "flocked to look at me," those who spent half their time in Rome counting the cats at the Pantheon and others like the pilgrims who had visited Voltaire. Just so, in Florence, they flocked to see Berenson when the initials "B.B." had become as well known as "G.B.S."

*

* *

"I was just thinking," said Mrs. Blake, in Edith Wharton's *Roman Fever*, "what different things Rome stands for to each generation of travellers. To our grandmothers, Roman fever; to our mothers, sentimental dangers,—how we used to be guarded! ——to our daughters, no more dangers than the middle of Main Street. They don't know it—but how much they're missing!" And how much everyone missed in Rome, missed in Italy on all sides, when the poetry of the Dream of Arcadia dwindled into prose!—when the "picturesque" fell into contempt, when even the word "signorina" became, with the usage of soldiers, a sort of byword and the *Roman Spring* of Mrs. Chanler became the *Roman Spring of Mrs. Stone*. There were travellers in Venice, in the new realistic age, who remembered only dead cats floating in canals and pigeons disgracing themselves on a yellow-back novel; and few found any longer in Italy that "remote dreamlike Arcadian charm" of which Hawthorne had written in *The Marble Faun*.

The romantic century drew to a close only with the first World War, but how much happened then, in America and in Italy, to change the mental climate of the new generation! Five years earlier, Marinetti had founded the Futuristic school with its contempt for "moonshine," "cemeteries," "museums," and with its ritual of "the fisticuff, the sprint and the kick" that accompanied the dehumanization of art. The aim of Futurism was to play havoc with tradition and taste, substituting the "delirious noise of the machine-gun," in harmony with D'Annunzio who said that he "smelt the stench of peace" and loved what he called "the round mouth of the cannon." Then Mussolini, preaching the sanctity of violence and the educational force of castor oil, silenced or banished all those in whom the Mazzinian vision survived, with the great humane cause of the Risorgimento. Toscanini, Borgese, Salvemini, Ferrero recalled the romantic Milanese exiles of old, while scholars who remained were reduced to secrecy as they had been when Austria ruled the country. Even Berenson, who stood for humanistic values, was obliged to go into hiding and conceal his name. The dreams of the nineteenth century could scarcely survive the twentieth-century contempt for the "cult of the past," while, for the rest, much of Italy came to the United States, thanks to the great collectors and builders of museums. One no longer had to cross the ocean to see Botticelli, Raphael, Tintoretto and Titian. In other respects the new age was sufficiently prosaic. There were countless peasants in southern Italy who might have been regarded, a century before, as Theocritean but who had returned from America and spoke voluble English,—when they were addressed by travellers,—with a Bowery accent. More-over, the new apartment-houses rising in Rome and in Florence took one back to Denver or the Bronx.

The Fascist regime had been less than agreeable for imagina-tive spirits. But after the fall of Mussolini the gates were sud-denly open again as they had once been after Napoleon's fall, and the Americans came flocking back to an Italy that was "all brand new, as if it had never been heard of before." So said Eleanor Clark in *Rome and a Villa,* adding that "now the tourist or student or wandering intellectual . . . comes in like a wisp of fog in a fog bank, with his *angst* and his foggy mod-ern eye." Gone were the old cosmopolitan days of the so-called classical education when everyone was brought up on Cicero and Plutarch,—and on Goethe, Ruskin, Hawthorne and John Addington Symonds,—and when everybody had known by heart, before he ever saw them, the landmarks of the ancients and the Renaissance. Ignorance and ridicule, thriving in the war years, had ravaged the old nineteenth-century culture; yet who could say that the newcomers, turning now from Paris to Rome, were insensitive either to history or to art? Of culture, in the older sense, few were more devoid than Theodore Dreiser, the novelist, for one example, yet the mere thought of St. Francis made his hair "tingle to the roots" when he first visited Assisi. Dreiser had "wild thoughts" of writing the "splen-did panegyric of Venice" that Mary McCarthy was to write many years later, enchanted as he was by the little canals wind-ing like ribbons flung broadcast with exquisite bridges crossing in delightful arches. He was enchanted again by the mountains one saw from Perugia fading into lavenders and purples, scarlets and blues as the evening fell or the dawn brightened; and who, in fact, was more responsive to this lordly land than the so-called barbarian from Indiana? Like Cooper and Howells,

Dreiser felt that Italy, dull at the moment perhaps, might well be magnificent again in the future.[2]

There had been, after the first World War, Americans who published little magazines not only in Paris and Vienna but in Rome as well, as Byron, Shelley and Leigh Hunt had established in Pisa their English liberal review. There were, for the rest, young girls studying to be singers and other young girls in love with Keats who haunted the Protestant Cemetery and the Piazza di Spagna, and there were young men, or men not so young,—Hemingway perhaps,—who lived again the Byronic life in Venice. There were others like the young man in Sinclair Lewis's *World So Wide* who "hunted for Michelozzos instead of mallards," and there might have been a Professor Lundsgard who was planning in Florence a lecture-tour to be "tied in with a feature movie about the Medici." Why not even a Miss Annie Spragg from Winnebago Falls who had received the stigmata, as her followers thought? There were certainly more painters and sculptors than ever, more students of mediæval hymns, or of tenth-century folkways and twelfth-century churches, more scholars studying the history of Siena or Arezzo, more girl-professors working on Machiavelli; and it was an everyday event for a novel to be written in "Provincetown, Rome and Portofino." How could there not be more travellers from a land where everything changed to the timeless world of the Pantheon, the Capitol, St. Peter's, where one could sit, in the Caffé Greco, at the table where Benjamin West had sat in the yesterday of Gibbon and Piranesi? In Rome, the Marble Faun still stood on the same spot in the same room where it

[2] "Trust the Italian of an older day to do well whatever he did at all; and I for one do not think that this instinct is lost. It will burst into flame again in the future; or save greatly what it already possesses."— Theodore Dreiser, *A Traveller at Forty*, p. 314.

had stood in the days of Hawthorne. Not far away, within the Baths of Diocletian, the cypresses of Michelangelo still flourished, and one day a new shoot suddenly appeared at the foot of Tasso's blasted oak.

INDEX

INDEX